EARLY CHRISTIANS AND ANIMALS

EARLY CHRISTIANS
AND ANIMALS

Robert M. Grant

London and New York

First published 1999
by Routledge
11 New Fetter Lane, London EC4P 4EE

Simultaneously published in the USA and Canada
by Routledge
29 West 35th Street, New York, NY 10001

Routledge is an imprint of the Taylor & Francis Group

© 1999 Robert M. Grant

The right of Robert M. Grant to be identified as the Author of this Work has
been asserted by him in accordance with the Copyright, Designs and Patents
Act 1988

Typeset in Garamond by
J&L Composition Ltd, Filey, North Yorkshire
Printed and bound in Great Britain by
Biddles Ltd, Guildford and King's Lynn

British Library Cataloguing in Publication Data
A catalog record for this book is available from the British Library

Library of Congress Cataloging in Publication Data
Grant, Robert McQueen.
Early Christians and animals/Robert M. Grant.
p.   cm.
Includes bibliographical references and index.
1. Animals–Religious aspects–Christianity–History of doctrines–
Early church, ca. 30–600.   I. Title.
BT746.G73 1999   98–48279
241'.693'09015–dc21

ISBN 0–415–20204–3

CONTENTS

LIST OF PLATES

ABBREVIATIONS

AAA	(Lipsius-Bonnet) Acta Apostolorum Apocrypha
AASS	Acta Sanctorum
AB	*Analecta Bollandiana*
Aelian	*Nature of Animals*
Aristotle	*Gen(eration of Animals)*; *Hist(ory)*; *Parts*; *Progr(ess)*; *Resp(iration)*
Aulus Gellius	*Attic Nights*
BZ	*Byzantinische Zeitschrift*
CCA	Corpus Christianorum Apocryphorum
CCL	Corpus Christianorum, Series Latina
CD	(Augustine) *City of God* (*De civitate dei*)
CSEL	Corpus Scriptorum Ecclesiasticorum Latinorum
Epiphanius	*Against Heresies*
Etym	*Etymologies*
Eusebius	*Church History*
FVS	(Diels–Kranz) *Fragmente der Vorsokratiker*
GCS	Die griechischen christlichen Schriftsteller der ersten drei Jahrhunderte
GL	(Augustine) *Genesis to the Letter*
Hex	*On the Hexaemeron* (Ambrose or Basil)
HTR	*Harvard Theological Review*
Hippolytus	*Refutation of All Heresies*
Irenaeus	*Against Heresies*
JBL	*Journal of Biblical Literature*
JTS	*Journal of Theological Studies*
KP	*Der Kleine Pauly*
LCL	Loeb Classical Library
N–H	Nag Hammadi (codices and pages)
OECT	Oxford Early Christian Texts
Origen *Celsus*	*Origen Against Celsus*
PG	(Migne) Patrologia Graeca
Phys	*Physiologus*

PL	(Migne) Patrologia Latina
Pliny	*Natural History*
PTS	Patristische Texte und Studien
RAC	*Reallexikon für Antike und Christentum*
RE	(Pauly-Wissowa) *Realencyclopädie der classischen Altertumswissenschaft*
SC	Sources Chrétiennes
Serv *Aen*	Servius on the *Aeneid* of Vergil
Serv *Ecl*	Servius on the *Eclogues* of Vergil
Serv *Georg*	Servius on the *Georgics* of Vergil
Sbordone	F. Sbordone, *Physiologus*
SVF	von Arnim, *Stoicorum Veterum Fragmenta*
Tatian	*Oration to the Greeks*
Theophilus	*To Autolycus*
Theophrastus	(*Enquiry into*) *Plants*
Thompson, *Birds*	D'Arcy Thompson, *Glossary of Greek Birds*
Thompson, *Fishes*	D'Arcy Thompson, *Glossary of Greek Fishes*
TU	*Texte und Untersuchungen*
VC	*Vigiliae Christianae*
ZNW	*Zeitschrift für die neutestamentliche Wissenschaft*

ACKNOWLEDGEMENTS

I am especially grateful to Michael Allen, Henry Chadwick, Matthew Dickey, Bishop Frank Griswold, John Helgeland, Martin Marty, Bernard McGinn, Eleanor McLaughlin, Bruce Metzger, Patricia Miller, Michael Murrin, Richard Pervo, John Priest, and I. Trencsényi-Waldapfel for their assistance.

1

BIBLICAL ANIMALS

1 Origins. 2 The snake in Eden. 3 Moral exegesis of the snake. 4 The snake as the Devil. 5 Gnostic exaltation/denial. 6 Paul forbids animal worship. 7 Dogs and pigs. 8 The allegorized ox. 9 Animals irrational or not? 10 Vegetarianism. 11 Dietary laws and exegesis.

1 Origins

For early Christians, animals originated on the fifth day of creation, when God (Elohim) made the great sea-monsters and all living creatures that move and swarm in the waters, and every kind of bird, urging them to be fruitful and increase. On the sixth day he made wild beasts, cattle, all the reptiles, and finally male and female human beings, to rule over the fish, birds, and every living thing that moves upon the earth. He blessed the human couple and gave them all the seed-bearing plants and fruit-bearing trees; green plants were for the wild animals, the birds, and the reptiles to eat (Gen. 1:20–31). In the second creation story, Yahweh Elohim "formed out of the ground all the wild animals and all the birds of heaven," bringing them to the man (still solitary, without a partner) to give them names (2:19–20). Animals frequently appear in the Old Testament and the New. For example, some of the plagues in Exodus include insects. The prophet Isaiah uses examples from the animal world when he describes the present or predicts the future. Job discusses the wonders of the animal world, ending with the crocodile, which is "king over all proud beasts." Psalm 102 compares the wretched author to "a desert owl in the wilderness, an owl that lives among ruins," while Psalm 104 relies on an Egyptian model to depict the marvels of animal life.

The Gospels frequently refer to animals, especially in comparisons. Thus men are called to be "wise as snakes and sincere as doves" (Matt. 10:16; cf. Ignatius *Polycarp* 2.2). Generally, however, snakes express wisdom less than hostility. God's angels protect disciples from asp and cobra, snake and serpent (Ps. 91:13). Matthew 7:10 also views snakes without enthusiasm: "What man of you, if [his son] asks for a

1

fish, will give him a snake?" – to which Luke 11:11–12 adds, "or if he asks for an egg, will give him a scorpion?" Disciples have the power to tread on snakes and scorpions (Luke 10:19) or pick snakes up (Mark [16:18]). Jesus denounces opponents as a "brood of [poisonous] vipers." He tells of birds that devour the seeds sown along a path (Mark 4:4). A cock's crowing marks the denial by Peter (14:72). A camel is mentioned just because of its size as contrasted with the eye of a needle (Mark 10:25). Domesticated animals named in early Christian tradition include those that stood by the crib of the baby Jesus, whose manger is mentioned in Luke 2:7 and 16. They were first named as ox and ass in the rather late *Gospel of Pseudo-Matthew* because they were thought to fulfill Isaiah 1:3 ("the ox knows its owner and the ass its master's stall") and Habakkuk 3:2 LXX ("between two animals you will be known").

2 The snake in Eden

The most important animal in Genesis or, indeed, in the whole Bible, appears toward the beginning of things. It is a snake, wise and/or subtle or crafty,[1] in the garden of Eden, abruptly trying to persuade Eve to disobey the command of Yahweh Elohim. After she and her husband do disobey and are found out, the snake receives the curse of moving on its belly, eating dirt, and being bruised by human feet (3:14–15). Ancient exegetes naturally concentrated on Eve's disobedience to God, but they also discussed the snake's activities. Two problems arose: how could the snake talk? Did it walk before it was cursed and had to glide? A few passages in early Greek literature could serve as parallels: a talking horse in the *Iliad*, a hawk in Hesiod (who calls his account a fable), and an asp in Aelian, who cites Euripides for nature's indifference to laws.[2] There was also Balaam's ass in Numbers 22:28, and perhaps we could adduce the apocryphal *Acts of Thomas*, which describe a "great snake" that comes out of its hole and tells the apostle that it had recently killed a young man by the road because he had seduced "a certain beautiful woman." Its motive was suitably ascetic, but after it admits to being the devil Thomas commands it to suck out the poison and restore the youth to life. The snake itself swells up, bursts, and dies. The *Acts* also tell how this twin brother of Jesus met a loquacious and Satanic snake and also a "colt of an ass." After a lengthy conversation with the colt, the apostle finally consented to ride it (thus imitating his brother). Unfortunately it then died, and Thomas refused to raise it up.

> I could indeed raise it through the name of Jesus Christ, but this is not expedient. He who gave it speech that it might speak was

able also to make it not die. I do not raise it, not because I am unable but because this is what is useful and helpful for it.[3]

But questions arose about snakes' linguistic ability.

3 Moral exegesis of the snake

Philo of Alexandria, the great first-century Jewish exegete, influenced Christians at least from Clement of Alexandria onward; Origen said explicitly that his treatise *On Dreams* was "worthy of intelligent and wise study by those who wish to know the truth."[4] In his rather literal *Questions on Genesis* Philo explains that the snake is called "wiser than all the beasts" first because it really is wiser, second because it was going to lead humanity astray through sexual passion. Its success proves, however, that the word "wiser" must apply to this particular serpent, not to snakes in general. Did it really talk? Plato had already held that in the golden age no creature was wild nor did they eat one another. Men and beasts all spoke the same language.[5] Philo is less sweeping. Discussing Genesis, he claimed that at the beginning all animals could probably speak somehow, though human beings spoke more clearly and distinctly. Second, God could change the serpent miraculously. Third, the senses of Adam and Eve were keener than ours are, made necessary because of their gigantic bodies; therefore they could distinguish the sounds the snake made. Finally, the story about the curse on the snake is confirmed by the testimony of experience. It does crawl on its breast and belly, with insatiable desire for food and drink. "Whatever has to do with food is altogether earthy; therefore he is said to eat dirt." (Here Philo turns toward allegory.) So there is a plain meaning and there is a deeper meaning. The deeper meaning is that the snake is a symbol of desire for food, drink, and sex.[6] That is to say, it is a moral allegory.

Philo also speaks of the literal reality of the snake in his allegorical treatise *On the Creation of the World*, "It is said that in ancient times the venomous earthborn crawling thing could send forth a human voice, and that one day it approached the wife of the first man." After retelling the Genesis story, Philo adds that "these are no mythical fictions such as poets and sophists delight in, but modes of making ideas visible, bidding us turn to allegorical interpretation guided by what lies beneath the surface."[7] A mythical fiction seems to differ from a mode of making ideas visible because of content, not form. We know that some did call the story a mythical fiction, notably Celsus, the later opponent of Christianity. Answering Celsus, Origen like Philo replied that the story "has a not undignified metaphorical meaning."[8]

Philo continues with a lengthy denunciation of pleasure, of which the snake is a symbol. It "carries its poison in its teeth," thus symbolizing gluttony, and it emits a human voice because pleasure is so often defended in words, for example by Epicureans.[9] The allegory has spread even farther.

Finally, in his treatise *On the Allegory of the Sacred Laws* Philo states even more explicitly that "the prophet" Moses gave pleasure "the symbolical name of snake," for it "glides with many coils" about each part of the irrational soul.[10] But there was another path for allegorizers to take, identifying the snake with the devil.

4 The snake as the devil

In Judaism there are at least two references to the snake as the devil. "It was the devil's spite that brought death into the world" (Wisdom of Solomon 2:243, New English Bible); similarly the Apocalypse of Enoch (69.6) claims that the heavenly power Gadriel brought death and seduced Eve. In the New Testament the apostle Paul tells the Corinthians of his fears that he cannot present the church as a pure virgin to her husband Christ; she may have been corrupted like Eve, led astray by the snake in its craftiness (2 Cor. 11:2–3).[11] In the Book of Revelation a cosmic serpent appears, with seven heads and ten horns, and it tries to kill a woman who is wearing the sun. Presumably this is a futuristic presentation of the struggle between the serpent and Eve, for after warring with Michael and his angels it is cast out of heaven and identified as "the great dragon, the ancient snake called devil and Satan" (Rev. 12:9). It still wars on "those who keep the commandments of God and bear testimony to Jesus" (12:17) and it can emit "spirits of demons" (16:13–14). In the future it will be bound on earth for a thousand years (20:2–3), then cast into eternal fire (20:10).

Justin, a leading apologist, provides more detail about the names. The devil is called "snake" by Moses (Gen. 3:1), "devil" in Job (2:1) and Zechariah (3:1–2), and "Satan" by Jesus (Matt. 4:10 etc.); the name in Syriac and Hebrew means "apostate" (*satan*) and "serpent" (*naas*).[12]

Another second-century apologist, Melito of Sardis, must have discussed these passages in his lost treatise *On the Devil and the Apocalypse of John*.[13] He held that when Absalom resisted David he was prefiguring "the devil who rebelled against the kingdom of Christ."[14] The rather literalist Christian exegete Theophilus of Antioch repeats Philo's literalist claim when he argues that "facts prove the truth of the statements" about the curses laid on the serpent and Eve. Women do suffer in childbirth, and the hateful snake does "creep on its belly and eat dirt," thus "demonstrating to us the truth of what has been said."[15] The demonstration is not very strong, but Theophilus is basically concerned with Satan, not snakes. Like Melito he uses the Apocalypse of John.[16]

> The maleficent demon also called Satan spoke to Eve through the serpent and is still at work in people possessed by him. He addressed her as Eve. She was led astray by the serpent and became the pioneer of sin. He is also called demon and dragon.
>
> (Rev. 12:9)

For Theophilus the snake spoke, but only because of Satan's ventriloquism. The problem did not really concern him greatly.

Irenaeus often followed Justin, sometimes Theophilus, but did not go into the details of the names, since he does not know Hebrew. He does insist that the real punishment for the snake was eternal fire, as in Revelation, not the punishments mentioned in Genesis, since in the gospel the Lord spoke of such a fire as prepared for the devil and his angels (Matt. 25:41).[17] He thus interprets the Old Testament in the light of its later completion or "fulfillment."

We shall discuss Clement, Origen, and Didymus more fully in Chapter 4 on the Alexandrians. Here it is enough to say that they regarded the snake as the devil, who was actively tempting Adam and Eve, but not as a zoological phenomenon.

Both literalists and allegorizers thus insisted on the theological importance of the snake, an importance that goes beyond the question of the factuality of the story. Those who claimed the serpent as fact and those who claimed it as fiction had to ask why the story was there at all. What comes out clearly is that there is remarkable variety in both literal and allegorical interpretation.

5 Gnostic exaltation/denial

Gnostic groups tended to deny the power of the Creator and reject his judgments, often by exalting the snake. Indeed, Hippolytus describes a group called Naassenes, from the Hebrew word *naas* or "snake." The primeval snake, not hostile to humanity, was worshiped by all everywhere, for *naos*, "temple," points toward *naas*; all temples, rites, and mysteries belong to him.[18] In another system Naas, the third angel of Eden (bride of Elohim), approached Eve (daughter of Eden and Elohim) and seduced both her and Adam. The same Naas, hostile toward the messengers of Elohim, tried to have Jesus crucified.[19]

In an unusual instance, Apelles rejected the snake story in his *Syllogisms*, asking "How can the snake, created voiceless and mindless in nature by God, speak reasonably and vocally?" If it ever did so, it would not have stopped conversing with human beings.[20]

6 Dogs and pigs

Dogs and pigs, often mentioned together, were usually viewed without favor. The worst thing the witch Circe in the *Odyssey* could do was change men into nine-year-old pigs,[21] while Sextus Empiricus called the dog "the most worthless of animals," though without explaining why.[22] Dogs, along with poisoners, fornicators, murderers, and idolaters, are excluded from heavenly abodes (Rev. 22:15). Like the beggar Lazarus (Luke 16:21), dogs eat scraps from the table (Matt. 15:26–27, Mark 7:27–28) – and thus are like pigs that will eat anything (Luke 15:16). A papyrus gospel-fragment tells of a bad high priest who bathes in water in which "dogs and pigs lie night and day."[23] Paul warns against dogs, and they are viewed unfavorably in Revelation (22:15) and by Ignatius. The dog proverbially turns back to its own vomit, and the pig is washed only to wallow in mud again (2 Pet. 2:22). Jesus drives a "legion" of unclean spirits from a demoniac into about two thousand pigs that leap off a cliff into the Lake of Galilee and drown, thus proving the reality of the exorcism.[24] They deserve their fate, for pigs prefer mud to clean water.[25] Besides, they are lustful.[26]

Dogs and pigs appear again in a gnomic saying in Matthew. "Do not give what is holy to dogs or cast your pearls before pigs" (Matt. 7:6).[27] The Didache (9.7) treats these dogs as the unbaptized, not to be admitted to the holy eucharist. Irenaeus views such animals as moral symbols and says that carnal men live like pigs and dogs.[28] Gnostics agreed with him. Basilides taught that "we are men; all the others are pigs and dogs."[29] When Naassenes claimed that the work of pigs and dogs is the intercourse of woman with man,[30] they apparently relied on a vulgar use of "pig" (as in Aristophanes[31]) to support their point. Elchasaite Gnostics noted that not all men are trustworthy or women upright, and urged devotees to treasure the mysteries like precious pearls.[32]

Second-century Christians were even accused of using dogs at their nocturnal meetings. Tied to the lamp, the dog would jump for food and overturn the lamp, freeing any human participant from blame.[33] Clement assigns such activities to the Carpocratian Gnostics, as well as to dogs, pigs, and goats.[34]

Egyptians too criticized the pig. Herodotus notes that they regarded it as unclean. Anyone who touches one has to bathe in the river at once, and swineherds marry only swineherds.[35] Philo believes that the pig excites pleasure: pork, he knows at second-hand, is the most delicious kind of meat. Elsewhere he interprets pigs as hair-splitting and licentious sophists.[36] The Epistle of Barnabas gives an anthropomorphic condemnation of the pig: while eating, it is silent and does not know its master, but when hungry it cries out.[37] Plutarch explains that the pig is unclean "because it seems to copulate especially as the moon wanes, and because the bodies of those who drink its milk break out with leprosy and scabby itching."[38] Clement of Alexandria rejects this in favor of an even more invidious explanation. "The pig refers to pleasure-loving and unclean desire for food and lewd and defiled license in sex, always itching for matter and lying in mud, fattening for slaughter and destruction."[39] He is not following Philo here, and later he gives other explanations. Jews avoid pork because the pig roots up and destroys the fruits of the earth. The comic poet Plato said pigs should be killed because their meat tastes so good and otherwise they are nothing but bristles, mud, and oinking. Clement concludes that "some eat them as useless, others as destructive of fruits, while still others do not eat because the animal is given to sex."[40]

7 Paul forbids animal worship

Like many other authors,[41] the apostle Paul emphatically denounced the notorious Egyptian worship of animals.[42] In a homiletic passage in Romans he remarked that immoral men

> exchanged the glory of the imperishable God for the likeness of an image of mortal man, birds, quadrupeds, and reptiles. They exchanged the truth of God for a lie and revered and worshiped the creation instead of the Creator, who is blessed for ever, Amen.

God therefore handed them over to various sexual sins (Rom. 1:23–28).[43] Sixty years ago my teacher A. D. Nock was struck by this passage. He wrote of Paul that

> he set out into the wider world with a fixed idea that Gentiles were idolaters and idolaters were immoral. He never abandoned this simple equation. The opening chapter of *Romans* possesses precisely the historical value of a mediaeval sermon on ritual murder as practised by Jews.[44]

We add a minor detail. The book of Wisdom denounced idolatry and explained that it led not only to ritual murder etc., but on to "sexual perversion, breakdown of marriage, adultery, and debauchery" (Wisd. 14: 23–27). The author insisted that the Egyptians worshiped the "most hateful" animals and therefore were oppressed by creatures such as vermin and snakes (15:18–16:1,5). Paul presents a more general form of the picture.

Christians and others continued to denounce Egyptian worship of animals. The apologist Aristides complained about worship of no fewer than twenty-three of them, while Justin denounced "Greek" worship of trees, rivers, mice, cats, crocodiles, and many other "irrational animals"; Athenagoras decried Egyptian worship of cats, crocodiles, snakes, asps, and dogs; and Clement attacked Egyptians for worshiping cats and weasels or, in another place, cats, crocodiles, and indigenous snakes.[45]

8 The allegorized ox

Paul's rejection of animals led him to allegorize the Mosaic legislation that deals humanely with oxen. The Deuteronomic code allows the eating of oxen, sheep, and goats (14:4), but does not allow domestic animals to work on the Sabbath (5:14). It forbids inhumane treatment of birds (22:6–7) and the boiling of a kid in its mother's milk (14:21). In addition, "You shall not plow with an ox and an ass together" (22:10)[46] and "you shall not muzzle an ox when it treads out the grain" (25:4).

Allegorizers were eager to find deeper meanings in such prescriptions. Philo referred the yoking of ox with ass to "unlawful mating" contrary to "the decree of nature" or "the law of nature." Josephus too upheld nature's intention.[47] Likewise Paul treated the ox and ass "unevenly yoked" as symbols of believers and unbelievers (2 Cor. 6:16). He also identified the ox treading out the grain (1 Cor. 9:8–10) as the Christian missionary. Indeed, the words of scripture could not possibly refer to animals. "Does God care for oxen?" No, the words were written on our account, not about oxen but about the plowman, who "should plow in hope and the thresher thresh in hope of a share in the crop."[48] For Paul the ox is not even a co-worker.[49] His allegorical exegesis thus agrees with the moral interpretation in the *Epistle of Aristeas*.[50] Moses, says this document, did not legislate with curious regulations for the sake of mice and weasel,[51] animals that head the list of unclean creatures in Leviticus 11:29–30. Aristeas thus agrees with both Epicureans and Stoics. Epicurus held that the question of just or unjust does not arise with animals that cannot engage not to harm or be harmed,[52] while the basic idea that animals exist for the convenience of men is Stoic.[53] Philo wanted to allegorize because "the law does not prescribe for irrational creatures."[54] His treatise *On Animals* begins with conventional Academic arguments for the rationality of animals (chapters 10–71) but ends by refuting them with examples borrowed from the Stoics (77–100).[55]

In an apologetic mood, however, Philo could claim that "Moses extended the duty of fair treatment even to irrational animals" and cited "the kindly and benevolent regulation about oxen," which showed how humane the law really was.[56] Hesiod had already spoken of feeding farm animals when threshing was done. "Unyoke the oxen," he said.[57] Something similar underlies Aristoxenus' account of Pythagoras, who supposedly ate animals except for "the plowing ox and the ram."[58] Josephus speaks of not muzzling the oxen and adds, obviously referring to them, "It is not just to exclude from the fruit your fellow workers who have labored to produce it."[59] Pliny too calls the ox "a partner in labor and agriculture."[60] The young Plutarch reflected a similar attitude when he denounced primitive men for not just killing dangerous wild beasts but harming "the worker ox."[61] Aelian devotes a chapter to praise of the ox, and its "share in farming." Though he describes smearing its nose with dung to keep it from eating, he notes that the Phrygians executed anyone who killed a plowing ox.[62]

Plutarch also tells how the Athenians rewarded the diligence of an aged mule that had carried stones for building the Parthenon. After retirement it encouraged its younger fellows at work and had free meals assigned to it, "as though to an athlete who had succumbed to old age."[63] Aelian, like Aristotle, praises the same mule for its love of work.[64] And Plutarch himself comments thus:

> If for no other reason than for practise in kindness to our fellows we should accustom ourselves to being mild and gentle with animals. I certainly would not sell even an ox that had been a worker, just because he was old.[65]

Plutarch held an exceptionally high, anti-Stoic view of animals.[66] Paul disagreed. If he wrote 2 Thessalonians, he insisted that "if anyone will *not* work, he must *not* eat" (3:10). Presumably, then, the worker deserves his food – as in Matthew 10:10 (cf. Luke 10:4). But Paul recognized no bond between human beings and oxen. He does not explain why God does not care about animals. (In Acts 10:2 and 11:6 it is Peter, not Paul, who dreams about animals, reptiles, and birds.) Paul does not appeal to Jesus' sayings about a man as much more valuable than a sheep (Matt. 12:12) or than many sparrows (10:31). Is there some basis for his attitude?

9 Animals irrational or not?

The question of animal rationality was vigorously debated in antiquity, and two rather late New Testament books, Jude and 2 Peter, call them "irrational." Jude 10 attacks unreasoning heretics who "know by instinct just as irrational animals do," while the parallel 2 Peter 2:12 refers to them as "like irrational animals, creatures of instinct, born to be caught and killed." Such heretics follow Balaam, rebuked when God made a mute ass speak with a human voice to restrain his master's madness (2:16).

Greek and Roman authors often discussed the rationality/irrationality of animals.[67] The Roman Varro, for example, insisted that ravens, crows, and infants may seem to talk but are not really communicating, and Seneca likewise held that wild animals lack reason and have only impulses.[68] Galen began his *Exhortation* by stating that the question is "obscure" but suggests that though animals do not speak with a voice (the "expressed logos"), all share to some extent in reason (the "internal logos") and imitate human crafts with spiders' webs and the honeycombs of bees.[69] Sextus Empiricus insisted more firmly on animal rationality, concentrating on the example of the dog, "held to be the most worthless of animals," while Porphyry presented the argument more fully in his *Abstinence from Animal Flesh*.[70] Philo of Alexandria sums up both sides in his treatise *On Animals*, and Plutarch like Philo gives both sides, though in his own opinion animals are intelligent.[71]

Philo listed some animals that had "instinctively learned the self-taught art of healing." These were deer that ate hops against spider bites, Cretan goats that ate dittany to heal wounds from arrows, and tortoises that ate marjoram after injudiciously devouring asps.[72] Likewise, the Christian Tatian tells of animals that by instinct, not reason, cure their ailments and cites dogs that eat grass, deer that eat vipers, pigs that eat river crabs, and lions that eat monkeys.[73] His source lies in the pseudo-scientific literature *On Sympathies and Antipathies* ascribed to the philosopher Democritus; in fact, he mentions such a work.[74] His examples appear specifically in the fragment of a certain Nepualius *On Antipathies and Sympathies* edited by Gemoll,[75] where Tatian's animals and cures stand at the beginning of a longer list. Similar questions arose about insects. According to Cicero, the Academic philosophers argued that ants have sense, mind, reason, and memory.[76] Evidently they could use a calendar too. Nepualius' comment about ants — that they abstain from work on the Sabbath — suggests that he may have been Jewish.[77] But since Aelian knows that they also stay home on the first day of the month[78] this kind of information may be non-sectarian in origin.

Around Tatian's time the anti-Christian author Celsus used stock examples of the rationality of ants and bees as he reworked a study like that by Philo.[79] Bees are rational, Celsus claimed, because they have a leader, attendants and servants, undertake wars and conquests, kill the losers, have cities and suburbs, pass work from one to the next, and drive out and punish drones. Ants save for the winter, help others, have graveyards, and discuss routes with one another.

Origen replies with the equally traditional claim that their activities are instinctive, not rational. To be sure, he has to admit that according to Proverbs 24:59–60 ants are included among the "wiser than the wise" (though they have no strength, they prepare their food in summer), but he insists that the ants are allegorical, perhaps because no one can be wiser than the wise, perhaps also because the snake in Eden was said to be wiser than the rest.

10 Vegetarianism

Paul was convinced that the Jewish laws about eating certain animals were obsolete. Genesis showed that dietary prescriptions changed. While the original diet of human beings and others was to be vegetarian, and animals, birds, and reptiles themselves were to have "every green plant for food" (1:29–30), after the deluge God told Noah that "every creature that lives and moves shall be food for you; as I gave you the green plants, I give you everything." The only exception is "flesh with its life, that is, its blood" (9:3–4). Perhaps the so-called "apostolic decree" refers to this prohibition when it requires abstinence "from food sacrificed to idols, from blood, from the meat of strangled animals" (Acts 15:28–29).[80] When Paul speaks of animals sacrificed to idols, meats which Christians can eat (1 Cor. 8–10), he does not mention the decree. He speaks only once of a few Christian vegetable-eaters at Rome, whom he calls "weak in faith" (Rom. 14:1–2). They are hard to identify.

He wanted to unify the church, not describe varieties of Christian experience. "If a man is weak in his faith you must accept him without attempting to settle doubtful points." Similarly, "let us pursue the things that make for peace and build up the common life" (14:19).

After his time there were Jewish Christians who twisted texts to make Jesus himself a vegetarian[81] and even deleted the "locusts" eaten by John the Baptist, making his diet one of "wild honey tasting like manna or a cake dipped in oil."[82] Some said that James the Lord's brother avoided meat or claimed that the apostle Matthew ate seeds, nuts, and vegetables.[83] A century later the dualistic Manichees (like the dualistic Marcionites) firmly rejected the eating of meat;[84] not everyone shared their view of animals as cognate with human beings. Ambrose explicitly says that "beasts share no common nature with us and are in no way subdued by brotherly justice. If they harm men they harm them as unrelated, and do not violate any natural rights."[85] The young Augustine agreed. He argued against the Manichees that "Christ showed there is no community of right (*ius*) between us and beasts and trees when he sent demons into a herd of swine and by a curse withered the tree in which he did not find fruit."[86]

Such a vegetarian ideal was found among Orphics in the Graeco-Roman world. Plato, Euripides, and Plutarch agree that the Orphic life included abstinence from animal food.[87] Diogenes Laertius, Philostratus, and Iamblichus report that Pythagoreans too were vegetarians and give various explanations of their diet.[88] Diogenes says they refused to kill or eat animals which like us have souls, but that was only an excuse. Their real goal, he says, was to provide a healthy body and a keen mind.

Tatian, whom Irenaeus calls a vegetarian who was the first Encratite, obviously regarded plants as created good. He wrote that "if there is anything poisonous in plants it is due to our sinfulness."[89] In other words, harmful plants such as thorns and thistles originated only after Adam's fall (Gen. 3:18). Theophilus too assigns a "fall" to animals, but not to the vegetable world. Wild animals, he writes, "were not originally created evil or poisonous, for nothing was originally created evil by God; everything was good and very good (Gen. 1:31). The sin of man made them evil, for when man transgressed they transgressed with him.[90] If the master of a house acts properly, his servants necessarily live in good order, but if the master sins his slaves sin with him.[91] Just so, it turned out that man, the master (Gen. 1:28), sinned and the slaves sinned with him. When man returns again to his natural state and no longer does evil, they too will be restored to their original tameness." This means a return to God's first command for man and animals to eat "from the fruits of the earth and seeds and herbs and fruit trees."[92] Irenaeus similarly insists that the diet of animals, and presumably man, will return to what it was in the beginning.

> When the world is restored to its primeval state all the animals must obey and be subject to man and return to the first food given by God, just as before the disobedience they were all subject to Adam and ate the fruit of the earth.
>
> (Gen. 1:28–30)[93]

The more practical Clement of Alexandria allowed abstinence from meat but favored moderation. In a moral discussion he cites Paul as saying, "It is good not to eat meat or drink wine" (modified from Romans 14:21), in agreement with the Pythagoreans, who held that "meat, appropriate for wild animals, darkens the [human] soul." Clement adds, however, that he who eats meat sparingly does not sin.[94] In his view the best diet consists of bulbs, olives, herbs, milk, cheese, fruits, and "all kinds of cooked food without sauces." But he is willing to include meat, preferably roasted, not boiled. He adduces the frugal disciples, who offered the risen Lord "a (small) piece of broiled fish, which he ate before them" (Luke 24:42–43).[95] In a later work Clement reflects more philosophical and literary concerns. Christians can abstain from meat on reasonable grounds, not the Pythagorean dream of the transmigration of souls. One might abstain because animal meat has "already been assimilated to the souls of irrational creatures." Furthermore, wine and meat do harm the mind, as the Pythagorean Androcydes said.[96] Similarly one of the late second-century *Sayings of Sextus*, authoritative for both Clement and Origen, claims that though abstinence is more rational, eating animate beings is really a matter of indifference.[97]

11 Dietary laws and exegesis

Hebrew dietary laws, notably in Leviticus 11 and Deuteronomy 14, required selective abstinence and some zoological knowledge. Leviticus allows one to eat animals that have a parted foot or a cloven hoof and also chew the cud ("clean" animals), while others, such as the camel, rock-badger, hare, and pig are off limits as "unclean" (11:2–8; Deut. 14:7–8). Marine life comes next, with the eating of what has fins and scales, not shellfish (9–12; Deut. 14:10). Various birds, such as vultures, falcons, owls, crows, and hawks, in addition to osprey, stork, cormorants, hoopoe, and bat, are forbidden (13–19; Deut. 14:13–18). Four-legged winged insects are forbidden except for locusts, with legs "jointed above their feet for leaping" (20–25); and small reptiles are forbidden too (29–30).

Such laws among Hebrews as among Pythagoreans needed explanation as circumstances changed.[98] Allegorical interpretation of the Pythagorean watchwords by a certain Androcydes[99] was continued by later Pythagoreans who promoted selective abstinence and gave "many sacred, physical, and soul-related explanations."[100] It was paralleled among Hellenistic Jews like the author of the *Letter of Aristeas*. Reasons, moral or philosophical, had to be given for prohibiting specific foods, as Philo of Alexandria testifies. First he explains historically that Moses simply opposes gluttony because the forbidden animals of land, sea, and air are those whose flesh is "the finest and fattest" (notably pork). Second, there are philosophical and moral lessons taught allegorically by the various species. A divided hoof and chewing the cud are symbols of teaching, fins and scales symbols of self-control, while reptiles are slaves of the passions. At the end of his discussion he returns to the literal and practical: the meat of carnivorous birds does harm to the human being who eats it.[101] (For the Christian *Epistle of Barnabas* see Chapter 4.)

The Christian apologist Justin gives a practical correction of the Old Testament law when he claims that Christians avoid some vegetables not because they are "common" or "unclean" but because in fact they are bitter or poisonous or thorny.[102] Origen attempts a rationale in his apologetic treatise *Against Celsus*, suggesting that "all the animals regarded by the Egyptians and others as having prophetic powers are unclean, while broadly speaking those not so regarded are clean." He adds that "among those which Moses calls unclean are wolf, fox, snake, eagle, hawk, and those like them . . . Not only in the Law but also in the prophets these animals are mentioned to illustrate the worst things, while a wolf or fox is never mentioned with a good connotation."[103]

Thus Jesus contrasted good Christian sheep with wolves or goats, as in Matthew's parable of the Last Judgment (Matt. 25), and in the words, "I send you out as sheep among wolves" (Matt. 10:16; lambs among wolves, Luke 10:3). Christ himself, the Lamb of God (John 1:29; cf. Rev. 5:6), is the good Shepherd who lays down his life for the sheep (John 10:11). Metaphorical wolves are feared, especially by metaphorical sheep (Matt. 10:16, Luke 10:3, John 10:12). They are figurative for Ignatius, who says that though Christians are sheep there are many plausible wolves among them (*Philad.* 2.2). So too in Matthew 7:15 there are wolves in sheep's clothing, while in 2 Clement 5. 2–4 there are lambs among wolves. In Didache 16. 3 sheep will even be turned into wolves. Acts 20:29 predicts the coming of wolves, and the second-century heretic Marcion is called the wolf of Pontus. Such terms are not specifically Christian. Dio reports that a captured Dalmatian rebel blamed the Romans for his revolt: "You are to blame for this, for as guardians of your flocks you send not dogs or shepherds but wolves," and Suetonius tells how Tiberius rejected heavy provincial taxation, telling a governor that a good shepherd shears his flock but does not skin it. As for foxes, Jesus notes that "foxes have holes, but the Son of Man has nowhere to lay his head" (Matt. 8:20 = Luke 9:59), though in Luke 13:32 he condemns Herod as "that fox," a name abusively used by Solon.[104]

2

UNUSUAL ANIMALS

1 Dangerous lions. 2 Friendly lions. 3 The lion in the *Acts of Paul*. 4 Jonah and the sea monster. 5 Tobit's medicinal fish. 6 The greed of fish. 7 Catching fish. 8 Do fish breathe and/or think? 9 Christian fish. 10 Biblical and apocryphal birds. 11 Helpful insects. 12 Bugs in Bible and debate. 13 Did the Creator make insects?

Much early Christian literature is concerned with telling stories about life in the world rather than with analyzing meanings. Such stories involve the unusual if they are to be told at all. Classification is hardly ever involved.

1 Dangerous lions

Lions are fearful beasts for the prophet Amos, who offers the basic biblical, and normally human, comments on them. Their roar is so terrifying that it can be compared with the voice of God (3:8).[1] He also portrays a "day of the Lord" when a man running from a lion will meet a bear, or a man will touch a wall only to be bitten by a snake (5:19). A shepherd can recover "out of a lion's jaws two shin bones or the tip of an ear" (3:12).

The Christian Ignatius of Antioch would have appreciated the comparison of the lion's voice with God's.[2] He says that at Philadelphia he "cried out with a loud voice, the voice of God" (*Philad.* 7.1), but he was more concerned with the privilege of fighting wild beasts in the arena, claiming to the Ephesians that he hopes to obtain it by their prayers (1.2). He vividly expresses his concern to the Roman Christians.

> Let me be food for the beasts through which I can reach God. I am the wheat of God, and I am ground by the teeth of beasts so that I may be found pure bread of Christ. Entice them to become my tomb and leave no trace of my body.
>
> (*Rom.* 4)

15

Plate 1 David fighting with a lion, from the Breviary of Martin of Aragon, Catalonia, Spain, fifteenth century. BNF, ROTH 2529 fol. 17v, © Bibliothèque nationale de France.

"I long for the beasts prepared for me, and I pray that they may be found prompt for me" (5.2). "May fire and cross and struggles with beasts come upon me, and cutting and tearing apart and rackings of bones, mangling of members, crushing of the whole body, wicked torments of the devil – may I but reach Jesus Christ" (5.3).

Ignatius' model for dealing with the beasts is the apostle Paul, who claimed to "die daily." Unless the dead are raised, Paul asked, what had he gained or would gain – even if, humanly speaking, he fought with beasts at Ephesus (1 Cor. 15:31–32)? Yet Ignatius goes beyond Paul, who in fact did not face the beasts and did not mention them when listing his trials and tribulations (2 Cor. 11:23–27). Ignatius struggles to balance his natural fears of torture against his supernatural longing for a martyr's death. When he asks the rhetorical question, "Why have I given myself up to death, to fire, the sword, wild beasts?" he replies that "near the sword is near God, with the wild beasts is with God."[3]

He was terrified, however, by the prospect of being crunched by the jaws of wild beasts, though he had heard of beasts that out of fear refused to touch Christians (Rom. 5.2). Had he conceivably heard some version of Paul's encounter (see below)? The late Latin *Martyrdom of Ignatius* tells of the lions that simply lay on him and crushed him so that his body could be preserved intact.[4]

Roman spectacles made lions fearsome, since they fought men in Roman arenas, sometimes with manes gilded. Seneca noted that "in the morning they throw men to lions and bears, at noon, to the spectators."[5] According to the apocryphal *Gospel of Thomas* (Saying 7) Jesus mysteriously referred to such experiences when he said, "Blessed is the lion which becomes man when consumed by man; and cursed is the man whom the lion consumes, and the lion becomes man." Both kinds of circumstances were possible. Though Pliny assigns "purely imaginary regions" toward the Sahara to people "who live chiefly on the flesh of panthers and lions,"[6] Galen knows real people who eat bear, lion and leopard and find that their meat and their fat are drier and warmer than mutton or even than human flesh.[7] The lion itself eats raw meat (but not the spleen), while human beings eat cooked foods.[8]

2 Friendly lions

Toward Jews and Christians, however, lions were not always hostile, as Daniel found out in the lions' den. The beasts did not touch him, for God sent an angel to him in spite of a stone over the mouth of the pit. The next day they "crunched up" his accusers with their wives and children, "bones and all." In later times an old man who lived in a Palestinian cave gladly received lions there and took them into his bosom, "so full of divine grace was the man of God." Another helpful lion helped a monk dig the grave of Mary of Egypt.[9]

Early in the third century Hippolytus of Rome knew of doubts about Daniel in the lions' den, but he insisted that the lions "rejoiced by shaking their tails as if submissive to a new Adam; they licked the holy feet of Daniel and rolled on his footprints in their desire to be trodden by him." After all, "if we believe that when Paul was condemned to the beasts the lion released against him lay down at his feet and licked him, how can we not believe the events told of Daniel?"[10] Jerome clearly indicates that the story about the lion appeared in the second-century *Acts of Paul* – a book whose Asian author, according to Tertullian, was deposed from the presbyterate for writing it "for the love of Paul."[11] Less credulous than Hippolytus, Jerome rejects "the *Travels of Paul and Thecla* and the whole fable of the baptized lion." The story obviously described the lion as not only friendly toward Paul but actually a Christian. In fact, the *Acts of Paul* do include a remarkable encounter between the apostle Paul and a lion (whom he cannot remember baptizing[13]).

Stories about lions and their humane relations with human beings were not uncommon in the first century. Pliny tells of a Syracusan traveling in Syria who was stopped by a lion so that he could pull a thorn out of its foot. A painting at Syracuse attests the story, he says. Again, a native of Samos when landing on the African coast met a lion which persuaded him to extract a bone caught in its teeth. As long as he remained in the vicinity the grateful animal brought meat to him.[14] Both lions were less rational than the thinking dog of Sextus Empiricus, which removes a thorn by rubbing its foot against the ground and by using its teeth.[15]

The most famous story of the first century dealt with Androclus and the lion. Seneca tells it in its simplest form. "We have seen a lion in the amphitheater who recognized one of the *bestiarii* as his former keeper and protected him from the attack of the beasts."[16] The name Androclus first appears in the lost *Aegyptiaca* by the polymath Apion, especially famous for his claim to have been everywhere and seen everything. This literary personage was in Rome not only under Caligula, when he headed an anti-Jewish embassy from Alexandria,[17] but earlier under Tiberius and later under Claudius. He seems to have inscribed his name on the right instep of the "speaking" statue of "Memnon" (Amenophis III) at Thebes in Egypt, with the testimony that "I heard [the sound] three times."[18] In his writings too Apion claimed he was setting forth his own eyewitness testimony, especially for most improbable events. He told the young Pliny about an herb with magical powers he had used to call up ghosts and ask Homer traditional literary questions about his native country and his parents' names (he did not dare repeat the answers).[19] He had seen that in a Sicilian spring everything floats and nothing sinks, and that in the "Egyptian labyrinth" (temple of Amenemhet III at Hawara) there "still exists" a 14-foot statue of Serapis.[20] Aelian thought perhaps he was "romancing" when he spoke of deer with four kidneys or, from the remote past, a two-headed crane and some other bird with four heads. Wellmann detected his work underlying Aelian's whole chapter, for the claim "I myself have seen an ox with five feet at Alexandria,"[21] cannot come from Aelian himself, who "used to say he had never traveled to any part of the world outside Italy, had never embarked on a ship or known the sea."[22] The further remark, "These phenomena seem not to conform to nature at all, but I have spoken of what reached my own sight and hearing," therefore also comes from Apion. Occasionally he criticized statements made by others, considering the claim of immortality for the ibis by priests of Hermopolis as "far indeed from the truth." Aelian echoed his judgment, holding that the story is "absolutely false."[23] On the other hand, Apion said he had witnessed the love affair between a dolphin and a boy to whom he gave rides off Puteoli for as long as 200 stadia. After the boy died the dolphin came looking for him and then pined away and died. "He was found lying on the shore by those who knew the story and was buried in the same tomb with his favorite."[24]

Aulus Gellius, another polymath a century later, relates how Apion (like Seneca) claimed to have seen Androclus and the lion in the Circus Maximus at Rome, on an occasion when "Caesar" was present. "Since I happened to be at Rome," said Apion, "I was an eyewitness of that event." A slave named Androclus had escaped from his master at Carthage and in a lion's den removed a large thorn from the beast's paw. They lived in the cave for three years but then Androclus was captured and taken to Rome. Condemned to the beasts, he escaped death when the lion recognized him. "Androclus was freed, acquitted, and given the lion by a vote of the people." Afterwards "we used to see Androclus with the lion, attached to a modest leash, going about the shops in the whole city."[25] Similarly Aelian, possibly relying on Apion, names Androcles (*sic*), a household slave of a Roman senator, who escaped to Libya and there removed a sharp stake from a lion's paw. Recaptured and sent to Rome, he was condemned to the beasts, but the lion refused to attack him. The spectators demanded liberty for man and beast. Aelian defends the story on the ground that "memory is indeed one of the attributes of animals." In fact, he has just told a story to show that lions have specific memories of those who mistreat them.[26]

3 The lion in the *Acts of Paul*

Positive evidence for the Christian story finally appears in two papyrus fragments of the *Acts of Paul*. A Bodmer papyrus in Coptic tells how Paul was praying when a lion approached and lay down at his feet. Filled with the Spirit, Paul asked what he wanted and the lion replied, "I want to be baptized." After the apostle took it to a large river and immersed it three times in the name of Jesus Christ, it greeted Paul with "Grace be with you." The apostle replied, "And also with you," as the beast ran away into the country.[27] The Berlin Greek papyrus of the late third century tells how Paul and the lion were in the arena at Ephesus[28] and recognized each other when the lion said, "Grace be with you," and Paul returned the salutation. Paul asked, "Lion, was it you whom I baptized?" When it agreed that it was, the proconsul sent more beasts against Paul and archers against the lion, but hail drove them off as the people cried out, "Save us, O

God, save us, O God of the man who fought with the beasts!" Paul left Ephesus by ship and the lion withdrew into the mountains.[29]

After Hippolytus the lion appears again when Commodian insists that God's power to do anything includes making mute animals speak, and cites as examples Balaam's ass (Num. 22:28–30), the dog that spoke to Simon Magus,[30] and finally, after a reference to Paul's preaching, the lion that spoke with a "divine voice." The heresy-hunter Filastrius also dipped into the apocryphal acts to find "talking cattle and dogs and beasts."[31] Paul's companion Thecla dealt with a friendly lioness that licked her feet and drove off a bear but later died with a lion,[32] but the story is derivative, as are the legends about how Jerome and the abbot Gerasimus took thorns from lions' paws, and how a lion licked the hands and feet of St. Eleutherius.[33]

4 Jonah and the sea monster

The most famous fish in the Bible and the early church is the "great fish" which God "ordained" to swallow Jonah, en route from Joppa to Tarshish (Jon. 1:3) so that "for three days and three nights he stayed in its belly" (1:17). After Jonah prayed within the fish, "the Lord spoke to the fish and it spewed Jonah out onto the dry land" (2:10). When Josephus retells the narrative he is rather non-committal, simply saying that

> the story is that he was swallowed by a sea monster and after three days and as many nights was cast up on the shore of the Euxine Sea, alive and without bodily harm . . . I have gone through the narrative about him just as I found it recorded.[34]

Irenaeus admits that "it seems incredible that men came out safely from the belly of the sea monster and the fiery furnace," but claims that "they were led out as by the Hand of God to show his power."[35]

Jerome is aware that "some will find it incredible that a man could be preserved for three days and nights in the belly of a great fish," but he believes that two sets of analogies may convince them. First, Christian believers will recall the young men in the fiery furnace (Daniel), the opening of the sea in Exodus, and the reluctant lions in Daniel. Second, non-believers presumably believe in the metamorphoses described by Ovid and others, such as Daphne turning into a laurel or the sisters of Phaethon turning into trees, not to mention Jupiter's transforming himself into a swan or a flow of gold or a bull. (It is hard to see why these analogies are relevant to Jonah's case.) Another problem arises from Jonah's "call" to God. Perhaps he saw the monster as he entered the sea and was terrified by the mass of its body or the awful gape of its mouth, opened to take him in; or else the waters gave way and there was room for his call inside; or else the call was "inward" as in Romans 8:23. Jonah calls either from "the belly of the fish" (2:1) or from "the belly of Sheol" (2:2) because it was so big that it was equal to Sheol.[36]

Jerome (*On Jonah*) notes that at Joppa "today the rocks to which Andromeda was bound before she was freed by Perseus are shown on the shore." Though this too may not seem to the point, it is true, according to Pliny, that "the skeleton of the monster to which Andromeda was said to be exposed was brought by Marcus Scaurus from the town of Joppa in Judaea and shown at Rome" in 58 BC; it was 40 feet long, with a spine $1\frac{1}{2}$ feet thick.[37] Some have thought Jonah's monster was a whale, and Juba, cited by Pliny, said a whale with a length of 600 feet and a breadth of 360 feet was killed in a river in Arabia.[38] The early Christian *Physiologus* also emphasizes size, as we shall see.[39]

In the New Testament the "sign of Jonah" is offered to "an evil and adulterous generation." "As Jonah was three days and three nights in the belly of the sea monster, so the Son of Man will be three days and three nights in the heart of the earth" (Matt. 12:39–40; cf. Luke 11:29–30).

5 Tobit's medicinal fish

In the Apocrypha Tobit went blind because of white patches that appeared after sparrows defecated on his eyes in the night. Fortunately, four years later his son Tobias took a trip with an angel and

Plate 2 Walrus, from *Der Physiologus: Tiere und ihre Symbolik*, © Artemis Verlag AG, Zurich, 1995, p. 79.

was washing his feet in the Tigris when a huge fish jumped out and tried to swallow his foot. The angel told him to drag the fish on to the bank, then split it and take out its bile, heart, and liver. The bile was to be applied to white patches on the eyes, and he later cured his father with it.

6 The greed of fish

Matthew 17:24–27 tells how Jesus criticized the temple tax but paid it for Peter and himself by having the apostle catch a fish with a coin in its mouth. Is this from Greek folklore? An old story about Polycrates of Samos tells how he tried to avoid the jealousy of the gods by casting away his most valued treasure, a gold ring with an emerald. Unfortunately a fisherman gave him a fine fish in whose belly the ring turned up.[40] Another parallel comes from Augustine, who tells how a poor old Christian lost his coat and after prayer at the Twenty Martyrs in Hippo found a large fish on the shore. The purchaser found a gold ring inside and gave it to the man.[41] The later biography of Kentigern may be more secular. After a queen gave her husband's ring to an admirer he lost it in the river Clyde, but thanks to the saint it turned up in a Scottish salmon.[42] The ring thus originates not specially among Jews or Greeks but generally in folklore. Lagrange noted the ground common with other stories: the fact that fish will eat almost anything.[43]

Indeed, the greed of fish is so great that they eat one another. This point is found in a wide range of pagan authors including Hesiod, Aristotle, Polybius, Varro, Plutarch, Oppian, and Sextus Empiricus.[44] Two Christian apologists suggest that adulterers and pederasts "live like fishes," and many later patristic authors follow their lead, as W. Parsons notes.[45]

Perhaps the greediest fish is mentioned by Clement of Alexandria. This is the hake, according to Aristotle the only animal to have its heart in its stomach, according to Epicharmus possessing an extraordinary paunch. Aelian refers only to Aristotle, but Athenaeus like Clement mentions both Aristotle and Epicharmus.[46] Clement's moral judgment about the fish seems to be his own.

7 Catching fish

Early in the Gospel of Mark (1:16–20) Jesus calls his first disciples to leave their calling as fishermen to become "fishers of men," and Mark tells no fish stories. On the other hand, a few fish stories appear in Matthew and Luke, though precise details about quantities or species of fish are lacking. Matthew 13:47–48 describes fishing with a big net for "every kind." The point is that the good fish will later be separated from the bad.[47] This is reversed in the more Gnostic *Gospel of Thomas* (Saying 8):

> Man is like a wise fisherman who cast his net into the sea and drew it up from the sea full of small fish. Among them the wise fisherman found a large good fish. He threw all the small fish down into the sea; he chose the large fish without trouble.

Luke 5:4–7 tells how Jesus told Peter to head for deep water, where a great shoal of fish broke his nets but still overfilled two boats. John 21:4–14 provides what may be a variant version of the tale, with Jesus on shore directing the disciples to cast their nets to the right side of the boat, about 100 yards from shore, where they found a great quantity. Simon Peter hauled the net ashore, intact with its catch of 153 fish. The miracle lies either in Jesus' ability to locate the fish (hardly a miracle) or in his control over their position, perhaps implied by the question in Mark 4:41: "Who is this, that wind and sea obey him?" It is God who provides fish: the pseudepigraphical *Testament of Zebulon* claims that the Lord gave Zebulon huge catches because he shared them with strangers, the sick, and the aged.[48]

Jerome believed he knew why John mentioned a catch of 153 fish, and he says that Oppian listed this number of species in his *Halieutica*. There is every reason to suppose that Jerome had looked not at Oppian but at some Christian commentator on John.[49] Every ancient ichthyologian counted the number of species differently, and Oppian, who after all lived about a century after John, did not quite list 153 kinds of fish.[50] A. W. Mair's "zoological catalogue" for Oppian includes 122 fishes, 17 molluscs, 7 crustacea, 2 echinoderms and 1 sponge, a total of 149. This is only 4 off, if one counts crustacea, echinoderms, and sponge as fish, but we can reach even 152 only by adding 3 worms.[51] Oppian himself says only the gods know the number, while Pliny counts them as either 104 (including 30 crustacea) or 144.[52] According to Apuleius, Quintus Ennius "enumerated countless kinds of fish" – Ambrose too thinks the species cannot be counted – but these are not exact statements, any more than Josephus' remark that the lake of Gennesaret contains "species of fish different, both in taste and appearance, from those found elsewhere."[53]

8 Do fish breathe and/or think?

Aristotle's ideas about fish are not as clear-cut as they seem at first. He held that the senses of fish include taste, hearing, and smelling,[54] but began his scientific treatise on *Respiration* by denouncing the ideas about the breathing of fish set forth by all earlier philosophers. Pliny felt free to insist that "all creatures in the water breathe."[55] Like Aristotle, Galen insists that though fish have a head they lack neck and lungs; they have no voice or breathing or windpipe; they also have no feet or hands.[56]

Basil makes clear the fact that fish take in air from the water. Whereas human beings dilate the thorax and moderate internal heat, fish substitute the expansion and contraction of their gills for respiration. The description comes from Aristotle.[57]

As for fish thinking, Philo of Alexandria insists that there is a chain of being in which humanity is naturally at the top, fish at the bottom. Fish, created first, are corporeal rather than endowed with any soul beyond the simplest. In a way they are both animate and inanimate, lifeless but mobile. Their "soul" takes the place of salt to keep them from rotting.[58]

Only Philo, to judge from Pease's references, mentions the fish rather than the much more common "pig" in this connection, perhaps because of Jewish sensitivity.[59] If Clement of Alexandria is following Philo's discussion of tasty meats, even at some remove,[60] he is not following him for the salty soul, since he refers to a pig, with "some philosophizers" as his authorities.[61]

Plato had explained the fish situation differently. Fish gradually developed out of the most stupid and witless human beings and they live in "extreme witlessness."[62] Later authors often made distinctions. Thus Aristotle specifically refers to the stupidity of the octopus, while Athenaeus tells of the intelligence of the sea-bass.[63] Plutarch claims on the one hand that human beings owe no justice to marine and deep-sea creatures, which are unamiable and lack affection or sweetness of disposition. Indeed, stupid and ignorant people are reasonably called "fish."[64] But when he argues the other side of his thesis he reminds us that successful fishing has to rely on "clever and deceitful tricks," for fish use their intelligence ingeniously and subtly.[65]

The clearest Christian picture appears in the homilies of Basil. In his seventh homily on the creation he urged his congregation not to despise fish as "mute and irrational," for "they have the law of nature strongly imprinted in them, and it shows them what is to be done."[66] His classification of species and much description as well comes from Aristotle's *History of Animals* or, more probably, an epitome.[67]

In his homily the next day, however, Basil accentuated the negative. Fish have no memory, no imagination, nor any recognition of the familiar. They not only are mute but cannot learn or teach, and are incapable of any share in human life.[68] "The ox knows its owner and the ass the crib of its master" (Is. 1:3), but the fish cannot recognize the one who feeds it.[69]

9 Christian fish

Tertullian is the first to speak of Jesus as a fish, obviously in a baptismal context.

> We little fish (*pisciculi*) in accordance with our ICHTHYS Jesus Christ are born in water and are safe only if we stay in water. Therefore that monstrous woman [leader of a hostile sect], who does not even have the right to teach, well knows how to kill little fish by lifting them out of the water.[70]

The fish could also be eucharistic, as in the inscription of Abercius (*c.* 200), lines 12–16. "Faith led the way everywhere and set forth as food a fish great and pure, which a pure virgin caught from a fountain and gave to the friends to eat forever, giving the good cup with bread."

Some saints favored fish over birds. Martin of Tours observed birds gulping down fish in great quantities and ordered them to stop.[71] A rather more impressive fish story appears some centuries later. Antony of Padua, rejected by heretics at Rimini in 1222, went to a river flowing into the Adriatic and began his sermon thus: "Hear the word of the Lord, ye fishes of sea and river, for the faithless heretics despise hearing it." In great numbers, and of all colors, sizes, and shapes, fishes held their heads above the surface to hear his scriptural discourse. He told them that they multiplied by God's command and were saved during the deluge (Gen. 1:20, 7:22).[72] One of them had rescued Jonah and then cast him forth on dry land. Another provided a coin for the tax on the Lord Jesus Christ (Matt. 17:27). Both before and after the resurrection they served as food for the eternal King (John 6:11; 21:9–13) – perhaps not a wholly tactful statement. After Antony's testimonies, all the fishes bowed their heads in praise of the Most High while some spoke with their voices. More fishes showed up, finally emboldening him to proclaim the Catholic faith to the local populace. He converted all the heretics before the fishes applauded and returned to the sea.[73] The scene is depicted in a charming fourteenth-century fresco in the basilica at Padua. The fish are standing on their tails with mouths agape.

10 Biblical and apocryphal birds

Birds have served God and man since the deluge. Noah sent forth a raven and a dove to see if the waters had subsided, and the dove brought back an olive leaf; he knew that the waters had gone down. A week later she went forth and did not come back (Gen. 8:6–12).

Plate 3 Otter, woodcut from *Der Physiologus: Tiere und ihre Symbolik*,
© Artemis Verlag AG, Zurich, 1995, p. 38.

When the prophet Elijah was hiding from Ahab and Jezebel the ravens brought him bread and meat morning and evening (1 Kings 17:6).

Jesus illustrated his teachings with references to birds. He mentioned the significant Old Testament birds, treating the dove as the model of sincerity[74] and noting that ravens are fed by God (Luke 12:24). He compared God's care for birds with his care for human beings. Sparrows are a dime a dozen – priced at two for one *assarion* in Matt. 10:29–31 or five for two in Luke 12:6–7 – but none falls to the ground apart from the will of the Father, and "you are more valuable than many sparrows." So too in the Sermon on the Mount Jesus cites birds as objects of God's care. They do not sow, reap, or collect crops in barns, for "your heavenly Father" feeds them.[75] He will feed you also, for you are much better than they are (Matt. 6:26).[76] The *Gospel of Thomas* (Saying 2) rationalizes by claiming that if the "kingdom" is located in heaven "the birds of the heaven will precede you" into it. Since you are better than they, the kingdom cannot be located there.

Birds care for their young in both Testaments. In Deuteronomy 32:11 God's care for Israel is compared with that of an eagle for its nest. It "hovers above its young, spreads its pinions and takes them up, and carries them upon its wings." Jesus likewise prophetically calls to Jerusalem, "How often would I have gathered your children together as a hen gathers her brood under her wings, and you would not!" (Matt. 23:37 = Luke 13:34).

Such devotion to offspring raised doubts about the supposed immorality of the partridge, also devoted to its chicks. While Aristotle judged it harshly, insisting that "the bird has a bad character and wicked tricks,"[77] Aelian was ambivalent, praising protection of the chicks as good but criticizing partridges as "the most incontinent of birds."[78] Origen explicitly referred to writers on "the nature of animals," such as Aristotle (*History of Animals*), who treat it as incontinent, but like Aelian asked whether it is good or bad when it deceives hunters to protect the chicks.[79] Two different moral criteria were involved.

The synoptic gospels tell how the Holy Spirit descended upon Jesus at his baptism "like a dove," or according to Luke 3:22 "in bodily form like a dove." Two centuries later Roman Christians were gathered in order to elect a bishop when a dove settled on the head of a rural delegate, "providing an imitation of the descent of the Holy Spirit in the form of a dove on the Savior." The people responded with a shout of "Worthy" and Fabian became bishop.[80]

In addition, the Christian apocryphal *Infancy Gospel of Thomas* tells how when Jesus was five he made soft clay with brook water and fashioned a dozen sparrows with it. When Joseph complained, Jesus clapped his hands and cried to the sparrows, "Away with you!" The sparrows took flight and went away chirping.[81]

11 Helpful insects

Lastly, for insects we turn to the second-century *Acts of John* with its story about the apostle and the bedbugs. Pliny had apologized for discussing insects at all.

> I feel sure that some will be disgusted at the animals I shall treat of, although Vergil did not disdain to speak quite unnecessarily of ants and weevils (*Georgics* 1.185–86), and of "sleeping places heaped up by cockroaches that avoid the light" (4.243). Nor did Homer disdain among the battles of the gods to tell of the greed of the fly (*Iliad* 17. 570), nor did Nature disdain to create them because she creates man.[82]

This seems derived from Aristotle, who says he is not passing over any animal, "no matter how mean" and unattractive.

> If anyone holds that study of the animals is an unworthy pursuit, he ought to go further and hold the same opinion about the study of himself, for it is not possible without considerable disgust to look upon the blood, flesh, bones, blood-vessels, and the like parts of which the human body is constructed.[83]

Christian apocryphers did not apologize for their delight in stories of unusual animals.

Since we found a talkative baptized lion in the apocryphal *Acts of Paul*, we are not surprised that in the apocryphal *Acts of John* insects are respectful toward the apostle at an inn.[84] "I tell you, bugs," says John, "behave yourselves one and all; you must leave your home for tonight and be quiet in one place." The author of the *Acts* reports that "we saw a mass of bugs collected by the door of the room we had taken." In the morning John addressed the bugs again. "Since you have behaved yourselves and listened to my counsel, go back to your own place." The bugs came running from the door towards the bed, climbed up the legs, and disappeared into the joints.[85] (Obviously John did not worry about future hotel guests.)

His considerate companion was the *koris* or *cimex lectularius*, familiar in the world of Aristophanes.[86] In an admirable study of hotels, restaurants, and cabarets,[87] Kleberg refers to the "Augustan" life of Hadrian (16.4):

> I don't want to be a Florus,
> Stroll about among the taverns,
> Lurk about among the cook-shops,
> And endure the round fat insects,[88]

and to Pliny *Natural History* 9.154: "Even the creatures found in inns in summertime that plague us with a quick jump or hide chiefly in the hair live in the sea and are often drawn out of the water clustering around the bait." More than that, Petronius tells of a slave in an inn hiding under a bed and pressing his lips against the bugs in the bedding,[89] and Artemidorus notes that bedbugs in dreams are symbols of cares and anxieties. "For bedbugs like anxieties keep people awake at night." Moreover, they point to impending disgust and distress for one's relatives, especially female.[90]

Consideration by insects was not limited to apostles. Two Greek writers tell us that sometimes flies, if not bedbugs, exhibited similar sentiments. Pausanias reports simply that sacrifices to Zeus at Olympia drove flies out, but Aelian is more analytical.

> The flies of Olympia at the time of the feast make peace, so to speak, with visitors and the local inhabitants. In spite of the quantity of sacrifices, of blood shed, and of meat hung up, the flies voluntarily disappear and cross to the opposite bank of the Alpheus.

Afterwards "the flies come back, like exiles allowed to return by a decree."[91] Aelian's exiled flies thus resemble John's exiled bedbugs. (On the other hand the people of Elis sacrificed to the god Flycatcher and the flies there immediately died.[92])

In the year 346 the prayer of Jacob, Christian bishop of Nisibis, produced swarms of gnats and mosquitoes that clogged the trunks of elephants and the ears and nostrils of other animals serving the army of the Persian king Sapor against the Romans.[93] The much later account of Saint Leutfred (he died in 738) is simpler. One hot day he was troubled by flies and could get no rest, but when he folded his hands over his eyes and prayed all the flies disappeared, never to enter the house again.[94] Flies, after all, were almost universally disliked, though Lucian wrote a mildly amusing parody-encomium on them.[95]

12 Bugs in Bible and debate

Apart from such stories, insects were matters of concern for philosophers and theologians, as well as in the Bible itself. Some of them, after all, lead exemplary lives. The Solomon of Proverbs could say, "Go to the ant, thou sluggard" (6:6–11). Ants are among the "smallest on earth yet wise beyond the wisest." They "have no strength yet prepare their store of food in the summer" (30:24–25). The *Physiologus* (12) describes their order, frugality, and foresight, while the fourth-century monk Malchus was highly edified by the spectacle of ants working together in the desert.[96] In paganism ants were related to the divine. "Thessalians are reported to worship ants, for they have been taught that Zeus, in the likeness of an ant, had intercourse with Eurymedusa the daughter of Cletor, and begot Myrmidon." (She was the aged nurse of Nausicaa in the *Odyssey* [7. 7–13]).[97] According to slightly less sensational accounts, ants already in existence were changed into Myrmidons.[98] Strabo rejects any such stories and reports that

> the Aeginetans were called Myrmidons not, as the myth has it, because during a great famine the ants became human beings in answer to the prayers of Aeacus, but because they excavated the earth after the manner of ants and spread the soil over the rocks, so as to have ground to till, and because they lived in the dugouts, refraining from the use of soil for bricks.[99]

In Proverbs the Septuagint text adds the bee as a model, following ordinary Hellenistic ideas about model insects.[100] Sirach 11:3 tells us that while the bee is small, as winged creatures go, its product is very sweet. Plato spoke of bees, wasps, and ants as "social and gentle species,"[101] and might have agreed with Pliny: the bee "was given to man to supply honey."[102] Philo of Alexandria discusses three insects (spider, bee, and ant) in his treatise *On Animals* and repeats Academic criticisms of them before stating Stoic counter-arguments.[103] Clement of Alexandria is so fond of bees that he calls one of his teachers a "Sicilian bee"; according to Varro the best honey was Sicilian.[104] In 1958 Pope Pius XII insisted that bees were "a proof of the existence of God." Theirs is a "marvelous world," due to "a superior intelligence," but though they act intelligently they do not understand anything.[105]

In harmony with early Christian enthusiasm for monarchy, divine and human, Origen points out that as one among bees is the king, so the prince of the prophets is "my Lord Jesus Christ."[106] He reflects a recurrent error when he calls the leader bee a king, not a queen. In Aristotle's view there are three kinds of bees: kings or leaders, workers, and drones, generated apart from copulation, spontaneously from the corpses of oxen.[107] When Xenophon refers to the chief bee as feminine he has his mate in mind.[108] Indeed, bees were considered austere in matters of sex, presumably because they lacked distinguishing sexual characteristics.[109] Plutarch says they seem "irritable and bellicose toward men who have been with women," while according to the *Geoponica* they tend to attack women who have had sexual intercourse (Aelian had limited their targets to those who "come from licentious intercourse"). The bees are like "modest and refined girls" offended by bad odors and the smell of perfume.[110]

When Stoics and others defended the providential arrangement of the world, they had to take insects into account and thus led the way to apologetic entomology. The optimistic Stoic Chrysippus defended bedbugs as really "useful for waking us up," as well as mice for "making us attentive about putting things away carefully,"[111] not to mention cocks, which like mice wake us up and pluck out scorpions and arouse us for battle.[112] They can all be fitted into the providential scheme. Just so, the hermit Colman of Kilmacduagh "was waited on by a cock, a mouse, and a fly: the cock woke him for the night office, the mouse prevented him from going to sleep again, and the fly acted as an indicator and book-marker."[113] Specifically, the mouse gnawed at his clothing or bit his ears, while the fly buzzed over the book and at Colman's command landed on the line of text at which the saint had stopped reading.[114]

The Stoic view appears again when Clement of Rome lists the workings of divine providence. Providence provides for "the smallest animals to come together in concord and peace."[115] Waszink lists many patristic parallels, especially from Jerome and Augustine,[116] statements implying that these animals have moral goals and therefore reason. Beyond this, "the Rabbis say, 'Even things that you regard as completely superfluous to the creation of the world, for instance fleas, gnats, and flies, also fall into the classification of things that were part of the creation of the world.'"[117]

Significantly, Basil concludes a brief discussion of the wonders of insects with the statement, Peripatetic in origin, that "God created nothing unnecessary or lacking anything that is necessary."[118]

On the other hand, ancient Hebrews found flies annoying, alive or dead. ("Dead flies make the perfumer's sweet ointment turn rancid and ferment," Eccl. 10:1.) The dog-fly was one of the plagues against Egypt (Exod. 8:20–32).[119] Baalzebub, the name of a Philistine god at Ekron (2 Kings 1:2, etc.), means "lord of flies" in Hebrew, while in the synoptic gospels Beezeboul is prince of demons. William Golding thus followed tradition when he identified the two deities in his novel *Lord of the Flies*. Origen points out how minute the fly is but how unpleasant its sting.[120]

Leviticus 11:20 insists that "all winged insects that go on four legs are an abomination to you," while verse 22 lists four kinds of locusts (grasshoppers?) that can be eaten, including the "desert locusts" which John the Baptist presumably consumed in the desert. He combined them with wild honey (Mark 1:6; Matt. 3:4) since the ancients did not possess sugar as such. Some of his critics supposed that he did not eat or drink at all but was a demoniac (Matt. 11:18), but Luke (7:33) more accurately reports that he ate no bread and drank no wine.

Moths, of course, produced nothing but trouble since they were so damaging to clothes. Job mentions them four times (4:19; 27:18, 20; 32:22) and uses the word "moth-eaten" in 13:28. Moths appear three times in Isaiah (33:1; 50:9; 51:8), once in Micah (7:4), and once in Hosea (5:12). They are also found in Psalm 39:11, Proverbs 14:30 and 25:20, and Sirach 19:3 and 42:13. They obviously consume

Plate 4 Dolphins, from *Der Physiologus: Tiere und ihre Symbolik*, © Artemis Verlag AG, Zurich, 1995, p. 58.

"treasure" on earth, though not in heaven (Matt. 6:19–20 = Luke 12:33). James 5:2 is even more explicit about their destructiveness: "Your riches have rotted and your garments are moth-eaten" (the same word as in Job).[121]

13 Did the Creator make insects?

Criticism of providence because of insects appears in Porphyry's treatise *On Abstinence* (ultimately derived from the Academic philosopher Carneades).

> If God prepared the animals for human use, what use can we make of flies, mosquitoes, bats, Spanish flies, scorpions, vipers, some of which are ugly to view and foul to touch and unbearable to smell and make horrible and unattractive sounds, while others are deadly to those who encounter them?[122]

Later the dualist theologian Marcion and his followers went on to ascribe inconvenient insects to an inferior Creator. Tertullian says to Marcion, "You deride the more minute animals," and urges him to "imitate if you can the buildings of the bee, the stables of the ant, the nets of the spider, the threads of the silkworm." Doubtless Marcion's own examples continue when Tertullian says to "stop if you can the beasts of your bed and rug, the Spanish fly's poisons, the house fly's stinger, the gnat's buzz and sting."[123] H. J. Schoeps correlated Marcion's complaints with his well-known abomination of women and sex, and urged psychoanalysts, insufficiently analytic thus far, to investigate. "His vermin-phobia is in fact worthy of a psychiatric investigation."[124] I agree that the expressions about women sound shrill, but the complaints about bugs are merely conventional, coming from Marcion's predecessors. It was easy for theologians to ascribe insects' activities to an inferior Creator-god, for several of them took part in the biblical plagues brought on the Egyptians. Exodus 8 describes frogs first[125] but rapidly turns to maggots,[126] dog-flies, and locusts (10:4),[127] all of which reappear in Psalms 77 (78) and 105 (106).

Others wondered how the Creator could declare that his creation is "very good" (Gen. 1:31) in view of the insects presumably present in it. Where did they come from? Augustine subtly argued that the "natural power" of insemination from decaying matter (spontaneous generation) produced the wonders of minute insects like flies and ants, and that this aspect of the divine plan was present in the created world from the beginning although not worked out until later.[128] He is less positive about details in the plan: "I admit I am ignorant as to why mice and frogs were created, or flies or worms, but I see that all things in their kind are beautiful even though because of our sins many seem hostile to us." He analyzes further, classifying animals as useful or harmful or superfluous. The useful ones are obvious, while those that seem harmful are really beneficial because they punish us, vex us, or scare us so that we may look for a life better than this one. There is no reason to inquire about the superfluous ones.[129] The discussion and debate was inconclusive.

3

UNREAL ANIMALS

1 Palaephatus. 2 Centaurs. 3 Dragons. 4 The phoenix.
5 Other unreal beasts. 6 A sea monster on land.

1 Palaephatus

Not all animal stories were likely to be true, but one needed some standard by which to judge them. The influential Hellenistic handbook by a certain Palaephatus *On Incredible Matters* adopts an unusual scientific standpoint and tries to solve a wide range of mythological problems, including the existence of fabulous beasts. In the early second century Theon, a teacher of rhetoric, says that "there is a whole book by the Peripatetic Palaephatus entitled *On Incredible Matters*, in which such questions [as that about centaurs] are solved."[1] Jerome also used the book to explain myths.[2] We shall come to centaurs in a moment.

Palaephatus' preface justifies his attitude.

> I wrote this about incredible matters. More credulous people believe everything said, since they are not in touch with wisdom and knowledge, but people more acute by nature and more experienced do not believe that any of these things takes place. To me it seems that everything said does take place (for the mere names did not come to be, but no account of them existed; but first was the deed and then the account of them); but whatever forms and shapes were said to be and were then, but now are not, such things did not take place. For if they came to be at some other time, they exist now and always will. Indeed, I always praise the authors Melissus and Lamiscus of Samos, who said, "What came to be at the beginning is now and always will be."[3] But the poets and logographers changed some of what took place into what was more incredible and more miraculous so as to make people marvel. I know that such things cannot be as they are described; for I learned this: if it did not take place it would not have been mentioned. So traveling over many lands I asked the

34

older people what they heard about each matter, and I am writing down what I learned from them. I myself saw the lands as each is, and I wrote these things not as they were said but as I myself visited and described them.[4]

The Christian apologist Justin also questions reports about remote places.

If someone told you that in India there is an animal unlike all others – such and such, diverse and many-colored – you would not know it before seeing it, and you would have no account to give of it unless you heard from someone who saw it.[5]

The satirist Lucian, however, drew the opposite conclusion:

Suppose an Ethiopian, who had never seen other men like us because he had never been abroad at all, should state . . . that nowhere in the world were there any men white or yellow or of any other color than black, would he be believed by them?

He imagines that an older and more experienced Ethiopian might ask, "How do you know this? You have never left us to go anywhere else, and indeed you have never seen what things are like among other peoples."[6] But he parodies professions of personal witness in his *True Story*. "I am writing about things I have neither seen nor experienced nor learned from others – which in fact do not exist at all nor can come into existence."[7]

Pliny's view is less sceptical. "Who ever believed in the Ethiopians without seeing them? Or what is not judged miraculous when it first attracts attention? How many events are judged impossible before they take place?"[8]

At times Palaephatus reasons from what he knows about real animals. A fox cannot have grabbed and eaten sons of Cadmus, for there is no land animal that can grab and eat a man, and the fox is small and weak. Dogs cannot have eaten Actaeon, for they love their masters.[9]

2 Centaurs

Though Palaephatus discusses few legendary animals, he does include the non-existent centaurs. First the problem. "People say that they were wild beasts and had the appearance of a horse except for the head, that of a human being." Next come the basic objections.

Plate 5 Unicorn, woodcut from *Der Physiologus: Tiere und ihre Symbolik*, © Artemis Verlag AG, Zurich, 1995, p. 35.

If anyone believes that such an animal exists, it is really impossible; for the natures of horse and man are not in harmony, their diets are not similar, nor is it possible for the food of a horse to pass through the mouth and throat of a man. If such a form ever existed it would exist now.

Finally there is an etymological solution in the form of a story.

The truth is this. When Ixion was king of Thessaly there was a herd of wild bulls on Mount Pelion and they made the other mountains impassable, for when the bulls came down to inhabited regions they devastated the trees and fruits and killed the domestic animals. Ixion then announced that if anyone killed the bulls he would pay him a lot of money. Some young men in the vicinity, from a village named Cloud, thought of training horses (earlier they did not rely on riding horses but only used chariots). Thus mounting the horses they hastened to where the bulls were and shooting their arrows stabbed them. And when they were chased by the bulls the young men fled (for the horses were very swift), but when the bulls stood still they turned and stabbed them, thus killing them. They got the name of centaurs because they shot down (*katekentannusan*, from *ken-teō*) the bulls (*taurous*).[10]

36

Lucretius reports a similar criticism of centaurs (which "never were") though not the etymology.[11] And Galen resolutely rejects the centaur, first of all because the union of horse and man is by nature impossible.[12]

Aelian describes centaurs and defends their existence hesitantly.

> Anybody who has seen an onocentaur ("ass-centaur") would never have doubted that the race of centaurs once existed, and that artificers did not falsify Nature, but that time produced even these creatures by blending dissimilar bodies into one. But whether in fact they came into being and visited us at one and the same period, or whether rumor, more malleable than any wax and over-credulous, fashioned them and by some miraculous combination fused the halves of a horse and a man while endowing them with a single soul – let us pass them by.[13]

Clement of Alexandria resolutely refers to the centaur as "a fiction from Thessaly."[14]

On the other hand, the Christian *Physiologus* (see Chapter 4) boldly returns to earlier tradition. Centaurs are "half human, half – from the chest down – horse."[15] And Jerome forgets his Palaephatus when reporting that a centaur directed Antony to the hermit Paul.[16] Perhaps this is an example of what Joan Petersen calls "the special relationship with the animal creation" found in Jerome's lives of the miracle-workers.[17]

Explanations like those of Palaephatus naturally recur in the *Etymologies* by Isidore of Seville, especially in his discussion of portents (11.3). Fabulous stories are false but contain a bit of truth that can be sifted by using etymology as a strainer.

3 Dragons

In his *Commentary on John* Origen asked, "What sort of corporeal dragon was ever described as seen in the corporeal river of Egypt?"[18] Apollonius of Tyana, on the other hand, tells about hunting dragons in India,[19] while the fourth-century bishop Donatus of Euroea vanquished a dragon in Epirus. The beast was ravaging "sheep, goats, oxen, horses, and men" when the bishop made the sign of the cross and spat. His saliva fell on the dragon's mouth and it immediately died. It was assessed as larger than the dragons of Indian fable, for the natives needed eight oxen to drag the corpse to a plain where it could be burned without polluting the air.[20] In 1125 the Venetians took Donatus' body to the island of Murano for reburial in the church now of Santa Maria e Donato.[21] Four of the dragon's bones, recovered somehow, now hang on the wall behind the altar.

At Rome an old tradition held that virgins were offered to a dragon in the Roman Forum.[22] Perhaps Tertullian alludes to it when he mentions Vestals and a dragon, though his dragon may come from Revelation.[23] It is clearer in three fourth-century versions. First, a certain Antonius tells how Vestal virgins took meals to the dragon every five years before Christians stopped the practice, holding that the dragon either was non-existent or was the devil.[24] The *Life of St. Sylvester* claims that pagan priests asked Constantine to send food to the dragon, since 6,000 people were dying daily (none of them Christians). After the apostle Peter appeared to Sylvester of Rome and told him to go in with three presbyters and two deacons, they sealed up the lair of the dragon, in which Satan was active.[25] Pseudo-Prosper, more interested in pagan mechanical devices, treats it as one of these. He has already explained that an iron chariot seeming to float in the air in the temple of Serapis at Alexandria was really held up by a powerful magnet. Now he turns to the cave at Rome in which lived a huge dragon with flashing gems for eyes. Virgins were sacrificed to it every year until a monk went down and boldly sliced it up.[26]

We must also mention the dragon first captured by prayer and the sign of the cross, then slain, by George, a Christian knight from Cappadocia, even though the legend does not antedate the medieval period. One version says that "four ox-carts were needed to carry the carcass to a safe distance."[27]

At some time or other a certain Saint Margaret was in prison when

Plate 6 Snake, from *Der Physiologus: Tiere und ihre Symbolik*, © Artemis Verlag AG, Zurich, 1995, p. 19.

a horrible dragon suddenly came out of a corner of her cell. Its hair and beard were golden, its teeth seemed to be iron, its eyes gleamed like pearls, fire and smoke came out of its nostrils, its tongue panted. Above its neck it was a snake, a shining sword was seen in its hand, and it made a stink in the cell. It dragged itself to the middle of the cell and loudly hissed, and a light shone in the cell from the fire out of the dragon's mouth. . . . It opened its mouth and placed it over her head and stretched its tongue over her heel, and inhaling it swallowed her into its belly.

She had previously made a cross of Christ for herself, and

this broke in the dragon's mouth and split it into two parts. The blessed Margaret emerged from the dragon's belly without suffering pain. When she looked to the left she saw the devil sitting there and looking like a black man with hands bound to knees.[28]

Modern editors of the Lives of the Saints are severely critical of this episode.[29]

4 The phoenix

The fantastic bird the phoenix appears in Christian literature of the late first century, when Clement of Rome used the phoenix as a "paradoxical sign" of the resurrection. Every 500 years, somewhere near Arabia, the unique phoenix builds a sepulchre with frankincense and myrrh and dies in it. Its decaying flesh spontaneously generates a worm which develops into another phoenix. The new bird takes the sepulchre, with its predecessor's bones, to the altar of the sun at Heliopolis in Egypt, where priests check registers and confirm the time interval.[30] This legend is true because attested not only by these priests but by God, "who shows us the greatness of his promise [of resurrection] through a bird."[31]

Several Roman authors had thought the phoenix was important. Discussing spontaneous generation, Ovid tells the story, ascribes it to "the Assyrians," and claims that "if there is any wondrous novelty here," the hyena's change of sex is equally marvelous (see Chapter 4).[32] Seneca refers in passing to its birth once in 500 years.[33] Tacitus mentions the appearance of the bird in Egypt in the year AD 34, after either 500 or 1,461 years. He says that "the details are uncertain and heightened by myth, but there is no question that the bird sometimes appears in Egypt."[34] In fact, however, the story did not go unquestioned. Pliny describes the bird and its spontaneous generation from ashes and shares important details with Clement, but

Plate 7 Vulture, woodcut from *Der Physiologus: Tiere und ihre Symbolik*,
© Artemis Verlag AG, Zurich, 1995, p. 32.

adds ambiguously that 11 years after arriving in Egypt it was taken to
Rome for the 800th year of the city (AD 47) "and displayed in the
Comitium, a fact attested by the Records, though no one would
doubt that it was false."[35] Aelian says the story is "common knowledge"; he summarizes details to emphasize the miracle. Priests at
Heliopolis in Egypt argue about the 500-year period, but then "the
divine bird" appears after miraculously guessing the period by signs,
finding Egypt and Heliopolis, taking its father to a definite location,
and knowing what kind of coffin to make.[36] In any event, Clement
must have heard that the phoenix was at Rome about a generation
before he wrote.

Attitudes toward the phoenix vary among Hellenistic Jewish
authors. The tragedian Ezekiel gladly included an appearance of
the phoenix among the miracles at the Exodus,[37] but neither Philo
nor Josephus mentions it. Patristic attitudes also vary. No second-
century Christian mentions the bird, and at a point where Theophilus

was copying Clement's analogies for resurrection he left it out. Clement (24–25) had noted the "resurrection" of day and night, seeds and fruit, and the phoenix. Theophilus spoke first of the resurrection of seasons, days, and nights, and seeds and fruits. Then he referred to a bird as excreting a seed that grew into a tree, and added the resurrection of the moon and the restoration of weight in healthy human beings.[38] Evidently he was trying to provide analogies of a more rational character. Irenaeus did not mention it at all; in his opinion no one knew even where birds generally go in winter.[39] In his *Miscellanies* Clement of Alexandria paraphrases much of the letter of "the apostle Clement,"[40] but not the section about the phoenix, a bird he mentions elsewhere only as an Egyptian astrological symbol.[41] Presumably he did not accept the story. The anti-Christian author Celsus definitely refers to it as "the Arabian bird, which after many years visits Egypt, and brings its dead father . . . and puts him in the shrine of the sun," but Origen hesitates over the truth of the story ("if he made a unique creature") and wants Celsus to marvel at the Creator, not the "unique animal" (a phrase from 1 Clement).[42] It appears, however, in Tertullian, Cyril of Jerusalem, Epiphanius ("it has come to the ears of many believers and unbelievers"), Ambrose, Rufinus, and the liturgical *Didascalia Apostolorum* and *Apostolic Constitutions*. Fortunately, Eusebius hesitated ("they say"), as did Gregory of Nazianzus and Augustine, and Photius finally said No, though at the same time he mistakenly rejected Clement's notion that there are lands beyond the Ocean.[43] How could he tell?

5 Other unreal beasts

In his early treatise *On First Principles* Origen discusses Hebrew dietary laws that cannot be kept and claims that no one would ever eat a vulture (Lev. 11:14); the goat-stag (Deut. 14:5 in Codex Alexandrinus) cannot exist; and there is no evidence for the griffin (Lev. 11:13; Deut. 14:12).[44] Plato had cited the goat-stag as an invention of painters.[45] Herodotus, however, describes gold-mining ants "bigger than foxes," and Aelian was willing to rely on what he had heard or read about griffins, winged quadrupeds of India that dig up gold and guard it against men.[46] Clement of Alexandria after Herodotus knows that ants mine gold but adds that griffins guard gold while the sea hides pearls.[47] When opposing Celsus several decades later, Origen more credulously stated that irrational griffins, as well as elephants, surpass human beings in size, strength, and length of life.[48] The Byzantine redaction of the *Physiologus* says, as one would expect, that the griffin is an enormous bird of the East.[49]

41

The chimaera also deserves attention. Homer tells about "the raging chimaera, of divine race, not of men; in face a lion, in after parts a dragon, a she-goat in between, breathing the dread might of blazing fire, which Bellerophon slew, trusting the wonders of the gods."[50] Plato refers to it, along with Scylla and Cerberus, as derived from ancient myth about many ideal forms grown into one,[51] and this passage is included in a short Gnostic tractate (6.5) from Nag Hammadi.[52] The late third-century Christian Methodius allegorizes the many-headed and many-faced beast, quoting *Iliad* 6.181–83 but substituting the wonders of "the Father" for the wonders of "the gods," and Christianizing two more verses.[53] Long before, Palaephatus had suggested that the chimaera was a volcano in Lycia.[54]

Aristotle had discussed something like the unicorn,[55] but while pagans were concerned with an animal said to be real, most Christians relied exclusively on biblical references and took them allegorically. Justin, using Deuteronomy 33:17 LXX for the plural "horns" of the singular unicorn, treated it as a figure of the cross.[56] Clement and Origen, followed by Eusebius, found an allegory of Christ in it.[57] Tertullian too found Christ in the unicorn, and while he also identified it as a rhinoceros, the reference presumably comes from Aquila's Greek Old Testament.[58] The more literal-minded Arian historian Philostorgius is the first to give it the head of a dragon, the body of a deer, and the feet of a lion. It lives in Arabia, he says, where you also find huge elephants, dragons, the cameleopard (giraffe), the sphinx (here a kind of monkey), and the phoenix.[59] Emphasis on the single horn appears in the *Physiologus*, along with further legends

Plate 8 Whale, from *Der Physiologus: Tiere und ihre Symbolik*, © Artemis Verlag AG, Zurich, 1995, p. 29.

(section 22). Ambrose appeals to "experts" who reject the unicorn as "not found in nature."[60] Cosmas Indicopleustes admits he has not seen one, but he knows of four bronze images of it "in the four-towered palace of the King of Ethiopia." Cosmas did not actually view every strange Indian animal he describes in his eleventh book; he says he saw the rhinoceros in Ethiopia, saw and ate the pig-deer (*choirelaphos*) in India, and saw many hippopotami in Ethiopia and Egypt. At Alexandria he even sold some big hippopotamus teeth that weighed 13 pounds.[61]

A beast rarely seen was the satyr, usually confused with Silenus. This wild spirit of woods and hills, always sexually excited, supposedly misbehaved on islands in "the outer sea." Hesiod called them "worthless and unfit for work." Centuries later, one was caught by a Thessalian shepherd and brought to the Roman general Sulla. After linguists questioned it, it gave a cry between a whinny and a bleat and was released.[62] According to Pliny the Indian satyr was extremely fast, running sometimes like a quadruped, sometimes erect.[63] Jerome tells how one was shown at Alexandria but died in captivity and in a hot summer was embalmed in salt for shipment to Antioch, where the emperor Constantius could view it. The ascetic Antony, when directed to Paul the hermit by a centaur, encountered a satyr in the desert.[64]

6 A sea monster on land

According to the fourth Vision of the *Shepherd* of Hermas, Hermas himself was going from Rome into the country along the Via Campana when he went into a trance and out of a cloud of dust there appeared a "great beast like some sea monster," 100 feet long with a pottery head of four colors: black, flame-blood, gold, and white. Fiery locusts were going out of its mouth. When Hermas approached, the beast simply lay down and stuck out its tongue. An envisioned virgin explained to him that the beast was "a type of the great persecution which is to come." She added that its colors were meaningful: the black meant this world, flame-blood referred to the destruction of this world, gold was the Christian, purified in the flames, and white was the world to come. Hermas does not attempt a realistic definition of the animal, but says only that "the Lord sent his angel named Thegri, who is over the beast . . . and shut his mouth so that he would not hurt you" (ending with Dan. 6:22 in the version of Theodotion). The context is apocalyptic. Jerome adds only a little confusion by denouncing an apocryphal book, presumably Hermas, in which "Tyri" is the lord of reptiles.[65]

4

ALEXANDRIANS AND
THE *PHYSIOLOGUS*

1 Philo of Alexandria. 2 The beasts of Barnabas. 3 Clement.
4 Origen. 5 Dionysius. 6 Didymus. 7 The *Physiologus*.

In the Hellenistic age the allegorical method was linked with literature, philosophy, and theology at Alexandria, especially in the exegesis of Homer and the Bible. For the Bible we find it in the fragments
of the Jewish teacher Aristobulus and the so-called *Letter of Aristeas*.

1 Philo of Alexandria

The most famous Jewish allegorizer was Philo of Alexandria, an older
contemporary of Jesus, whose treatise *On Animals* is a conventional
dialogue in which his nephew first argues for the rationality of
animals (cc. 1–72) and Philo himself then rejects it (cc. 73–100).
In the first part he lists some animals that had "instinctively learned
the self-taught art of healing." These were deer that ate hops against
spider bites, Cretan goats that ate dittany to heal wounds from
arrows, and tortoises that ate marjoram after injudiciously devouring
asps.[1] These were conventional, and their like would recur with the
Christian author Tatian.

He naturally touches on animals again when discussing the
prohibition of specific foods. First, he explains that Moses opposes
gluttony because the forbidden animals of land, sea, and air are
those whose flesh is "the finest and fattest" (notably pork). Second,
there are philosophical and moral lessons taught symbolically by the
various species. A divided hoof and chewing the cud are symbols of
teaching, fins and scales of self-control, while reptiles are slaves of
the passions. At the end of his discussion he returns to the literal
and practical: carnivorous birds are bad for the human being who
eats them.[2]

Proverbial wisdom is expounded by talking animals in the fables
ascribed to Aesop. As Philo's nephew puts it, "though animals lack

the ability to speak, no fable [of Aesop] is created but that it substantiates their wisdom and knowledge in many ways." Philo agrees but is unenthusiastic. "I was nurtured on such instructions throughout childhood, on account of their certainty, intriguing names, and easy comprehension."[3]

The statements by Philo and his nephew are of course conventional. Aesop's fables had a part to play in Greek and Latin rhetorical education. Early on, Aristotle mentioned them, and so did the teachers of the second through the fifth century A.D.[4] A little after Philo, Quintilian urged beginners to "learn to paraphrase Aesop's fables, which come very close to the fables told by nurses, in simple language without anything immoderate."[5] Few authors discussed their verisimilitude or lack of it.

2 The beasts of Barnabas

The Christian apocryphal letter of Barnabas comes from the late first century and probably from Alexandria, where allegorical exegesis of the Old Testament continued to flourish.

The dietary laws of the Pentateuch remained hard to fathom, and most Christians, who did not observe them, looked for allegorical interpretations.[6] Barnabas treats some of the animals involved as immoral.[7] First comes the pig (Lev. 11:7–8; Deut. 14:8), greedy for food. Next there are four birds which rob others: eagle, hawk, kite, and crow (Lev. 11:13–16). Barnabas mentions three kinds of fish without scales (Lev. 11:10; Deut. 14:9–10), but not one is specifically named in the Old Testament: the lamprey, octopus, and cuttlefish, which do not swim but live at the bottom of the sea.[8] The most immoral animals of all, he claims, are the hare (Lev. 11:5),[9] the hyena, and the weasel (Lev. 11:29). Barnabas' statement presents at least two problems.[10] First, Moses does not mention the hyena or any of the fish in question. Second, Barnabas oddly claims that the hare grows a new anus annually,[11] while the hyena changes sex every year[12] and the weasel conceives through the mouth.[13] These notions were sometimes found in collections of animal lore, but the authoritative Aristotle had explicitly rejected two of them. For Barnabas the animals are equivalent to various kinds of sinful men, for after "Moses received three decrees concerning food and spoke thus in the Spirit [allegorically]," the Jewish people took them literally of food because of "the lust of the flesh." Only David in Psalm 1 set forth the true understanding of the three decrees: "Blessed is the man who has not gone in the counsel of the ungodly" (fish) "and has not stood in the way of sinners" (pig), "and has not sat in the seat of the scorners" (birds). Swine while eating do not recognize their masters but later cry out for food and again turn to silence. So human beings forget the Lord in time of plenty but recognize him in time of want. The four birds do not work for a living but plunder the property of others. The fish live in darkness on the bottom of the sea. Such crude moralisms serve only to bypass the dietary laws.

3 Clement

The primary work of Clement of Alexandria, in eight books, was his *Stromateis* or *Miscellanies*. Like Aelian, he used a good source (an epitome of Aristotle's *History of Animals* by Aristophanes of Byzantium), but added a good deal of erudite nonsense. As an Alexandrian, Clement is naturally concerned with Egyptian matters. He refers to "the gods of Egypt such as cats and weasels," as well as "cat or crocodile or native snake."[14] On a literary level he analyzes Egyptian writing as epistolographic (= demotic) or hieratic or hieroglyphic. There are two kinds of hieroglyphs, literal and symbolical, while the symbolical in turn is divided into three: (1) literal by imitation (the sun is a circle, the moon looks like a moon), (2) figurative, and (3) allegorical using enigmas. He illustrates the third type by stars depicted as snakes because of their oblique orbits, the sun as a beetle because it fashions a ball of ox-dung and rolls it before its face.[15] Later he discusses the symbolical meanings of animals in the hieroglyphs. Some Egyptians show the sun on a ship, others on a crocodile; they mean that the sun generates time, or else that the crocodile symbolizes time. On the sacred Pylon at Diospolis there was a boy, the symbol of generation, and an old man, decay. A hawk was the symbol of God, a fish of hatred, while the crocodile can mean shamelessness. Taken together, the symbols mean this: "You who are born and die, God hates shamelessness." (This last account is close to Plutarch, except that he locates the carving in the temple of Athena at Sais and identifies the shameless animal as the hippopotamus.[16]) In addition, the lion symbolizes strength and vigor; the ox, agriculture and nourishment; the horse, courage and boldness; the sphinx, strength with understanding, for it has the body of a lion, the face of a man. A man symbolizes intelligence, memory, power, and art. In the processions of the gods they carry gold images: two dogs, one hawk, and one ibis. The dogs symbolize two hemispheres; the hawk the sun, the ibis the moon; or else the dogs are the tropics, the hawk the equinoctial line, and the ibis the ecliptic.[17] The errors in this exegesis are comparable only to those in the *Hieroglyphics* of Horapollo,[18] who wrote several centuries after Clement, but relied on similar sources. Both authors took the symbols seriously but did not know what they meant.

When Clement attacked anthropomorphists who held that God literally enjoys smelling the smoke of sacrifices (Gen. 8:21), he turned to natural history for analogies. Do insects breathe or not? Clement marshalled a scientific account of breathing, to combat the idea that God breathes. Aristotle (*On Respiration*) had argued that insects do not breathe because when centipedes are cut up the parts stay alive, and flies and bees can swim in liquid for a long time.[19] On the other hand, in his *History of Animals* he noted that all insects die if covered with oil, a point suggesting that they do breathe.[20] Clement deals with the question by defining terms. Plants are nourished from the density of the air,[21] while hibernating bears are nourished from the exhalation arising from their own bodies.[22] Demons ventilate internally (*diapneitai*).[23] Fish inhale (*empneitai*) through the dilation of their gills.[24] Insects circumspire (*peripneitai*) through pressure of membranes on the waist.[25] Finally, there are creatures that inhale (*anapnei*) by rhythmic beats corresponding to the counter-dilation (*antidiastolē*)[26] of the lungs against the chest. A little later, Clement notes that land animals and birds inhale as human beings do, though fish breathe the air infused into the water at the creation. Theophilus too had remarked on this infusion.[27]

Clement dealt with diet from points of view both moral and philosophical. He quoted Paul as saying, "It is good not to eat meat or drink wine" (shortened from Romans 14:21), in agreement with the Pythagoreans – for whose opinions he quotes the Stoic Musonius Rufus: "meat, though appropriate for wild animals, darkens the soul." He adds, however, that he who eats meat sparingly does not sin.[28] In his view the best diet consists of bulbs, olives, herbs, milk, cheese, fruits, and "all kinds of cooked food without sauces." (The list comes from Plato through Plutarch.) But Clement is willing to include meat, preferably roasted, not boiled. He cites the frugal disciples, who offered the risen Lord "a piece of broiled fish, which he ate before them" (Luke 24:42–43).[29]

In a later work Clement reflects deeper concerns. Christians can abstain from meat on reasonable grounds, not the Pythagorean dream about the transmigration of souls. One might abstain because animal meat has "already been assimilated to the souls of irrational creatures." In addition, wine and meat harm the mind, as (the Pythagorean) Androcydes said.[30] Similarly one of the late second-century *Sayings of Sextus*, authoritative for both Clement and Origen, claims that though abstinence is more rational, eating animate beings is really a matter of indifference.[31]

Egyptian priests in their purifications abstain from meat and fish, for "such food makes the flesh flabby."[32] Elsewhere Clement lists a few fishes "venerated" at various places: one kind at Syene, another at

Elephantine, yet another at Oxyrhynchus.[33] This kind of information reflects the interests of the age, not those of Christians generally save for the literary-minded author himself.

He also tells how some Phoenician Syrians "venerate" fishes, while Porphyry mentions Syrians in general, as well as initiates into the mysteries at Eleusis. The Christian apologist Athenagoras says Syrians "venerate" fish because of the mythical Derceto (who had a fish's tail).[34] "Venerate" again means "not eat."

Clement identifies the serpent with the devil but usually, after Philo, relates his work to pleasure.[35] He adds that the serpent is now the cause of idol-worship, and acts like barbarians who bind their captives to corpses. The simile comes from the *Exhortation* of Aristotle, but Clement obviously makes it his own.[36]

Since Clement knew something of zoology he could question animal lore, either tacitly or explicitly. In his *Miscellanies* he paraphrases much of the letter of "the apostle Clement,"[37] but not the section about the phoenix, a bird he mentions elsewhere only as an Egyptian astrological symbol.[38] Presumably he did not accept the story. When he commented on Barnabas, whom he regarded as an apostle,[39] he relied on Aristotle for questioning the story about the hyena, though without naming either the apostle or the philosopher. He agreed with Barnabas that Moses spoke allegorically but rejected his ideas about what he meant. "I do not agree with this exegesis of what was said symbolically."[40] Closer to Aristotle than to Barnabas, Clement says the hare really has a bifurcated uterus.[41] And as for the weasel, the Hellenistic Jewish *Epistle of Aristeas* said that the weasel conceives through the ear and gives birth through the mouth; Plutarch states that "many suppose and say that the weasel conceives through the ear and gives birth through the mouth."[42] Harnack and others thought Zeno of Verona was expressing a like thought when he said that "Christ enters Mary through the ear."[43] They did not notice that Zeno was simply giving allegorical exegesis of the angel's speaking a word to her, just as when he said that the devil crept into Eve through her ear.[44] This was not Barnabas' notion.

The author of the *Clementine Recognitions* rather sensibly supposed that these unusual habits prove that the Creator specifically chose the usual modes of conception and birth as norms.[45] The *Physiologus*, as usual, went back to gossip, claiming that the hyena is androgynous, alternating sexes,[46] while the weasel conceives through the mouth and gives birth through the ears.[47] The latter statement simply reverses Aristeas' notion.[48]

4 Origen

In his early theological work *On First Principles* Origen denied the literal veracity of the whole creation story.[49]

> Who is stupid enough to think that like a farmer God planted a garden in Eden to the east and in the garden made a tree of life, visible and perceptible to the senses, of such a kind that he who ate its fruit with his physical teeth would receive life? And again, that anyone would participate in good and evil by having eaten fruit taken from this tree? If God is represented as walking at evening in the garden and Adam as hiding under the tree, I believe one cannot doubt that all this signifies certain mysteries, expressed in a historical narrative that seems to have taken place but did not take place corporeally.

Origen sees in the serpent not a zoological phenomenon but – like his predecessors – the devil, who was actively tempting Adam and Eve.

This is not to say that on Origen's view nothing really happened in Eden, or that the snake was not the devil in disguise.[50] Nature also gave him an analogy to the conception of Jesus from a virgin.

> The Creator showed in the birth of various animals that what he did in the case of one animal he could do, if he wished, also with others and even with human beings. Among the animals there are certain females that have no intercourse with the male, as writers on animals say of vultures. This animal preserves the continuation of the species without any copulation.[51]

To be sure, Aristotle had already disposed of the fable[52] (though he did not reject all instances of spontaneous generation), and Pliny reported only that vultures "make their nests on extremely lofty crags."[53] Plutarch, however, says that in Egyptian myth vultures are female and conceive by breathing the east wind, and Aelian tells the same story.[54] Basil takes Origen's analogy and amplifies it slightly.[55]

Origen generally uses anecdotes about animals and birds to provide moral models.[56] Four examples will suffice.

1   The bad character of the partridge had appeared in writings on zoology, and Origen ultimately relied on Aristotle's *History of Animals* for the partridge's protection of its young by tricking hunters[57] and for the bird's lustfulness.[58]

2 Agreeing with Aristotle, Polybius, and Pliny, Origen held that the aged lion haunts towns to hunt men.[59] Fire comes out of its broken bones. Aristotle too had noted that the lion fears fire but not that fire comes out of his bones; the latter notion appears in Aelian as well as Origen.[60]

3 The name *dorkas* for deer "according to their physiology" (perhaps an allusion to *Physiologus* 41, which however lacks the etymology) comes from *derkomai*, "I see," in reference to their acute vision.[61] They are enemies of snakes, and by their breath drag them from their holes and eat them.[62] Those skilled in medicine say that the deer has a humor in its viscera that dispels mist before its eyes.[63] Origen thus refers his discussion of the deer not only to physiology and medicine but also to "the physiology of those who dispute on the natures of animals."[64]

4 The turtledove of the Song of Songs (2:13) is remarkable for its monogamy and love of solitude; when the female dies, the male's desire for intercourse dies too.[65]

Aristotle also wrote a short treatise *On Longevity and Shortness of Life*, and stated in his generalizing manner that the longest-lived of all were land animals with blood such as man and the elephant.[66] In replying to Celsus Origen named two long-lived animals, the griffin and the elephant.[67] We have already discussed his remarks on insects and instinct.

5 Dionysius

Origen's successor Dionysius, attacking Epicurean atomism, also discussed longevity and argued that Epicurus' uniform atoms could not account for variations in the longevity of animals and plants. Dionysius began with animals, first such birds as eagles, ravens, and phoenixes, next land animals such as deer, elephants, and dragons, and finally one example of a marine animal, the whale. Among trees he lists date-palms, oaks, *perseai*, and evergreens, supposedly totalling fourteen.[68] Most animals and plants, he says, are short-lived. This kind of discussion shows how far Alexandrian Christians had gone toward zoology.

6 Didymus

Toward the end of the fourth century Didymus the Blind was a vigorous Origenist allegorizer. Rufinus and Jerome heard him comment on scripture in 374 and 386.[69] Pierre Nautin found that his commentary on Genesis, discovered in papyrus,[70] was deeply influenced by Origen, much less so by Theophilus. Didymus discussed

que eſt in ſupiombs galilee.

Plate 9 Tobias, advised by archangel Raphael, catching the fish. From the Breviary of Martin of Aragon, Catalonia, Spain, fifteenth century. BNF ROTH 2529 fol. 263v, © Bibliothèque nationale de France.

animals in relation to Gen. 1:20–25, mostly according to *anagogē* (papyrus p. 44, 12) and "the laws of allegory" (45, 4).[71] As with Origen, natural history corroborated the exegesis. "Scripture calls quadrupeds all that are gentle and serviceable for men, beasts the useless quadrupeds, and reptiles the serpent-like; these differences are not unknown to naturalists" (49, 13–16). If, however, we ask how scripture can say that savage beasts and poisonous reptiles are "good," we find that "the exact reason for their existence is hidden from us" (50, 9–12). His discussion is based on the letter, but he insists that we must go on to spiritual contemplation (50, 24–25), and allegorize all the examples (51, 18–53, 26).

Didymus like Origen treats the "serpent" as the devil; he was "the father of evil" or (after Philo) pleasure.[72] The serpent was not a reptile "of such a nature as to emit a false word that would invite God to punish it," and Paul shows in 2 Corinthians 11:3 that it must have been what the scripture calls the devil. It was not perceptible to the senses.[73]

7 The *Physiologus*

The *Physiologus* is an anthology, partly from the second century, that uses the traits of many animals in order to draw moral or theological lessons from their behavior or illustrate biblical texts.[74] The author/editor's constant comment, "The Physiologus spoke well about" the animals, might encourage separation of the older accounts from the newer allegorical additions (except where nothing older existed and the story was simply created as an allegory), but the book has little point without the allegories. After F. Sbordone in his great edition differentiated an "original" edition from at least two Byzantine revisions, D. Offermanns printed a text close to this original from the manuscripts G (Pierpont Morgan 397, tenth–eleventh century) and M (Ambrosianus graec., A 41 sup., eleventh–twelfth century).[75] My translation is based primarily on Sbordone, with occasional use of Offermanns.

1 The lion

We shall begin speaking with the lion, the king of beasts. For Jacob when blessing Judah said, "whelp of a lion is Judah, from a shoot, my son, you went up, etc." The Physiologus said of the lion that it has three traits. The first trait is this: when it walks on a mountain and the smell of hunters comes to it, it conceals its tracks with its tail so that the hunters will not follow its tracks, find its den, and capture it.[76]

Thus also our Christ, the spiritual lion, sent by the invisible Father, covered his spiritual tracks, that is, his divinity. With angels he became an angel, with archangels an archangel, with thrones a throne, with powers a power,[77] until his descent; and he came to the womb of the holy virgin Mary so that he might save the lost race of men; "and the Logos became flesh and dwelt among us" (John 1:14). Therefore in ignorance of him, those who descended from above said, "Who is this king of glory?" Then the Holy Spirit says, "The Lord of powers, he is the king of glory" (Ps. 23:10).

The second trait of the lion is that when it sleeps in its cave its eyes watch, for they are open.[78]

And in the Canticles (5:2) Solomon testifies, saying, "I sleep and my heart watches." Thus the body of my Lord sleeps on the cross, but his deity watches from the right hand of the God and Father: "For he who keeps Israel neither slumbers nor sleeps" (Ps. 120:4).

The third trait of the lion: when the lioness bears her cub she bears it dead, and she watches over the young until on the third day its father comes and breathes into its face and raises it.[79]

Thus our God the Almighty, the Father of all, on the third day raised from the dead his Son, first-born before all creation, our Lord Jesus Christ. So Jacob well said, "Falling he slept like a lion and a whelp; who will raise him?" (Gen. 49:9).

2 The solar lizard

There is a lizard called "solar," as the Physiologus says. When it grows old, its eyes are dimmed and it grows blind and it does not see the light of the sun. It seeks for a wall looking to the east and comes to a crack in the wall, and when the sun rises its eyes are opened and it becomes healthy again.[80]

In this way you too, O man, if you have the clothing of the old man and the eyes of your heart are dimmed, seek the rising sun of righteousness, Christ our God, and he will open the eyes of your heart.[81]

3 The plover

There is a bird called plover, as is written in Deuteronomy (14:18). The Physiologus said of it that the bird is all white, with no black at all. Its droppings heal cataracted eyes,[82] and it is found in royal palaces.[83] If anyone is sick, it is known from the plover whether he lives or dies; for they carry it before the sick person in his bed, and if the man's disease is for death, the plover turns its face from the sick one and all know that he is dying; but if the man's disease is for life the plover looks at the sick one and the sick one at the plover, and the plover consumes the disease of the sick one and flies up to the aether of the sun and burns the disease of the sick one and scatters it, and the plover and the sick one are preserved together.[84]

It is good to refer this to the person of the Savior, for our Lord is all white, with no black at all; for he said that "the prince of this world comes, and he will find nothing in me" (John 14:30). For when the Lord came from heaven to the Jews he turned away his divinity from them; but when he came to us gentiles and took our weaknesses and bore our diseases (Is. 53:4) he was raised up on the wood of the cross and he blotted out (Col. 2:14) all our weaknesses and sins. Ascending on high, he led captivity captive (Ps. 67:19). The Physiologus spoke well about the plover.

But you will tell me that the plover is unclean according to the law (Deut. 14:18) and how is it referred to the person of the Savior? But though the serpent is unclean, John testified that "as Moses lifted up the serpent in the desert, so the Son of Man must be lifted up" (John 3:14). For the creatures are twofold, to be praised and blamed.

4 *The pelican*

Well does David say, "I am become like a pelican of the desert" (Ps. 101:7). The Physiologus said of the pelican that it is devoted to its offspring. When it generates chicks and they grow a little, they strike their parents' faces and the parents beat the young and kill them. Later their parents take pity and mourn for three days for the offspring they killed. On the third day their mother strikes her side and her blood drips on the dead bodies of the chicks and raises them.[85] Thus also the Lord said in Isaiah, "I generated sons and raised them up, but they rejected me" (Is. 1:2). For the Fashioner of all creation generated us, and we beat him. How did we beat him? We worshiped the creation instead of the Creator. By coming to the height of the cross and opening his side, our Savior shed the blood and the water for salvation and eternal life: the blood because it says, "Taking the cup he blessed it"; the water at the baptism of repentance.

The second trait of the pelican.[86] It is a bird, and the snake is a great enemy of its chicks.[87] What does it do? It fixes the nest at a height, and guards it on all sides because of the snake. What does the maleficent snake do? It watches to see where the wind is from and thence breathes its poison on the chicks and they die. The pelican comes and sees that its offspring have died, and it flies to the height and beats its sides with its wings, and blood comes forth, and it bleeds on them and they are raised.

5 *The night owl*

The Psalmist said, "I became like a night owl in a house" (101:7). The Physiologus said of the night owl that this bird loves night more than day.[88]

So also our Lord Jesus Christ loved us who sat in darkness and the shadow of death, the people of the gentiles more than the people of the Jews, who inherited the promise of the fathers. Therefore the Savior said, "Fear not, little flock, for the Father has been pleased to give you the kingdom," etc.

But you will tell me that the night owl is unclean according to the law (Deut. 4:17), and how is it referred to the person of the Savior? Rightly; and how does the Apostle say, "Him who knew not sin, he made sin for us" (2 Cor. 5:21). He humbled himself so that he might save all and we might be exalted. The Physiologus spoke well about the night owl.

6 *The eagle*

David says, "Your youth will be renewed like the eagle's" (Ps. 102:6). The Physiologus said of the eagle that when it grows old its eyes and wings are weighed down and it is dim-sighted. What does it do? It seeks a pure spring of water and flies to the aether of the sun, burns its old wings and the feebleness of its eyes, descends to the spring and bathes three times, is renewed and becomes young.[89]

Thus you, O man, if you have the clothing of the old man and the eyes of your heart are dimmed, look for the spiritual spring, the Word of God, who says, "They abandoned me, the spring of living water" (Jer. 2:13); and fly up to the height of the sun of righteousness, Jesus Christ, and put off the old man with his deeds and wash three times in the ever-flowing spring, in the name of the Father and the Son and the Holy Spirit; and put off the old man, that is the old clothing of the devil, and put on the new, created in accordance with God, and the prophecy of David will be fulfilled in you: "Your youth will be renewed like the eagle's."

7 *The phoenix bird*

The Lord said in the Gospel, "I have power to lay down my life, and I have power to take it again," and the Jews were vexed by the word (John 10:18). There is a bird in India called phoenix. Every 500 years it comes to the forests of Lebanon and fills its wings with spices, and signals to the priest of Heliopolis on the new month, Nisan or Adar, that is, Phamenoth or Pharmouthi. The signalled priest comes and fills the altar with vine-wood, while the bird comes to Heliopolis, laden with the spices, and ascends to the altar, lights the fire, and burns itself up. The next day the priest, searching the altar, finds a worm in the ashes. On the second day he finds the chick of the bird, and on the third day he finds the mature bird and it greets the priest and goes to its own place.[90]

If then this bird has the power to kill and make itself alive, how are the stupid Jews vexed by the Lord's saying, "I have power to lay down my life and I have power to take it again"? The phoenix assumes the role of our Savior, for when he came from heaven, spreading his two wings, he carried them full of sweet scent, that is of virtuous heavenly words, so that we might extend our hands in prayer and send up a spiritual sweet smell through good lives. The Physiologus spoke well about the phoenix.

8 *The hoopoe bird*

It is written, "He who curses father or mother shall surely die" (Exod. 21:16), and how are some patricides and matricides? There is a bird called hoopoe whose offspring, if they see their parents aging, pluck out their old wings, lick their eyes, warm the parents under their wings, make a nest for them, so that their parents become young. They say to their parents, "As you nested us and labored, toiling and feeding us, so we shall do the like for you."[91]

And how can stupid men not love their parents? The Physiologus spoke well about the hoopoe.

9 *The wild ass*

It is written in Job, "Who let the wild ass free?" (39:5). The Physiologus said of the wild ass that it leads a herd and if the strays produce males, their father cuts off their genitals so they will not produce sperm.[92]

The patriarchs sought to sow a physical seed, but the apostles, spiritual children, exercised continence, seeking a heavenly seed, as it is written, "Rejoice, barren woman not bearing children, break forth and shout, you without birth pangs, for the children of the deserted one are more than those of her who has a husband" (Gal. 4:27). The old is the seed of promise, the new, of continence.

The Physiologus spoke well about the wild ass.

10 *The viper*

Well did John say to the Pharisees, "Generation of vipers, who showed you how to flee from the wrath to come?" (Matt. 3:7; Luke 3:7) The Physiologus said of the viper that the male has the face of a man, the female, the face of a woman. To the navel they have a human form, but they have the tail of a crocodile.[93] The female has no vagina, just the eye of a needle; the male expels his sperm in her mouth. If she swallows it she cuts off his testicles and he dies immediately. As the offspring grow they eat the mother's stomach and come out; thus they are patricides and matricides.[94]

Well, then, did John compare the Pharisees with the viper; as the viper kills father and mother, so they killed their spiritual fathers, the prophets (he said) and our Lord Jesus Christ and the church. How then will they flee from the wrath to come? The father and the mother live forever, but these died.

56

11 *The snake*

The Lord said in the Gospel, "Be wise as snakes and sincere as doves" (Matt. 10:16). The Physiologus said of the snake that it has two traits. Its first trait is this: when it ages, its eyes are impeded [by cataracts], and if it wants to become young, it fasts for forty days and forty nights (Matt. 4:2) until its skin becomes loose; then it seeks a rock or a narrow crevice, squeezes itself against it, bruises its body, casts off old age, and becomes young again. In this way you too, O man, if you wish to cast off the old skin of the world, through the strait and narrow way, through fasting, reduce the body, "for strait and narrow is the way that leads to eternal life" (Matt. 7:14).

The second trait of the snake: when it comes to drink water at a spring it does not bring its poison with it but leaves it in its hole. So we too, when hastening to the ever-flowing and innocent water, full of divine and heavenly words, should not carry the poison of malice with ourselves in the church but cast it away entirely from ourselves and come in purity.

The third trait of the snake: when it sees a naked man, it is afraid and turns away.[95] When it sees him clothed it leaps against him. And we understand spiritually that when our father Adam was naked in paradise, the devil could not bind him. If then you have the clothing of the old man, that is the fig of pleasure, as one grown old with evil days, it attacks you.

The fourth trait of the snake: when a man approaches it and wants to kill it, it delivers its whole body to death, protecting only its head.[96] So also we, in a moment of temptation, ought to deliver our whole body to death, guarding only the head, that is, not denying Christ, like the holy martyrs; "for the head of every man is Christ," as it is written (1 Cor. 11:3).

12 *The ant*

Solomon said in Proverbs (6:6), "Go to the ant, O sluggard." The Physiologus said of the ant that it has three traits. This is its first trait: when they walk in line, each carries a seed in its mouth, and the empty ones that have nothing do not say to those with loads, "Give us some of your seeds," nor do they rob forcibly, but go away and collect for themselves. One can find these words spoken about the wise and foolish virgins (Matt. 25:8).

The second trait of the ant: when they store the grain in the ground they divide the seeds in two so that when winter comes they will not sprout again and the ants starve. And the perfect ascetics (must note) the words of the Old Covenant concealed by the Spirit, lest the letter kill you; for Paul said that "The law is spiritual" (Rom. 7:14). For by holding to the mere letter the Jews were killed by pestilence and became killers of the saints.

The third trait of the ant: often it goes into the field at harvest-time and climbs on the sheaf and takes the seed, but first smells the stalk of the sheaf and from the smell knows whether it is barley or wheat. And if it is barley it does not come up, but if wheat, it comes up and consumes the grain, for the grain is food for animals,[97] as Job said: "In place of wheat may barley come forth for me" (Job 31:40).

Flee, then, from animals' food and take the wheat laid up in the heavenly granary. For the barley parallels the teaching of the heterodox, but the wheat the most orthodox faith of Christ.

13 *Sirens and hippocentaurs*

Isaiah the prophet said that "demons and sirens and hedgehogs will dance in Babylon" (13:21–22). The Physiologus said of sirens and hippocentaurs, that there are sea animals called sirens, which like Muses sing beautifully. If sailors hear their melodies they jump overboard and drown. Their upper half, down to the navel, has a human shape, while the other half has that of a goose. Likewise hippocentaurs have a human upper half, while the lower is that of a horse.[98]

So every double-minded man is unstable in all his ways (James 1:8). There are some gathered in the church who have the form of piety but deny its force, and though they are in the church as men, when they depart from the church they become beasts. Such men take on the appearance of sirens and hippocentaurs, I mean of hostile powers and deceptive heretics. Because of their gentle speech and blessings, like the sirens they deceive the hearts of the simple. "For evil communications corrupt good manners" (1 Cor. 15:33). The Physiologus spoke well about the sirens and the hippocentaurs.

14 *Hedgehogs*

Hedgehogs have the shape of a ball and are prickly.[99] The Physiologus said of the hedgehog that it goes up a vine and comes to a cluster, casts a bunch on the ground, and lies on it. The grapes cling to its quills, and it goes to its offspring, leaving the branches bare.[100]

And you, O Christian, stand by the spiritual and true vine to be borne to the spiritual winepress and kept in the royal halls and reach the holy judgment seat of Christ. For how do you keep the hedgehog, the evil spirit, from entering your heart and leaving you empty like a bunch of grapes, with no branch at all in you?

15 *The fox*

The Physiologus said of the fox that it is a crafty animal, for when it is hungry and does not find an animal to eat, it seeks to find a pond or a shelter for chaff and throws itself in, looking upward, and holds its breath and blows hard. The birds think it is dead and settle on it to eat it, and thus it rises, seizes them and eats them.[101]

So also the devil is completely crafty, as are his deeds. He who wants to share in his flesh will die. For these are his flesh: acts of fornication, avarice, pleasure, murder.

This is why Herod resembled a fox (Luke 13:22)[102] and the scribe heard from the Savior, "The foxes have holes and the birds of the heaven have nests" (Matt. 8:20). And in the Canticles (2:15) Solomon says, "Catch for us the little foxes, for they destroy the vineyards." And David says in the Psalms (62:11), "They will be the portions of foxes," etc. The Physiologus spoke well about the fox.

16 *The panther*

The prophet prophesied and said, "I became like a panther to Ephraim" (Hos. 5:14). The Physiologus said of the panther that it has this trait: it is the most friendly of all animals, an enemy only of the snake.[103] It is as variegated and beautiful as Joseph's coat, and is gentle and mild. After it eats and is filled, it sleeps in its hole, and on the third day it is raised from sleep and cries out with a loud cry.[104] Beasts far and near hear its voice, and from its voice comes forth all the sweet smell of aromas, and the beasts, following the sweet smell of the panther's voice, come close to it.[105]

So also our Lord Jesus Christ, when he rose from the dead on the third day, cried out, "Today is salvation for the world, whatever is

Plate 10 Fish eats fish (Ostia). Photo by the author.

visible and invisible" (cf. Luke 19:9), and every aroma came to us, far and near, and peace, as the Apostle said (Eph. 2:17). The spiritual wisdom of God is variegated (Eph. 3:10), as it was said in the Psalm (44:10) also: "The queen stood at my right hand, wearing a variegated golden robe." So the divine scriptures say nothing aimlessly about birds and beasts. The Physiologus spoke well about the panther.

17 *The* Aspidocelonē

Solomon in Proverbs (5:3–5) gives instruction, saying,

> Do not turn to a bad woman, for honey drips from the lips of a prostitute and for a while she oils your throat but later you will find her more bitter than gall and sharper than a two-edged sword. The feet of foolishness bear those who use her to Hades with death.

There is a big fish in the sea called *aspidocelonē*,[106] with two traits. The first trait is this: if it is hungry it opens its mouth and all the sweet smell of spices comes out of its mouth[107] and the little fishes smell it and pile into its mouth and it swallows them. I do not find the large and mature fishes approaching the big fish.

So also the devil and the heretics through gentle speech and deceit, the seeming sweet smell, entrap those who are childish and immature in understanding but leave the mature steadfast in mind, such as Job (the mature fish), Moses, Isaiah, Jeremiah, and the whole chorus of the prophets; as Judith escaped Holophernes, Esther Artaxerxes, Susannah the elders, Thecla Thamyris.[108]

The other characteristic of the big fish: it is very large, like an island.[109] Sailors ignorantly moor their boats to it as on an island, fixing their anchors and pins and kindling a fire on the fish in order to cook something for themselves. When the fish gets hot it dives deep and sinks the boats.[110]

And you, if you cling to the hope of the devil, he will sink you as well as himself to the gehenna of fire. The Physiologus spoke well about the *aspidocelonē*.

18 *The partridge*

Jeremiah (17:11) the prophet says, "The partridge called, it gathered eggs it did not lay, making its wealth unjustly; in half its days they will abandon it, and at its end it will be a fool." The Physiologus said of the partridge that it warms the eggs of others and hatches them;

when they grow, each kind flies to its own parents and they leave the foolish bird alone.[111]

So the devil attacks those who are infants in intelligence (1 Cor. 14:20); but when they come to a measure of age, they begin to recognize their heavenly parents, that is, Christ and the church and the holy prophets and apostles, and they leave him alone as a fool. The Physiologus spoke well about the partridge.

19 *The vulture*

Well did our Lord and Savior say in the Gospel, "Woe to those who are pregnant and nursing in those days" (Mark 13:17 and parallels). The Physiologus said of the vulture that it dwells in lofty places and heights and sleeps on high rocks or mountain peaks. If it becomes pregnant it goes to India and takes the stone that aids in birth.[112] This stone has a circumference like a nut,[113] and if you wish to move it, another stone within it jumps, knocking and sounding like a bell. If the pregnant animal takes it, she sits over the birthing stone and gives birth without pain.

And you, O man, becoming pregnant with the Holy Spirit, take the spiritual stone of birth, rejected by the builders, which became the head of the corner (Ps. 117:22), and sit on it, as Isaiah the prophet (26:18) said, and you will bear a spirit of salvation: "Because of your fear, Lord, we became pregnant and suffered pangs and gave birth to a spirit of your salvation, which we made on earth." For truly he is the birthing stone of the Holy Spirit, our Lord Jesus Christ, cut without hands, that is, born of the virgin without insemination, and as the birthing stone has another stone sounding within it, so the body of the Lord had deity sounding within it. The Physiologus spoke well about the vulture.

20 *The ant-lion*

Eliphaz king of the Temanites said (Job 4:11), "The ant-lion perishes because it has no food." The Physiologus said of the ant-lion that it is a lion before, an ant behind. The father is a carnivore but the mother eats pulse. When they generate the ant-lion they generate it with two natures. It cannot eat meat because of the nature of its mother, nor pulse because of the nature of its father, and it perishes from lack of food.[114]

So also every two-souled man is unstable in all his ways. He must not go on two paths or speak doubly in prayer; for "woe," it says (Sir. 2:12–13) "to the double and sinful heart that goes on two paths." It is not good to say Yes for No and No for Yes, but "let

Yes be Yes and No No," as our Lord Jesus Christ said (Matt. 5:37). The Physiologus spoke well about the ant-lion.

21 *The weasel*

The law says (Lev. 11:29), "Do not eat weasel nor what is like it." The Physiologus said of the weasel that it has this trait: her mouth conceives from the male, and when pregnant she gives birth through the ears.[115]

There are some who eat the spiritual bread in the church, but when they go out, they cast out the word from their hearing, being like the unclean weasel, and become like a deaf asp with its ears stopped. So do not eat weasel or what is like it.

22 *The unicorn*

The Psalm (91:11) says: "And my horn will be exalted like that of a unicorn." The Physiologus said of the unicorn that it has this trait: it is a little animal like a kid, but very clever. A hunter cannot get near it because it is very strong, and it has one horn in the middle of its head.[116] How is it hunted? They place a pure virgin before it and it goes to her bosom and the virgin suckles the animal and takes it to the palace, to the king.[117]

The animal is referred to the person of the Savior: "He raised up a horn in the house of David" (Luke 1:69) our father, and he became a horn of salvation for us. Angels and powers were not able to hold him, but he tabernacled in the womb of the true pure virgin Mary. "And the Word became flesh and tabernacled among us" (John 1:14).

23 *The animal beaver*

There is an animal called beaver, a very gentle and quiet animal. Its testicles aid healing.[118] When it is pursued by hunters and knows it is caught, it cuts off its testicles and flings them to the hunter.[119] If it later encounters another hunter and is pursued, it throws itself on its back and shows itself to him, and the hunter thus knows it has no testicles and leaves it.[120]

And you too, Christian, give back what is his to the hunter. The hunter is the devil, his are fornication, adultery, murder. Cut off such and give them to the devil, and the huntsman devil will leave you so that you too may say, "Our soul like a sparrow was delivered from the snare of the hunters" (Ps. 123:7). The Physiologus spoke well about the beaver.

24 *The hyena*

The law says, "Do not eat hyena or what is like it."[121] The Physiologus said of the hyena that it is bisexual, sometimes male, sometimes female. It is a polluted animal because it changes sex.[122]

Therefore also Jeremiah (12:9) says, "Not the cave of a hyena is my inheritance." So do not be like the hyena, sometimes accepting the male nature, sometimes the female – whom the Apostle blamed when he said, "Males in males worked deeds of shame" (Rom. 1:27). The Physiologus spoke well about the hyena.

25 *The otter animal*

There is an animal called otter, with the shape of a dog. It is the enemy of the crocodile, and when the crocodile sleeps with its mouth open, the otter comes and smears its whole body with mud, and when the mud dries it leaps into the mouth of the crocodile, and eats all its passages and consumes its entrails.[123]

The crocodile is like the devil; the otter assumes the person of our Savior. Our Lord Jesus Christ taking flesh of earth descended to Hades and loosed the pangs of death, saying to those in bonds, Come forth, and to those in darkness, Be uncovered. And again the Apostle (1 Cor. 15:55): "Where is your victory, O death? Where is your sting, O Hades?" And Christ rose from the dead on the third day, raising with him the earthy substance.

26 *The ichneumon*

There is an animal called ichneumon, especially hostile toward the asp. When it finds an asp, as the Physiologus says, it goes and smears itself with mud, and covers its nostrils with its tail until it kills the snake.[124]

So also our Savior assumed the nature of the earthy race until he killed the dragon of Pharaoh that sits upon the river of Egypt, that is, the devil. For if Christ were bodiless how could he destroy the dragon? The dragon would answer him, "You are God and Savior, and I can do nothing to you." But the one greater than all humbled himself in order to save all.

27 *The crow*

Jeremiah (3:2) said to Jerusalem, "You sat deserted like a crow." The Physiologus said of the crow that it is monogamous and when its mate dies it no longer joins any other male, nor the male crow another female.[125]

The synagogue of the Jews, the earthly Jerusalem, that killed the Lord [. . .] For Christ is no longer her husband, "for I betrothed you to one husband to present a pure virgin to the Lord" (2 Cor. 11:2), but she committed adultery with the wood and the stone. If then we have the husband in our heart, the adulterous devil does not enter; but if the male word leaves our soul, the adversary slips in. "For he who keeps Israel neither slumbers nor sleeps" (Ps. 120:4). The Physiologus spoke well about the crow.

28 *The turtledove*

In the Canticles (2:13) Solomon testifies and says, "The voice of the turtledove was heard in our land." The Physiologus said of the turtledove that it is monogamous[126] and very solitary. It lives in the deserts and does not love to be in the midst of a crowd.

So also our Savior stayed on the Mount of Olives, taking Peter and James and John, and there appeared to them Moses and Elijah, and a voice from heaven, saying, "This is my beloved Son, in whom I am well pleased" (Mark 9:27 and parallels).[127] The Physiologus spoke well about the turtledove.

29 *The frog*

There is a land frog and a marine frog. The Physiologus said of the land frog that it bears the heat of the sun and the flaming fire, but when harsh winter takes it, it dies. If the marine frog comes out of the water and the sun touches it, it dives back into the water at once.[128]

The most noble Christians are like the land frog, for they bear the heat of temptations. If then winter violently comes upon them, that is, persecution because of virtue, they will die. But those of the world are marine, for when a light heat of temptation or lust touches them they cannot endure it but dive again on to the same longing for sexual intercourse. The Physiologus spoke well about the frog.

30 *The deer*

David says (Ps. 41:2), "As the deer longs for the water brooks, so my soul longs for you, O God." The Physiologus said of the deer that it is highly hostile to the snake. If the snake flees from the deer into the crevices of the earth, the deer proceeds to fill the hollows with spring water, vomits on the crevices of the earth, and takes the snake, cuts it up, and kills it.[129]

Thus our Lord killed the great serpent by the heavenly waters which he had (theologically speaking, virtuous wisdom). For the dragon could not endure the water, nor the devil, the heavenly word.

31 *The salamander*

There is an animal called salamander. The Physiologus said of it that if it enters a furnace of fire, the whole furnace is extinguished, and if it enters the hypocaust of a bath, the hypocaust is put out.[130]

If then the salamander puts out the fire by natural causes, how do some still not believe that the three children cast into the furnace were not harmed (Dan. 3) but on the contrary put out the furnace? For it is written (Is. 43:2) that "even if you go through fire the flame will not burn you."

32 *The diamond stone*

The Physiologus said of the diamond that it is found in the East, not during the day but during the night. It is called "adamant" because it dominates all and is dominated by none.[131]

Also our Lord Jesus Christ judges all, but he himself is judged by no one (cf. 1 Cor. 2:15). For he himself said, "Who among you convicts me of sin?" (John 8:46).

33 *The swallow*

When winter is past the swallow appears with the spring and speaks in the morning, waking sleepers up for work.[132] It gives birth once and no more.[133]

And the perfect ascetics, when the winter of the body has passed, that is, all lust for sexual intercourse, remember their Lord, meditating on him at daybreak, awaking those burdened with sleep to do good, and shouting, "Awake, you who sleep, and rise from the dead, and Christ will shine upon you" (Eph. 5:14). The Physiologus spoke well about the swallow.

34 *The ambidextrous tree*

There is a tree in India called ambidextrous. Its fruit is very sweet and very good. The doves feed on the fruit of that tree, and dwell under it. There is a snake hostile to the dove, but it fears that tree, and its shadow, in which the doves live, and the snake cannot get near the dove or the shadow of the tree. If then the shadow of the tree inclines to the western regions, the snake flees to the east; if the shadow comes to the east the snake flees to the west. If the dove wanders away from the tree in the dark, the snake finds it and kills it.[134]

The tree is understood as the Father of all, as Gabriel said to Mary: "Holy Spirit will come upon you, and the power of the Most High will overshadow you" (Luke 1:35). "For the tree of life is for all who hold to it" (Prov. 3:18), "it will give its fruit in its season" (Ps. 1:3), and "we hope in the shadow of your wings" (Ps. 56:3). And the shadow of the holy Peter drove corrupting death from men (Acts 5:15). If then we cling to wisdom and eat the fruits of the Spirit, that is, love, joy, peace, continence, endurance, the wicked devil does not draw near us; but if we wander in the acts of darkness, which are fornication, adultery, idolatry, passions, wicked lusts and covetousness, the devil will find us not remaining by the tree of life and will easily destroy us. Therefore the Apostle, knowing that the wood of the cross was destructive of the devil, cried out, "Far be it from me to boast except in the cross of Christ, through which the world was crucified to me and I to the world" (Gal. 6:14). The Physiologus spoke well about the ambidextrous tree.

35 *The dove*

John said that

> I saw the heavens opened and the Holy Spirit coming down like a dove from the heavens and remaining on him, and a voice came from the heavens, saying, This is my beloved Son, in whom I am well pleased.
>
> (Matt. 3:16–17; cf. John 1:32)

The Physiologus said of the dove that if the dove-keeper sends out all the doves they bring none in nor allow the other doves to enter the nest except for the fiery one that brings and persuades the others.[135]

Before the incarnation of Christ the Father sent forth messengers like doves to call all to life: Moses, Elijah, Samuel, Jeremiah, Isaiah, Ezekiel, Daniel, and the rest of the prophets, and none was strong enough to lead men to life; but when our Lord Jesus Christ was sent from the heavens by the Father, by his own blood he led all to life, saying, "Come to me all who toil and are burdened, and I will refresh you" (Matt. 11:28). The Physiologus spoke well about the red dove.

36 *The antelope animal*

There is an animal called antelope, very subtle, which the hunter cannot get near; it has long horns in the shape of a saw, so that it can saw large and tall trees and bring them to the ground. When thirsty it goes to the Euphrates river and drinks, where there is light-twigged heather, and the animal starts to play with the heather with its horns and it is caught from below in the heather leaves, and it cries out, wanting to escape, but it cannot. When the hunter hears it calling, he comes and kills the animal.[136]

And you, Christian, having two horns, the Old and New Testament, by which you can gore your enemies, fornication, adultery, avarice, bragging, and all the material passions, do not be fashioned with them, which are far from heather honey, or the wicked hunter will destroy you.

37 *Fire-casting stones*

There are stones that when near to one another burst into flame and burn everything that encounters them; male and female are of this nature, with a great difference between them.

So you, most noble Christian, flee from the female so that you do not draw near and be set aflame for pleasure and burn up all the virtue that is in you. For Samson, nearing a woman, had his strength cut off; and many, according to what is written (Sir. 9:8), were led astray by the beauty of women.

38 *The magnet stone*

The Physiologus said of the magnet stone that it draws iron.[137]

If then created things draw one another, how much more the Creator and Fashioner of all, drawing heaven away from earth and spreading it out like a curtain? The Physiologus spoke well about the magnet stone.

39 *The sawfish*

There is a marine animal called sawfish,[138] which has long wings. If it sees boats sailing it imitates them and raises its wings and sails, rivaling the boats that sail. After racing thirty or forty stadia it gets tired and folds up the wings and the waves bear it back to its former habitat.[139]

The sea is taken for the world, and the boats for the person of the apostles and martyrs, who crossing something like a sea and bathed in the business of life, have reached a fair haven, the kingdom of heaven. This animal is compared to beginners in the life of asceticism who turn around again to their former life in the world. The Physiologus spoke well about the sawfish.

Plate 11 Pygmy evades crocodile (Merida). Photo by author.

40 *The ibis*

The ibis is unclean according to the law (Lev. 11:17). It does not know how to dive but lives by the mouths of rivers and lakes. It cannot enter the depths where the clean fish swim, but goes where the unclean minnows congregate.[140]

You must learn to swim spiritually, so that you may come to the spiritual deep river, to the depth of the riches and wisdom and knowledge of God. For unless you extend both hands and make the sign of the cross, you cannot cross the sea of life. For the figure of the cross extends to all creation.[141] The sun, unless it extends its rays, cannot shine; the moon, unless it extends its double horn, does not shine; a bird, unless it extends its wings, does not fly. Moses by extending his hands destroyed Amalek, Daniel the lions; Jonah was in the belly of the great fish; Thecla was cast into fire and to beasts and seals, and the figures of the cross saved her. Susannah was saved from the elders, Judith from Holofernes, and Esther from Artaxerxes, and the three children in the fiery furnace; and, inferior to all, the ibis [. . .] What are begotten by sinners are sins.

41 *The gazelle*

There is an animal called gazelle (*dorkas*). The Physiologus said of it that it especially loves the highest mountains, finds food on the plains

Plate 12 Crocodile eats pygmy (Merida). Photo by the author.

of the mountains, sees from afar all who approach it, and knows whether they come with guile or with friendship.

It is a model of the wisdom of God, which loves the highest mountains, as it (Cant. 2:8) said: "Behold, the [beloved] of my sister comes upon the mountains, bounding on the hills."

Since then the deer is sharp-sighted (*oxy-dorkikos*) it signifies that the Savior sees all that is done (for he is called God [*theos*] because he sees [*theōrein*] our deeds and knows "those who come to him from afar with guile," as he knew Judas, who betrayed him with a kiss). For David said, "The Lord knows those who are his" (Num. 16:5) and John (1:29) said, "Behold the Lamb of God that takes away the sin of the world."

42 *The diamond stone*

There is another trait of the diamond stone: when struck it does not fear iron or fire, nor does it take on the smell of smoke. If it is in a house no demon enters there nor is evil ever found, but the man who holds it conquers every diabolic power.

The diamond is our Lord Jesus Christ. If you have him in your heart, O man, nothing evil will ever befall you.

43 *The elephant*

There is an animal called elephant on the mountain. In this animal there is no desire for intercourse. If it wants offspring it goes to the east, near paradise, where there is a tree called mandrake. The female and the male go there and the female first partakes of the tree, offering it to her male, and plays with him until he takes and eats and has intercourse with the female and she conceives at once. When the time comes for her to give birth, she goes to a lake until the water comes over her teats, and bears her offspring on the water, and this reaches her thighs and sucks its mother's teat. The elephant guards the pregnant female because of the snake, since the snake is the elephant's enemy, and if the elephant finds it, it treads on it and kills it. The trait of the elephant is this: if it falls, it cannot get up, for it does not have joints in its knees. How does it fall? If it wants to sleep it leans on a tree and sleeps.[142] Hunters, knowing the trait of the elephant, come up and saw the tree nearly through. When the elephant reclines it falls with the tree[143] and begins to cry out in lament. Another elephant hears, and comes to its aid but cannot raise it. Both cry out and twelve elephants come but even these cannot raise the fallen one. Then all cry out, and finally a little elephant comes and puts its trunk under the elephant and raises it.[144]

The elephant and its mate personify Adam and Eve. When they were in the delight of paradise before the fall they did not know intercourse and had no thought of union. But when the woman ate from the tree, that is the spiritual mandrake, and gave it to her husband, then Adam knew the woman and she bore Cain on the blameworthy waters, as David (Ps. 68:2) said: "Save me, O God, for waters have risen up to my soul." Then the great elephant, that is, the law, came and was not able to lift him; then came twelve elephants, the chorus of the prophets, and they too could not raise the fallen one; last of all came the spiritual and holy elephant [our Lord Jesus Christ] and raised man from the earth. He who is greater than all [as Christ and new Adam] became the slave of all; for he humbled himself, taking the form of a slave in order to save all (Phil. 2:7). The Physiologus spoke well about the elephant.

44 *The agate and the pearl*

When divers seek the pearl they find it through the agate. They tie the agate to a strong cord and drop it into the sea. When the agate comes upon the pearl it stands still and does not move. Divers note the spot and by following the cord they find the pearl. How is the pearl generated? Listen. There is a shell in the sea called oyster, and it comes up from the sea in the early morning hours. Opening its mouth, it swallows the dew from heaven as well as the ray of the sun and the moon and the stars, and makes the pearl out of the luminaries above. The shell has two wings, between which the pearl is found.[145]

The agate is understood as John, for he showed us the spiritual pearl, saying, "Behold the Lamb of God that takes away the sin of the world" (John 1:29). The sea refers to the world and the divers to the chorus of the prophets. The two wings of the shell refer to the Old and New Testament.

45 *Wild ass and monkey*

There is another trait of the wild ass:[146] it is found in palaces and on the 25th day of the month Phamenoth they know from the wild ass that it is the equinox, for if it brays twelve times the king and the palace know that it is the equinox. Likewise, if the monkey urinates seven times in the night, it is the equinox.[147]

The wild ass is the devil, since night, that is, the people of the gentiles, became equal to day, that is, the prophets who believed. And the monkey assumes the role of the same devil, for he has a beginning but no end, that is, a tail, just as at the beginning the devil was one of the archangels, but his end was not found. The Physiologus spoke well of the wild ass and the monkey.

46 *The Indian stone*

There is an Indian stone, with this trait: if a man has dropsy, the physicians look for this stone and tie it to the dropsical man for three hours, and the stone absorbs all the waters of the man. Then they untie the stone and weigh them both, and the little stone weighs more than the man's body. If the stone is left out in the sun for three hours, all the foul water that it took from the man's body flows out and the stone becomes clean, as it was before.[148]

The stone is our Lord Jesus Christ, the perfect love casting out fear (1 John 4:18). Since we were afflicted with dropsy, with the waters of the devil in our heart, the Lord came and being bound through the cross to our hearts he healed our flood of waters. For he carried our weaknesses and bore our diseases. The Physiologus spoke well about the Indian stone.

47 *The heron bird*

The Psalmist said (103:18), "The dwelling of the heron directs them." The Physiologus said, this bird is much more prudent than many birds. It has one nest and one enclosure, it does not seek for many beds but wherever it dwells, there it feeds and sleeps, though it never eats a dead body nor flies to many places. Its bed and its meal occur in one location.[149]

And you, O Christian man, do not seek many places of the heretics; let there be one bed, the holy church of God, and one meal, the bread that came down from heaven, our Lord Jesus Christ. Do not touch dead teachings, so that the heavenly bread may be conspicuous for you, and do not seek many places of the heterodox. The Physiologus spoke well about the heron bird.

48 The fig tree

The blessed Amos says (7:14): "I was no prophet or a prophet's son, but I was a herdsman dressing mulberries." The herdsman shepherds goats. Well, then, does Amos assume the role of Christ. To say "dressing mulberries" is a spiritual expression, and Zacchaeus climbed a sycamore (Luke 19:4). You know that before the sycamore is dressed there are fleas called gnats within it, dwelling in darkness, not seeing light, saying in themselves, "We inhabit a great space," but they are seated in darkness. When then the sycamore is dressed and they come out, they see the brightness of sun and moon and stars and they say in themselves, "We were sitting in darkness before the sycamore was dressed." It is dressed on the first day, ripe on the third, and becomes food for all.

The side of our Lord Jesus Christ was dressed with a spear, and blood and water came forth, and on the third day, when he rose from the dead, we saw the spiritual luminaries, like fleas when the sycamore is dressed, and I saw the immortal luminaries. "The people that sat in darkness has seen a great light, and light arose on those sitting in a place and the shadow of death" (Matt. 4:16). When the sycamore is dressed, it becomes food on the third day; thus also our Lord Jesus Christ was dressed in his side and rose from the dead on the third day and became life and food for us all.

5

ANTIOCHENES AND BASIL
THE GREAT

1 The study of animals. 2 Tatian. 3 Theophilus. 4 Irenaeus of
Lyons. 5 Epiphanius of Salamis. 6 Basil of Caesarea.

At Antioch and in its sphere of influence, largely because of Jewish
exegesis and Aristotelian philosophy, biblical exegesis was generally
more literal, ideas about animals less fanciful than at Alexandria. The
contrast was not absolute but the concerns of Antiochene theologians
were often different. Ideas about real animals were likely to accom-
pany a more literal exegesis.

1 The study of animals

Graeco-Roman study of zoology had begun with some of the Hippo-
cratic treatises and with Aristotle and his works on animals. Toward
the beginning of his *Parts of Animals* (645a15) Aristotle announced
that he would not leave out any of the animals even if they were more
or less insignificant. "We must not feel childish disgust when obser-
ving the more insignificant animals, for there is something wonderful
in everything natural." His pupils Theophrastus and Clearchus continued his concern with animals. Eventually the question of animal
intelligence became a set subject for debate between Academic and
Stoic philosophers. The Academics used Aristotle's materials. In first-
century Rome, Pliny the Elder was concerned chiefly with presenting
"facts" in a more or less systematic form and knew some of Aristotle's
writings through epitomes. Similarly Oppian described real animals
and fishes in his treatises on hunting and fishing, though animals
supposedly thoughtful and talkative appear in the fables ascribed to
Aesop. Enthusiasm for interesting fiction continued to spread, earlier
with Apion and even Pliny, later with Nepualius and Aelian. Though
Aelian used an epitome of Aristotle's *History* by Aristophanes of
Byzantium, he added a good deal of nonsense. In addition, he set
forth his varied descriptions in a random order to avoid tedium. He

wanted his work "to resemble a meadow or a crown of flowers beautiful with many colors."[1] He thus shared the intention of Clement of Alexandria, who prepared a "meadow" with blooming flowers and claimed that his lack of order was a virtue.[2]

2 Tatian

Around 175 a certain Tatian, who called himself an "Assyrian," produced a convoluted attack on Greek culture. In it he noted that he had already written *On Animals*, a lost treatise intended to show that true "man" could be differentiated from animals not by his mind and reason but by his not acting like an animal. As the image and likeness of God he has advanced far beyond humanity to "attain to God himself."[3]

We have already seen (p. 10) how Tatian thought that the self-cures of animals were instinctive, not rational. Indeed, he claimed that a Cynic philosopher, who does not know God, simply imitates "irrational animals" (specifically, just the dog).[4] And he asked if it was not foolish to believe Herodorus' books about Heracles when they proclaim that there is an earth above, from which the lion killed by Heracles came down.[5] But it would be pointless to synthesize doctrine from Tatian's rhetorical flourishes. As Abderos "was consumed by the horses of Diomedes,[6] so he who boasts of the magician Ostanes will be delivered at the last day to consumption in eternal fire."[7] Did Tatian suppose that the horses really ate Abderos? Or that his comparison has any force?

The traditional topic of the rationality of animals had the contemporary anti-Christian author Celsus claiming that "everything was made just as much for the irrational animals as for men." In reply Origen took up the position already set forth by Tatian, saying that animals use "instinct." The arguments and examples on both sides were conventional.[8]

In another treatise Tatian attacked the animal names of the constellations.[9] The planets are demonic gods who diagrammed the arrangement of the Zodiac, based on animal life.[10] In the diagram the pagan gods have paid heavenly honors to "reptiles, marine animals, and quadrupeds on the mountains" so that they themselves "might be thought to dwell in heaven and might represent irrational life on earth as rational through the constellations."[11] Tatian proceeds to list constellations, many of which were *not* named after animals.

3 Theophilus

Among Christians, Theophilus of Antioch was the first to produce a continuous interpretation of the creation story in his apologetic treatise *To Autolycus*, around 180.[12] He seems to bear witness to the so-called "hexaemeral literature" on the six days of creation.[13] It originated with Hellenistic Jews like Philo, whose *Questions and Answers on Genesis* are rather literal, while his work *On the Creation according to Moses* is more allegorical. What little Theophilus has to say about animals lies in two chapters of his exegesis. There were innumerable animals and species from the waters, and God blessed them in anticipation of his blessing through the water of baptism. Second-century theologians were likely to discuss vegetarianism in relation to the biblical story of creation and the fall. Thus Theophilus explains the existence of wild animals and poisonous snakes and then alludes to diet (see Chapter 1).

God originally commanded mankind to have a diet of fruits, seeds, herbs, and fruit trees, and the animals were to share this diet.[14] But when Theophilus turns to a more allegorical exegesis of Genesis he finds some difficulties. Marine animals and birds have the same "nature"; that is, they were made on the same day; God saw that they were good, and he blessed them. Some retain their original goodness and do not harm the weak but "keep the law of God and eat seeds from the earth." Others, however, transgress. "The great fish and the carnivorous birds are in the likeness of greedy men and transgressors," for they eat meat and harm the weak. Robbers, murderers, and the godless resemble the great fish (and wild beasts, Theophilus adds) and carnivorous birds. They virtually gulp down those weaker than themselves. (Could Theophilus have Jonah in mind? The Greek version of Jonah refers to a great fish [*kêtos*] that "gulped down" the prophet.) Indeed, there are two kinds of birds. Some inferior specimens have wings but are unable to fly because they are weighed down by sins and therefore "unable to run the upward course to the divine nature." This is so, in Theophilus' view, in spite of the fact that all were created good, and fell only when their master Adam fell. The whole question is complicated by the existence of the snake, which was responsible for the fall of Adam and Eve and then of wild animals. It too must have been created good, for he was originally an angel but turned away (*apodedrakenai*) from God and became a snake (*drakôn*).[15] Only after being cursed by God, however, did the snake become "hateful" and creep on its belly and eat dirt.[16] According to Theophilus, "there is much to say about it [or him], but for the present I am passing over the narrative of these matters; the statement about him has been given to [or by] us elsewhere."[17] He may refer to the apocryphal literature he usually ignores, or to Genesis.

75

Theophilus repeats Philo's literalist claim when he argues that "facts prove the truth of the statements" about the curses laid on the serpent and Eve. Women do suffer in childbirth, and the hateful snake does "creep on its belly and eat dirt," thus "demonstrating to us the truth of what has been said."[18]

Giet has argued that *To Autolycus* 2. 13 is a source of Basil, who appeals to a Syrian's statement that in Genesis 1:3 the word "borne" (*epephereto*) in Syriac (close to Hebrew) means that the Spirit "warmed and made alive" the substance of the waters, like a bird that sits on its eggs and by warming them infuses a certain vital power. The difficulty with the comparison is that Theophilus betrays no knowledge of Syriac. While he may have encouraged Basil's literalism, Basil goes well beyond the earlier simple and conventional comments on the variety of fishes and the voracity of marine monsters, and relies on better sources.[19]

4 Irenaeus of Lyons

Theophilus influenced Irenaeus of Lyons, who frequently followed his theology and exegesis and, though no Antiochene, explicitly rejected allegorization. He was chiefly concerned with animals not in the present but in the eschatological future taken literally.

> When the world is re-established in its primeval state all the animals must obey and be subject to man and return to the first food given by God, as before the disobedience they were subject to Adam and ate the fruit of the earth (Gen. 1:28–30).[20]

5 Epiphanius of Salamis

Epiphanius belongs with the Antiochenes not only because of occasional allusions to Theophilus but also because of his intense hostility toward Origen and Origenists. In his attack on the heresies he tries to correlate each one with a kind of snake,[21] and at the beginning he refers to Nicander, who wrote on beasts and reptiles, as well as to Dioscurides and others who discussed roots and plants.[22] He really used a "zoological-pharmacological manual" that went beyond Nicander, as Dummer pointed out.[23] Indeed, Nicander describes only a dozen poisonous snakes.[24]

6 Basil of Caesarea

We have seen several Alexandrians reproducing "facts" about animals in their treatises, and the *Physiologus* tries to discuss them systematically. A more analytical approach, however, appears at Antioch and Caesarea, where greater use is made of Greek zoological works.

Basil "the Great," bishop of Caesarea in Cappadocia who died early in 379, was certainly interested in the classification of animals before 364, when he wrote his *Epistle* 188. In it he explains that scripture correlates the birds of the heaven with the fish of the sea because both come from the waters and swim, fish in water, birds in air.

> What lives in water is not necessarily a fish, for example sea monsters, whales, sharks, dolphins, seals, and also hippopotami, dogfish, sawfish, swordfish, and ox-fish, and if you will, nettles, cockles, and all shellfish — none of which are fish, though all pass along the paths of the seas.[25]

He discussed animals in greater detail in the last three of his nine homilies on the Hexaemeron or Six Days of Creation. The seventh, entitled "On reptiles," also deals with fish and was delivered on the evening of the fifth day of the cycle. The eighth considers "birds and marine animals" and was given on a morning in a time of fasting. The ninth, on "land animals," was delivered that evening.

Basil's homilies contain no trace of the *Physiologus*, but this is not surprising when we recognize his rejection of allegory and affinities with Antioch. In any event, the homilies reveal Basil's systematic and rather rigid literal exegesis, close to the Antiochenes of his time. He often attacks allegorizers[26] and insists that the scriptural "darkness" was real (*Hex* 2.5) and that "authors of the church" wrongly took texts in an "anagogical" (allegorical) sense. "Such interpretations are nothing but tissues of dreams and old wives' tales. Let us reject them and understand water as water" (3.9).

One might contrast the homilies with Basil's statement in his commentary on Isaiah that flies are born out of manure. But Aristotle held this view of the fly,[27] and Basil follows him for most of his information about insects, not directly[28] but relying on an epitome close to Aristophanes of Byzantium.[29] The homilies are thus based partly on Aristotle and partly on the lore gathered by Plutarch, Aelian and others, all put together for homiletical presentation, Basil's real forte.[30]

Criticism soon arose. Basil's younger brother Gregory of Nyssa defended the homilies as a whole,[31] but his friend Gregory of Nazianzus had to admit that Basil knew rhetoric, grammar, and philosophy much better than astronomy, geometry, and arithmetic.[32] This judgment suggests that he was a reliable reporter on ancient views of animals, since information about them would normally be presented in the fields he knew best, not mathematical sciences. Basil gave impetus to the work of his principal Roman readers. Ambrose built allegorizations on Basil's animals, while Augustine relied on them for his *Genesis to the Letter*, using a Latin version by a certain Eustathius.[33]

We should add the literalism of a homily wrongly ascribed to Basil. It says that at first even the panther and the lion ate fruits, but after men fell and God allowed them to eat meat the animals took the same liberty. The lion turned carnivorous and vultures began to eat cadavers.[34] (Earlier there were no cadavers anyway.)

Homilies 7, 8, and part of 9

I translate the seventh and eighth homilies with part of the ninth (before the creation of man) in order to give an example of moderate non-allegorical exegesis. The notes lay emphasis on the contributions of Aristotle and (as a representative of non-scientific stories) Aelian, though without denying that Basil used epitomes for the former or even compends for the latter. The homilies are cited by number, chapter, page of Amand de Mendieta-Rudberg (GCS N.F. 2, 1997).

Homily 7

7.1 (110,2) "And God said, 'Let the waters bring forth reptiles with living souls after their kind, and birds flying in the firmament of heaven after their kind'" (Gen. 1:20).

Water and fish

After the creation of the luminaries the waters were finally filled with animals, so that this part too might be adorned. For the earth had received its adornment from the plants it produced, and heaven had received the flourishing of the stars and, like rays of twin eyes, was adorned with the pair of great luminaries. It remained to give the waters their own adornment. There came a command, and at once rivers were at work and marshes, each productive of their natural kinds. And the sea gave birth to every kind of aquatic animal; not even the waters in mud and swamps remained idle or lacked a share in completing the creation.[35] Frogs, gnats, and mosquitoes obviously emerged from them. What we still see is proof of what happened. Thus every water drove itself to serve the creative command, and the great and invisible power of God suddenly bestowed an active and mobile life on beings whose species could not be numbered, as soon as

Plate 13 Lion eats prey (Tolmeta, Libya). Photo by Tolmeta Expedition, 1957; Oriental Institute of the University of Chicago; reproduced by permission.

the divine command had given the waters the power of producing living beings. "Let the waters bring forth reptiles with living souls." Now for the first time an animal with soul and sense-perception is created. Plants and trees, if they should be said to live by sharing in the ability to feed and grow, are not animals and do not have soul.

Therefore, "Let the waters bring forth reptiles." Everything that swims, either on the surface of the water or through the deep, is by nature reptilian, crawling along the body of the water. Certainly there are marine beings with feet and able to walk (most of these are amphibious, like seals, crocodiles, hippopotami, frogs, and crabs), but they are especially eager to swim. This is why [it says] "Let the waters bring forth reptiles."

In these brief words what kind is omitted? What is not included in the command of creation? Viviparous animals, like seals and dolphins and torpedoes and the animals like them called rays? Or the oviparous, like almost every species of fish? Those covered with scales? Those with a wrinkled skin? Those that have fins and those that do not?[36]

The sound of the command was slight, or rather it was not a sound but an impulse of the will; but the thought contained in this command is as rich as are the varieties of fishes and their shared traits. It is as difficult to enumerate all of them as to count the waves or to measure out the water of the sea. "Let the waters bring forth reptiles." Among them are those of the sea, of the shore, of the deep, of the rocks; those that live in shoals or are solitary, sea monsters, the largest and the smallest fishes. For it is the same power and an identical command that makes them share in being, great and small. "Let the waters bring forth." He has shown you the physical affinity of swimming animals with water, and therefore fish perish if separated from water, for they do not have respiration in order to draw in air, but such as air is for land animals, such is water for the fish. The reason for it is clear. With us, there are lungs, which by dilation of the thorax take in the air and disperse and cool the internal heat, but for them there is the expansion and contraction of their gills, admitting and discharging the water and accomplishing the function of respiration.[37] Fish have a peculiar lot, a peculiar nature, a life separate from others, a unique way of life. Therefore no marine animal can be domesticated nor can it endure the touch of a human hand.[38]

Varieties of fish

7.2 (114,4) "Let the waters bring forth reptiles with living souls, after their kind." These are now the first fruits of each kind, which he orders produced like seeds of nature; their "multitude" is saved up for the subsequent succession, when they must increase and multiply. One kind is called testaceous, such as mussels and scallops and sea mussels, snails and the countless varieties of oysters. Another kind is called crustaceous: crayfish and crabs and the like. Yet another consists of molluscs, so called, whose meat is soft and spongy: polyps and octopuses and the like. Then among these there are countless varieties: dragons and lampreys and eels that live in rivers and marshes and are closer to venomous snakes by the likeness of their nature than to fish. A further kind is oviparous, and another is viviparous. Sharks, sea-dogs, and generally those called cartilaginous are viviparous.[39] Most large sea animals are viviparous too: dolphins and seals, which are said to conceal in their belly their offspring while still small, when they are frightened for some reason.[40]

"Let the waters bring forth after their kind." One kind is sea monsters, another is little fish. Furthermore, fish are divided into countless varieties in each kind. They have particular names and special food, and form and size and qualities of flesh, all separated from one another by the greatest differences and constituted in various forms. Who are the lookouts for tunnies who can count the differences in kind for us? And yet it is said that they can announce even the number of the fish in great shoals. Who among those who watch by banks and promontories can tell us accurately his observations of all? Those who sail the Indian sea? Those who fish the Egyptian gulf? Islanders? Mauretanians? But that first command and that invisible power produced all the fish, small and great.

Reproduction by fish

The particulars of their lives are many, and many are the differences in the reproduction of each kind. Most fishes do not brood like birds, build nests, or take pains to feed their offspring; the water receives the egg that falls and makes an animal of it. For each kind there is an immutable succession, not mixed with another nature. Their unions are not like those of mules on the land, or the couplings of some birds that counterfeit the kinds.

The teeth of fish

No fish is armed with a half-round of teeth, like the ox and the sheep with us, for none chews the cud except (as some say) the parrot-wrasse;[41] all are thickly planted with very sharp teeth so that the prey will not escape during prolonged mastication. For if this were not promptly cut up and sent to the stomach it would risk being carried out by the water during chewing.

Fish eat fish

7.3 (116,10) Each kind of fish has its own defined food. Some feed on mud, others on seaweed; others are content with the grasses that grow in the water. Most fishes eat one another, and the smaller among them is food for the larger. If it happens that one of them after overpowering a smaller one becomes the prey of yet another, they fall together into the belly of the last.

Moral exegesis

What else do we men do in tyrannizing over inferiors? What is the difference between this last fish and the man who with voracious cupidity hides the weak in the insatiable bowels of his avarice? This man had what the poor man possesses; and you have taken him to make him an element of your own wealth. You have shown yourself more unjust than the unjust, more avaricious than an avaricious man. See that the lot of the fishes does not overtake you: the hook or weel or net. It is likely that after following a road with many injustices we may not escape the final punishment.

The crab and the oyster

Now I want to show you how to escape the example of the wicked by learning craftiness and treachery from a weak animal. The crab wants the meat of the oyster, but catching it is difficult because of the covering shell. Nature protects the tenderness of the meat with this unbreakable defense, and therefore it is called hard-shelled. And since these two shells, exactly fitting each other, surround the oyster the pinchers of the crab are necessarily useless. What then does it do? When it sees an oyster warming itself in places without wind and opening its shells to the rays of the sun it furtively casts a pebble, keeps the oyster from closing, and obtains by a trick what it lacked strength for.[42] Such is the malice of animals without reason or voice.

Moral exegesis

But I want you, though rivaling the resourcefulness and ingenuity of crabs, to avoid harming your neighbor. One like them approaches his brother with craft and attaches himself to the brother's troubles, and delights in the misfortunes of others. Flee from imitating these wretched animals. Be content with what is yours. Poverty with true sufficiency is preferable for the wise to all other enjoyment.

The octopus

I should not like to pass over the craftiness and theft of the octopus. It takes on the color of whatever rock it attaches to. Thus many fishes that negligently swim by fall in with the octopus as with a rock, and become a catch ready for the crafty one.[43]

Moral exegesis

Such is the character of those who fawn upon those who happen to be in power and transform themselves according to circumstances without standing on the same principles but easily passing from one to another; honoring chastity with the chaste, libertines with libertines, and changing opinions to please each one. It is not easy to avoid these people nor to be preserved from harm from them, for in the guise of friendship lies concealed their permanent wickedness. The Lord called such characters "ravening wolves" appearing "in sheep's clothing" (Matt. 7:15). Flee from this manifold and subtle conduct; pursue truth, simplicity, singleness of character. The snake is subtle; therefore it was condemned to creep. The just man is unaffected, as Jacob was (Gen. 25:27). And that is why "the Lord made those who were solitary live in a house" (Ps. 67:7).

Limits of habitation

"The sea is great and vast; there are the countless reptiles, animals small with great" (Ps. 103:25). Yet there is a certain wise and well-ordered arrangement with them. For we find not only subjects of blame among the fishes but also those worthy of imitating. How do the kinds of fishes, after dividing up the areas suitable for them, not infringe on one another but remain within their own limits? No geometer among them assigned their abodes or surrounded them with walls or limits; spontaneously what is useful has been assigned to each. This gulf feeds these kinds of fishes, that one others; those that multiply here are lacking elsewhere. No mountain raises sharp peaks to divide them, no river bars their passage, but a law of nature assigns to each, equally and justly, the abode that is useful to each one.

Moral exegesis

7.4 (119,8) We are not like them. Why? We constantly change the eternal boundaries that our fathers set (cf. Prov. 22:28). We divide up the earth; we add "house to house and field to field" (Is. 5:8) in order to take something from our neighbor. The great fish know the life fixed for them by nature; they occupy the sea beyond inhabited lands, without islands, not limited by any continent. There is no sailing, no investigation, nor any need that would persuade sailors to venture there. The great fish, in size like the greatest mountains (as those who have seen them say), have taken possession of it and remain within their proper limits and do not damage islands or coastal cities.

Migration of fish

Thus each kind, as if in cities or villages or ancient countries, is established in the parts of the sea appointed for them. But there are also migrant fishes that seem to be sent to foreign regions as if by a common decree, all leaving upon a single signal. When the appointed time of conception has arrived, migrating some from one gulf, others from another, aroused by a common law of nature they hasten to the Black Sea. And at the time of their ascent you may see the fishes united like a torrent, flowing through the Sea of Marmora to the Black Sea.[44] Who moves them? What king's command? What edicts posted in the market indicate the set day? Who guides them in a foreign country? You see the divine ordinance accomplishing everything, and extending to the smallest. A fish does not oppose the law of God, and human beings do not accept the salutary teachings. Do not despise the fish, even though they are mute and irrational, but fear to be less rational than they are, when you resist the command of the Creator. Listen to the fish: they lack only speech, their actions tell you, We set out on such a long journey for the preservation of our species.[45] They do not possess reason, but they have the law of nature strongly imprinted in them, and it shows them what is to be done. "Let us go," they say, "to the Black Sea." Its water is sweeter than elsewhere because the sun remains more briefly over it and its rays do not draw up all the drinkable water. Even the fish of the sea enjoy sweet waters and so they often ascend rivers and go far from the sea. This is why they consider Pontus preferable to other gulfs as more suited for bearing and nourishing their offspring. But when their goal is sufficiently achieved they all return home together. And why? Let us hear from these mute creatures. "The Black Sea," they say,

> is shallow and overturned by the force of the winds, with few points and coves. So the winds easily stir it up from the bottom so that the bottom sand is mixed with the waves. In addition, it is cold in winter, filled by many great rivers.

That is why the fishes, after enjoying it as long as possible during the summer, when winter comes hasten toward the warmth of deep waters and sunny regions. Escaping the north winds, they enter the less agitated gulfs. 7.5 (121,4) I have seen this spectacle and I marveled at the wisdom of God in everything.

Moral exegesis

If irrational animals think and provide for their own safety; if the fish knows what it must choose and reject, what shall we say who are honored with reason, instructed by the law, led on by the promises, made wise by the Spirit, but then act more unreasonably than fishes? They know how to make some provision for the future, but we from lack of hope for the future use up our lives through bestial pleasure. A fish crosses so many seas in order to find some advantage; what will you say as you live in idleness? Idleness is the source of wickedness. Let no one allege ignorance as an excuse. An innate reason shows our attraction to the good and repulsion from harmful actions.

The sea-urchin

I am not digressing from marine examples; they are the subject of our investigation. I have heard from a shore-dweller that the sea-urchin, a very small and contemptible animal, often instructs sailors about calm and storm. When it foresees a disturbance of the winds it finds a great stone and rests firmly on it as on an anchor, kept by its weight from being easily tossed by the waves.[46] When the sailors see this sign, they know that they must expect the violent turbulence of the winds. No astrologer or Chaldaean, taking the rising of the stars as an indication of turbulence in the air, has taught the sea-urchin, but the Lord of sea and winds (cf. Matt. 8:27) has set a clear imprint of his own great wisdom in the tiny animal. There is nothing unforeseen, nothing neglected by God. His sleepless eye watches everything. He is present with all, procuring salvation for each. God has not excluded the sea-urchin from his oversight; does he not watch over your concerns?

Moral exegesis and the viper

"Husbands, love your wives" (Eph. 5:25), even if you were strangers when you came together in the fellowship of marriage. Let the bond of nature and the yoke imposed by the [nuptial] blessing be the union of the two beings. The viper, most wicked of reptiles, advances to wed the sea eel and by a whistle indicating its presence calls it from the deep to conjugal union. The eel obeys and unites with the venomous beast.[47] What do I want to show by this account? That no matter how hard or violent the character of the husband may be, it is necessary to endure him and not accept any excuse to sever the union. Brutal? But a husband. Drunkard? But united by nature. Hard and peevish? But he is now one of your members, and the most valuable of all. 7.6 (122,17) Let the husband listen in turn to the exhortation that fits him. The viper disgorges its poison because it respects marriage; and do you not put away the rude and inhuman aspects of your soul out of respect for your union? Perhaps the example of the viper will offer us yet another useful teaching. Nature presents us with adultery in the embrace of the viper and the eel. Let them learn, therefore, who plot against the marriages of others, what sort of reptile they are like. I myself have one goal, from every side to edify the church. May the passions of the licentious be contained, chastened by the examples from land and sea.

Peroration (123,1)

Here I must stop, for the weakness of my body compels me, and the lateness of the hour, though I had many further examples worthy of admiration to set before attentive hearers, concerning marine animals and the sea itself.

More examples

How does water become solid with salt?[48] How is the most valuable stone coral a grass in the sea that when brought into the air solidifies with the hardness of stone? Why did nature place the most valuable pearl inside the cheapest animal, the oyster? – for what the treasuries of kings covet are scattered about shores and on coasts and sharp rocks, enclosed in oyster shells. How do the pinnas produce the golden wool which no dyer has thus far imitated? How can shells give kings purples that surpass the flowers of the field in brightness?

"Let the waters bring forth." And what necessary thing has not come to exist? What valuable thing has our life not been given? Some

Plate 14 Frog, woodcut from *Der Physiologus: Tiere und ihre Symbolik*, © Artemis Verlag AG, Zurich, 1995, p. 42.

are for serving us, some for viewing the marvel of the creation. Some are fearsome, instructing our carelessness.

God made the great sea monsters. They are called "great" not because they are larger than a shrimp or a sprat but because in the size of their bodies they equal the greatest mountains. When they swim on the surface of the waters one often sees them appear like islands.[49] But enormous as they are, they inhabit not coasts and shores but the so-called Atlantic Ocean. Such are the animals created to inspire fear and astonishment.

If you hear that the greatest ships, sailing with full sails, are so easily stopped by a very small fish, the "remora" (*echeneis*), that it keeps the ship motionless for a long time as if rooted in the sea, do you not have also in this little being the same proof of the power of the Creator?[50]

Swordfish, sawfish, dogfish, whales, hammer-heads, all are fearsome, but the sting of the sting-ray (even a dead one) and the sea-hare are no less fearsome, bringing swift and inevitable death. Thus the Creator wants you to be always on guard so that in the hope you put in God you may escape harm from them.

Peroration (125,1)

But now let us rise up from the depths and take refuge on dry land. For one after another the wonders of the creation, like waves with their constant alternating ebb and flow, have submerged our discourse. And yet I should be amazed if our thought would not encounter greater marvels on land, and like Jonah take refuge at sea.

It seems, however, that my discourse, encountering a myriad of marvels, has forgotten its symmetry and has had the experience of sailors who at sea lack a fixed point to calculate their speed and therefore often do not know how far they have run. So it has probably happened in our case, that while our discourse runs through creation we do not notice the amount that has been said. But attentive as this reverend assembly is, and sweet as the account of our Master's wonders is to the ears of us slaves, let us raise anchor and wait for day to complete our account.

So let us all arise and give thanks for what has been said, and ask for the completion of what remains. And may you, at the reception of food, discuss at table everything that our discourse has treated from morning to evening, and bound in sleep with thoughts about them, may you even when asleep enjoy the pleasure of the day so that you may say, "I sleep but my heart watches" (Cant. 5:2) because it meditates night and day on the law of the Lord; to whom be glory and might to the ages of the ages. Amen.

Homily 8

8.1 (126,2) "And God said, Let the earth bring forth a living soul after each kind: quadrupeds, reptiles, and wild beasts after their kind. And it was so" (Gen. 1:24). The divine command continued to go its way and the earth received its proper adornment. Formerly God had said, "Let the waters bring forth reptiles with living souls"; now, "Let the earth bring forth a living soul." So is the earth animate? Are the stupid Manichees right when they assign a soul to the earth? Since God did not say, "Let it bring forth," so that it brought forth what was concealed in it, but he who gave the command also gave it the power to bring forth. For when the earth heard, Let it germinate a plant of grass and fruit trees, it did not have the grass hidden within, nor did it bring to light the palm tree, nor the oak, nor the cypress, hidden beneath in its sides; but the divine Word is the "nature" of what comes to be. "Let the earth bring forth," not "Let it make what it possesses come forth," but "Let it acquire what it does not possess when God gives the power to act." So also here, "Let the earth bring forth a soul," not one lying within but the one given by God through the command. Then the word will be turned to oppose them [the Manichees]; for if the earth brought forth the soul, it would leave itself destitute of soul. But their abominable notion is obviously wrong.

Animals on sea and land

Why were the waters commanded to bring forth living reptiles, and the earth, a living soul? We think that nature seems to have given fish an imperfect life because they live in the density of water. Their hearing is harder, and they see with difficulty because they look through water, and they have no memory or imagination or recognition of the familiar.[51] Scripture practically indicates that the physical life of fish governs their psychic movements, while for land animals, whose life is more perfect, the soul is in charge of everything. Their senses are keener, and with most quadrupeds there are sharper perceptions of the present and accurate memories of the past. That is probably why the bodies of aquatic animals were created with souls (for living reptiles came out of the waters) but for land animals it was commanded that a soul should govern their bodies because, living on earth, they would share more fully in vital power.

Of course the land animals too are irrational, but each of them, thanks to the voice received from nature, indicates many of the impressions in its soul. Joy and grief, recognition of the familiar, need of food, separation from companions, and countless other impressions, are revealed by their cry. Aquatic animals not only are mute but savage and unteachable, incapable of sharing life with men. "The ox knows its owner and the ass its feeder" (Is. 1:3), but the fish would not recognize its feeder. The ass knows a familiar voice. It knows the road it is accustomed to take. Sometimes it guides the man who is lost. The sharp hearing of the animal is shared with no other land animal. As for the memory of camels, their wrath and lasting anger, what sea animals could imitate it? The camel, though beaten long ago, preserves its resentment and when it gets an opportunity it repays the evil.

Moral exegesis

Hear, vindictive men, you who practise vengeance as a virtue, about the one whom you resemble when – like a spark hidden under the ashes – you keep your grievance against your neighbor to the point where you find wood for burning your anger like a flame.

8.2 (128,15) "Let the earth bring forth a living soul." Why does the earth bring forth a living soul? So that you may learn the great difference between the soul of an animal and the soul of a man. A little later (9.6) you will know how the human soul originated; now hear me on the soul of the irrational animals. Since, as it is written, "The soul of every animal is its blood" (Lev. 17:11 LXX), and blood solidified changes into flesh, but the flesh when corrupted dissolves into earth, presumably the soul of animals is of earth. "Let the earth bring forth a living soul." Observe the sequence: soul to blood, blood to flesh, flesh to the earth, and analyzing it again in reverse, flesh to blood, blood to soul; and you will find that earth is the soul of the animals.

Do not suppose that soul is older than the substance of their body or that it stays on after the dissolution of the flesh. Flee from the nonsense of the insolent philosophers, not ashamed to make their souls of the same form as those of dogs, saying that they were once women and bushes and fish of the sea.[52] I would not say whether they had once been fish, but I would strongly maintain that in writing these things they were more irrational than the fish. "Let the earth bring forth a living soul."

Why, when my speech was flowing rapidly, was I silent for a long moment, while most people probably wondered? Certainly the more attentive among my hearers were not ignorant of the cause of the silence. How could they be? Those who looked at one another, made signs for my attention, and recalled me to the thought of what I had forgotten. A whole kind of creatures, not the least, has escaped us, and my discourse almost passed by without any discussion of that.[53]

(129,19) "Let the waters bring forth reptiles with living souls after their kind, and birds that fly on the earth in the firmament of heaven." We have spoken of those that swim as time allowed us yesterday evening; today we have passed to investigate those on land. Between the two the winged kind has escaped us. So, like forgetful travelers who have gone far on their way but have left something important behind and retrace their steps, undergoing something like a penalty deserved for their negligence, we must go back over the same road. For our omission is not slight but covers a third of the animals of the creation, if it is true that there are three kinds of animals: land, winged, and in the water.

"Let the waters bring forth reptiles with living souls, after their kind, and birds that live on the earth, in the firmament of heaven, after their kind." Why did he take winged creatures from the waters and make them live? Because there is a relationship between what flies and what swims. As the fish cut through the water, by the motion of their fins pushing forward, and owe change of direction or straight movement to the mobility of their tails, so it is with the birds that one can see swimming across the air, in similar fashion, with their wings. This is why, since both have the ability to swim, they hold the same affinity from their origin in the waters.

Nevertheless, none of the birds lacks feet, for all find their nourishment on the land, and necessarily need help from their feet. The greedy ones received sharp claws for their hunting; the others, who have to procure their food and carry on their lives, necessarily use their feet. Some birds have bad feet, suited for neither walking nor hunting, for example swallows, which cannot walk or hunt, and the birds called "sickle-birds" (*drepanides*); they find their destined food in the air.[54] Besides, the swallow's flight near the ground compensates for the weakness of its feet.

Scripture better than Aristotle

8.3 (131,10) There are innumerable differences among birds. Whoever wants to go through them in detail, as we have attempted to do for fish, will find that the name "bird" covers innumerable differences in size, shape, and color; and that in their lives, actions, and customs there is an inexpressible variety among them. Some have even sought to use invented words so that as through brandings with unusual and strange nomenclature the traits of each kind might be recognized. They called some Schizoptera [with wings of separate feathers], like eagles, Dermoptera [with dermatous wings], like bats, Ptilotes [with membraneous wings] like wasps, Koleoptera [with sheath-wings], like beetles and all the insects that born in cabinets and garments can fly once they have broken their covering.[55] But for us common usage is a sufficient indicator of the peculiarities of kinds, and the distinctions between clean and unclean animals found in scripture.

Another kind is carnivorous birds, with another constitution suiting their way of life: sharp claws, curved beak, and rapid wing so that the prey may be swiftly lifted and when torn serve as food for the killer. Another is the constitution of seed-pickers; yet another, that of those that eat everything they find.

And among them there are many differences.[56] Some live in flocks, though not the rapacious, with which nothing is shared except union in couples. Countless others prefer collective life, such as doves, cranes, starlings, jackdaws. Again, some of them have no leaders and are so to speak autonomous, while others accept rule by a master, like cranes. Another difference is that some are sedentary and local, while others are accustomed to travel farther and at winter's approach generally migrate. Most birds when brought up become tame and domesticated, except for the weak ones which because of excessive fear and timidity cannot endure the trouble caused by constant contact with the human hand. Yet there are some birds that are domesticated and willing to share our abodes; others live in mountains, others love the desert.

There are very great differences in the characters of their cries. Some birds are vocal and talkative, others silent. Some sing on various notes, others are completely unmusical and incapable of song. Some are imitative, either by nature or from practise; others emit monotones and emit an unchanging sound. The cock is exultant, the peacock ostentatious,[57] doves and household birds are lecherous, always ready for intercourse. The partridge is deceitful and jealous, wickedly helping hunters take their quarry.

The politics, industry, and skill of bees

8.4 (133,10) We have said (131,10) that there are innumerable differences in animals' actions and lives. Among irrational animals some are political, if it is characteristic of social life to apply the energy of individuals to a common goal, as one can see in regard to bees. They share a common abode, common flight, and have one work. Most important of all, they work under a king or commander, and would not go into the meadows before seeing the king leading the flight. Their king is not chosen by vote (often the people's lack of judgment has promoted the worst to rule), nor by lot (for the irrational chances of lots often bring power to the last of all), nor by hereditary succession (for the heirs are uneducated and lack all virtue, generally spoiled by luxury and flattery). Instead, he has primacy over all from nature, surpassing others in size, appearance, and the gentleness of his character. Certainly the king has a sting but he does not use it for defense. These are like unwritten laws of nature, that those who attain the greatest powers should be slow to punish. In addition, bees who do not follow the example of the king quickly repent of their imprudence, for they die from the blow of their sting.

Moral exegesis

Let Christians hear this, commanded "never to return evil for evil but to overcome evil by good" (Rom. 12:17,21).

Imitate the life-style of the bee, which constructs honeycombs without harming anyone or spoiling a different fruit. For it manifestly gathers wax from flowers; as for the honey, this liquid spread on the flowers like dew, it sucks it in with its mouth and puts it in the hollows of the honeycomb. This is why it is first liquid, then with time thickens and acquires the consistency and pleasure proper to it.

Beautiful and suitable are the praises that the bee obtained from Proverbs, where it is called "wise and industrious" (6:8a LXX). As much as the labor that it uses to collect our food ("The fruits of its labor," it says, "kings and subjects apply to their health" [6:8b LXX]), so much ingenuity it also uses to fashion the containers for the honey. For it spreads the wax into a light membrane and with it constructs hollow cells connected with one another. All these little boxes, tightly attached to one another, become a solid support to the whole. Each cell is held to the next by a light partition that serves to separate and bind. By two or three stages the cavities are built on each other. The bee avoids making a single continuous hollow so that the liquid may not be dragged down by its weight and spread outside.

Learn how the discoveries of geometry are secondary for the most wise bee. For all the cavities of the honeycomb are regular hexagons and do not rest directly one on another, so that the bases may not be fatigued, fitted on to empty cells, but the angles of the lower hexagon may serve as a base and support for the hexagons placed above, so that they can bear the weight securely and that the liquid contained in each cell may be well guarded.

Birds: cranes

8.5 (135,14) How should I accurately enumerate all the traits of the life of birds? How do cranes maintain guard in turn during the night? Some sleep, while others go the rounds and provide total security for those asleep. Then when watch time is over, the guard raises a cry and turns to sleep, while the one relieving the first in turn provides the security it obtained. You will also observe their good

Plate 15 Deer, woodcut from *Der Physiologus: Tiere und ihre Symbolik,*
© Artemis Verlag AG, Zurich, 1995, p. 43.

order in flight. Sometimes one, sometimes another leads the way, and
the one that has directed the flight for a fixed time passes to the rear
and hands over the direction of the route to its successor.[58]

Storks

The way of storks is not far from rational intelligence; thus they all
come back to our regions at the same time, and all leave on the same
signal. Our crows escort them and send them on, it seems to me, to
provide some support against hostile birds.[59] Evidence? First, no
crows appear anywhere at that time, and further, they return with
wounds that provide proof of their fighting and alliance. Who pre-
scribed the laws of hospitality to them? Who threatened deserters
with pursuit so that nothing would be lacking from the escort? Let
the inhospitable hear, those who close doors and provide no shelter on
winter nights for strangers.

The care taken by storks for the aged would suffice to make our
children love their parents, if they wanted to pay attention. For no
one is so unintelligent that he would not be ashamed to lack virtue
compared with the most irrational birds. Storks gather in a circle
around their father whose feathers have fallen off with age; they warm
him with their wings and ungrudgingly supply food and in flight
provide all possible aid, bearing him gently up on both sides with

their wings. Their conduct is so famous among all that some give gratitude the name *antipelargōsis* (cherishing in turn).[60]

The swallow

No one should complain about poverty, or despair of his life, because he has no resources at home, but he should consider the industry of the swallow. For when she builds her nest she brings twigs in her beak. Unable to lift mud with her feet, she wets the ends of her wings in water, then envelops herself with the finest dust and thus plans the use of the mud. Bit by bit she binds the twigs together with mud as a kind of glue, and in this she feeds her young. If anyone puts out their eyes, she has a remedy from nature to bring back their sight.[61] May this instruct you not to turn to crime because of poverty, nor in the most difficult trials to reject all hope, remaining inactive and unenergetic; but take refuge in God, for if he gives such gifts to the swallow, how much greater ones will he not supply to those who call on him with all their heart (cf. Luke 11:13)?

The halcyon

The halcyon is a sea-bird. It is accustomed to hatch its eggs on the sand where it laid them. They hatch toward the middle of the winter, when the sea is agitated by many violent winds and breaks against the land. But all the winds grow calm, as do the waves of the sea, during the seven days when the halcyon sits on the eggs, for only for that many days does she hatch the young. Then, since they need food, the generous God allows this tiny animal seven more days for their growth. All sailors know this and call those days "halcyon."[62] God provided these examples of his providence for irrational animals to encourage you to ask him for what is salutary. What miracle would he not work for you, made after God's image, when for such a small bird the sea, great and fearsome, holds still in midwinter when ordered to maintain calm?

The turtledove

8.6 (138,6) They say that the turtledove, once separated from her mate, does not accept intercourse with another male but remains solitary, and remembering her former mate refuses intercourse with another.[63] Let women know the nobility of widowhood, which even among irrational animals is far preferable to the impropriety of successive unions.

The eagle

The eagle is most unjust in the upbringing of her young. When she brings forth two young, she pushes one to the ground, driving it out with blows of her wings; she accepts only the other and recognizes it while rejecting the other she generated, because of the difficulty of obtaining food. But the vulture, they say, does not let this one perish; taking it up into its own nest it brings it up with its own chicks.[64]

Moral exegesis

Such are the parents who on pretext of poverty expose their infants, or in dividing their estate are most inequitable toward the children. For it is just that after giving life equally to each they should also provide the means of living equally and with equal share.

Do not imitate the cruelty of birds with curved claws; when they see their chicks emboldened to fly they drive them out of the nest by beating them with their wings and pushing, and take no further care of them. The crow's love for its young is praiseworthy. As soon as they begin to fly it flies alongside, and feeds them and nourishes them as long as possible.

Vultures conceive without intercourse

Many kinds of birds have no need of intercourse with males for fecundation, but while in others the ungerminated eggs are infertile, they say that vultures mostly reproduce without coupling, to a very advanced age; for they usually live a hundred years. Pay attention to this point in the natural history of birds, so that if you see people ridiculing our mystery as impossible and outside the world of nature, that a virgin gave birth while preserving inviolate the signs of her virginity, you will remember that God, who "was pleased by the foolishness of the preaching to save those who believe" (1 Cor. 1:21), gave us in advance countless reasons from nature to accept the miracles of faith.

8.7 (139,17) "Let the waters bring forth reptiles with living souls and birds that fly on the earth in the firmament of heaven." It was commanded that they fly "on the earth," because food for all is from the earth, and "in the firmament of heaven." . . . "Heaven" (*ouranos*) receives its name because the air is visible (*horasthai*), and "firmament" from its density, greater than that of the etherial body, and from the greater pressure on the air above our heads because of the vapors borne from below.

Thus you have the heaven adorned, the earth beautified, the sea teeming with its own creatures, the air full of birds that fly through it. If you are an industrious student of the wisdom of God present in everything, you will have conjectured for yourself everything that was brought from non-being into being by the divine command, even if our address has neglected it for the moment, avoiding a longer account so as not to seem to exceed measure – then never stop admiring and glorifying the Maker through all his creation.

Night birds

You have nocturnal kinds of birds in the darkness, and birds of daytime in the light. Those that feed by night include bats, night-owls, night-ravens; when you are sleepless it will suffice for you to think of them and by recalling their qualities raise a doxology to their Maker.

How the cicada remains awake during incubation without inter-rupting its song all night long. How the bat is at once a quadruped and winged; how alone among birds it uses teeth and is viviparous like quadrupeds and flies in the air, not raised by a wing but by a membrane of skin; how by nature they have mutual affection and cling together by a kind of chain, one suspended from another – a thing not easy for human beings to achieve, for most men prefer a life separate and individual to one shared and united. See how those devoted to vain wisdom are like the eyes of the night-owl. For this bird's eyesight is strong at night but dim when the sun shines. So their intelligence is very keen for the study of vanity but very obscure for the understanding of the true light.

Day birds

During the day it will be very easy for you to collect reasons from all sides for admiring the Creator. How does the cock in your house rouse you to work, crying out with shrill voice and indicating in advance the approach of the sun, lying awake at dawn with travelers and bringing farmers to harvest? How vigilant are the geese, with a keen sense for what is concealed, so that they once saved the Queen City by indicating that enemies were entering through underground passages to take the citadel of Rome?[65] In what kind of birds does not nature indicate a special marvel? Who tells vultures in advance that men will die when they depart to war against one another? You may see countless bands of vultures accompanying armies and divining the outcome from the armament.[66] This is not far from human reasoning. How shall I tell you about the frightful expeditions of the locust? The whole troop rises at one signal and encamps on the breadth of the land, but it does not touch the fruits until the divine ordinance is given. How does the locust-eater follow them and remedy the plague, thanks to the limitless appetite with which the beneficent God made its nature insatiable, for the benefit of men?[67] How does the cicada produce its song? And how are cicadas more harmonious at midday, drawing in air by the dilation of their thorax, and emitting the sound?[68] It seems to me that I am farther from expressing the wonders of winged animals than if I tried to reach the speed of their feet.

Insects

When you see the winged animals called insects (*entoma*), such as bees and wasps (the name comes from the incisions [*entomai*] that appear everywhere on their bodies), consider that they have no respiration or lungs, but feed on air through their whole bodies.[69] Therefore they perish when covered with oil because their pores are blocked but revive when vinegar is poured on them and their pores reopen.[70]

Marine birds

Consider further the animals that love water, and you will find a different formation in them. Their feet are not divided like those of the crow, nor hooked like those of carnivores, but flat with membranes; they let them swim easily on the water, for they push the water using the membranes of their feet like oars.

And if you consider how the swan, extending its neck into the depths, brings up its food from below, then you will find the wisdom of the Creator who for this reason gave it a neck longer than its feet so that it might send it down like a line and bring up the food hidden in the depths.[71]

8.8 (143,4) Read simply, the words of the scripture are short syllables: "Let the waters bring forth birds that fly over the earth in the firmament of heaven." But once the real meaning in the words is discovered, then the great marvel of the Creator's wisdom appears. What differences did he not foresee among birds? What distinctions did he not establish among kinds? What special characteristics did he not impress on each? Daylight fails me as I describe for you the aerial marvels. The earth invites us to the spectacle of beasts, reptiles, and herds, ready to show us beings as honored as plants and the poisonous kind and all winged creatures: "Let the earth bring forth the living soul of animals and beasts and reptiles after their kind."

What do you say, you who disbelieve Paul on the change at the resurrection, when you see many aerial creatures changing their forms? Such, it is said, as that horn-bearing Indian worm, which first transforms itself into a caterpillar, then becomes a larva, and does not stay with this form but supplies itself with soft and broad wings. And when you, women, are seated at your work, unwinding the threads which the Chinese send you for making silk clothing, remember the transformations of the insect;[72] receive a clear idea of the resurrection and do not disbelieve the change that Paul proclaimed to all.

(144,4) But I perceive that my speech goes beyond all proportion. In fact, when I recall the abundance of things said, I see myself carried beyond measure, though when I consider the variety present in the works of wisdom, I think I have not even begun my account. But to hold you a long time was not useless. What would one do until the evening? You do not have guests pressing you; no banquets await. That is why, if you approve, we will profit from our bodily fast for the joy of our souls. You have often served the flesh for its enjoyment; today, remain in the service of the soul. "Delight in the Lord and he will give you the requests of your heart" (Ps. 36:4). If you love wealth, here is spiritual wealth. "The judgments of the Lord are true and just altogether, more to be desired than gold and precious stone" (Ps. 18:10–11a). If you seek enjoyment and love pleasure, you have the oracles of God, "sweeter than honey and the honeycomb" (18:11b) to one who has a firm spiritual sense.

If I dismiss and release the congregation, some will hasten to dice, where people will make oaths, quarrel, and suffer the pangs of avarice. Through the dotted bones the demon is present, arousing madness and moving the same money from one side of the table to another, now lifting this one in victory, and discouraging the other, again showing that one radiant and this one put to shame. Of what use is it to fast with the body when the soul is full of innumerable evils? He who does not play at dice uses his leisure differently, but how many vain words does he not utter? What is there immoral that he does not hear? Leisure without the fear of God teaches wickedness to those who lack time to think. Perhaps you will find some advantage in my discourse; otherwise, it is the case that you have not been sinning while you are here busy listening to me; and indeed keeping you still longer withdraws you from wicked deeds.

In any event, an equitable judge will find that I have said enough, if he considers not the richness of the creation but the weakness of our powers, and the satisfaction and joy of those assembled. The earth has welcomed you with its flowers, the sea with fish, the air with birds. The mainland is ready to show you beings not inferior to these. But let this be the end of the morning festival, lest a surfeit take away your appetite for enjoying the evening meal. May he who filled the universe of his creation and in everything has left clear evidences of his marvels fill your hearts with all spiritual joy in Jesus Christ our Lord, to whom be glory and power for ever and ever. Amen.

Homily 9

9.1 (146,2) How did the banquet of oratory this morning strike you? It has come to me that my zeal was like that of a poor man giving a feast. Eager to be among those honored for their generosity, he wears out the guests with the poverty of the service, covering the table with meager provisions so that his ambition turns out to be vulgarity. Such would be our situation unless you say otherwise. But whatever it is, despise nothing. For in the time of Elisha people did not refuse him as a bad host, even when he set wild vegetables before his friends (2 Kings 4.39).

Against allegory

I know the laws of allegory, not from inventing them myself but from encountering them in the labors of others. Those who do not accept the scriptures in the common sense say that water is not water but some other substance; they interpret plants and fish as seems good to them, and they explain the origin of reptiles and beasts by twisting them to their own understanding, like the interpreters of images appearing in sleep. But when I hear of grass I understand grass, and plant and fish and beast and cattle; I take everything as it was said. "For I am not ashamed of the Gospel" (Rom. 1:16).

The Bible is not cosmology

Those who have written about the world have discussed the shape of the world at length, whether it is a sphere or a cylinder or resembles a disc and is all round or is shaped like a cradle, hollow in the middle[73] (those who wrote about the world have been carried away to make all these conjectures, each destroying those of the others). But that will not make me speak disdainfully about our creation story, on the pretext that God's servant Moses said nothing of these forms, did not note the perimeter of the earth as 180,000 stadia,[74] did not measure how much the shadow of the earth is displaced in the air when the sun passes under it, and did not explain how this shadow projected on the moon brings about eclipses. Because he maintained silence on these points which have nothing to do with us, being useless to us, must I therefore consider the oracles of the Spirit less honorable than foolish wisdom? Or should we not glorify the one who did not amuse our spirit with vanities but cared to have everything written for edifying and restoring our souls? Some who did not understand have tried to attribute a depth of borrowing from themselves to the scriptures by alterations of meaning and allegories. But that is to make oneself wiser than the oracles of the Spirit and to introduce one's own ideas on the pretext of exegesis. Let them be understood as they stand written.

9.2 (147,23) "Let the earth bring forth the living soul of tame animals, beasts, and reptiles." Consider the Word of God that runs through the creation; it began the work then and is active after that and will continue to advance toward its goal until the world is complete. As a ball when pushed by someone encounters a declining slope and, because of its own structure and the disposition of the ground, is borne downhill, not stopping before some level surface receives it, so the nature of things, moved by a single decree, passes with steady steps through the creation subject to birth and decay, preserving through similarity the continuity of species until it reaches its end. For it makes a horse succeed a horse, a lion a lion, and an eagle an eagle, and preserving each animal in continuous successions it accompanies it until the end.[75] Time does not destroy or efface the particular characters of animals, but nature, ever young, as if it had just been constituted, follows the course of time.

Spontaneous generation

"Let the earth bring forth a living soul." This command remained inherent in the earth and does not cease serving the Creator. For some beings owe their existence to those who preceded them, but others even now are engendered by the earth itself. These are not only the cicadas that it produces during rains, nor countless other winged beings carried in the air, most of which have no name because they are so small; but also it produces mice and frogs from itself. Near Thebes in Egypt, when it has rained abundantly during the hot weather, immediately the land is full of field mice.[76] As for eels, we do not see them born except from mud; neither eggs nor any other mode provides succession, but their birth is from the earth.

Moral exegesis

"Let the earth bring forth a soul." The beasts are of the earth and incline toward the ground, but the heavenly plant,[77] man, is as much better than them in the fashion of his bodily formation as he is in the dignity of his soul. What is the attitude of quadrupeds? Their head is bent toward the ground; it looks at the belly, from which it seeks pleasure in every way. Your head is turned toward heaven; your eyes look up.[78] If you dishonor yourself in the passions of the flesh, serving the belly and what is below, "you have approached stupid animals and have become like them" (Ps. 48:13).

A different concern suits you, to "seek the things above, where Christ is" (Col. 3:1), to rise above earthly things by thought. As you were fashioned, so dispose your life; "you have a city in the heavens" (Phil. 3:20). Your true native city is the Jerusalem above; your fellow-citizens and compatriots are "the first-born, whose names are written in the heavens" (Heb. 12:22–23).

Traits of irrational animals

9.3 (149,11) "Let the earth bring forth a living soul." Not that the soul of the irrational animals appeared after being hidden in the earth, but that it came into existence along with the command. The soul of irrational animals is one. It has one trait, irrationality. Each of the animals is distinct, however, in different traits:[79] the ox is calm, the ass is slow, the horse is ardent in desire for the mare, the wolf is savage, the fox is crafty, the deer is timid, the ant industrious, the dog is grateful and mindful of friendship. For at the moment when each one was created, it brought with itself its natural trait.

Courage is innate for the lion, as well as its solitary life and unsocial attitude toward its species. Like a tyrant over the irrational animals, it is proud by nature and rejects equal treatment with others in the crowd. It rejects food a day old and never returns to the remains from its hunt. Nature has set such vocal organs in it that many animals that surpass it in speed are often caught just by its growl. The panther is impetuous and bounds rapidly; its body is nimble and light and follows the movements of its soul. The bear is lazy and its life-style is its own; it is treacherous and violently ravenous. Besides, it is clad in a body that is heavy, compact, crooked, suitable for one that freezes in a cave.

Spontaneous cures

If we proceed to consider how much untaught and natural care for their own life is in these irrational animals, either we shall be brought to watch over ourselves and to care about the salvation of our souls, or else we shall be condemned when we are found far from the imitation of even the irrational animals. Often a bear with many deep wounds heals itself when by every device it stuffs a naturally dry plant, the mullein, into the wounds. You may also see the fox healing itself with pine resin. The tortoise, afflicted in flesh by the viper, flees from the harm of the venomous animal by the antidote origany. The snake cures its sick eyes by eating fennel.

Animal prognostication

And do not the prognostications made by animals from changes in the air surpass rational understanding? The sheep, when winter approaches, throws itself on its food, as if providing provender for the future need. The oxen, long enclosed during winter time, know when spring returns, and by a natural sense expect the change; from their stables they look toward the doors, all changing their appearance by one command. And some diligent students have remarked that the hedgehog has two airholes in its hiding place; when the north wind is going to blow, it stops up the northern one, and when it changes again, the southern.[80]

Moral exegesis

What do these things show us men? Not only that the Creator extends his care to everything, but that even among irrational animals there is some sense of the future, thus inviting us not to be attached to the present life but to have complete zeal for the future age. Will you not be industrious, O man, and in the present will you not put aside the repose of the future, considering the example of the ant?[81]

The ant

In summer it saves up its food for winter. Though the distresses of winter have not yet arrived, it does not give itself to idleness but with wise understanding it works as hard as possible for a sufficiency. With its claws it cuts grains in the middle so that they will not germinate and become useless as fruit. And it dries them out when it senses that they are humid, and exposes them, not all the time but when it anticipates that the weather will remain fair. At any rate, you will not see rain falling from clouds as long as ants leave their wheat outside.[82]

Moral exegesis

What discourse will express it? What ear will hold it? What time will suffice to tell and discuss the marvels of the Artisan? Let us say with the prophet, "How great are your works, Lord; you made everything with wisdom" (Ps. 103:24).

[9.4 (152,13–23) = Stoic discussion on the natural knowledge of duty and the cardinal virtues.]

Moral exegesis

(152,24) Children, love your parents.[83] "Parents, do not provoke your children to anger" (Eph. 6:4). Does not nature say the same (cf. 1 Cor. 11:14)? Paul gives no new counsel but strengthens the bonds of nature. Since the lioness loves her young and the wolf fights for its cubs, what can a man say who disobeys the commandment and debases nature, when the child dishonors a father's old age or a father forgets his children through second marriages?

There is a remarkable love of offspring and parents for one another among irrational animals because the God who created them compensated for their lack of reason by the abundance of their perceptions. Whence comes it that among countless sheep the lamb that leaps out of the fold knows the color and voice of its mother, and hastens to her and seeks its own streams of milk? And should it encounter poor maternal teats it is satisfied with them and passes by many heavy udders. And does not the mother recognize her own among countless lambs? The same voice, the same color, a similar smell with all as far as our sense judges; but they have a certain perception keener than our intelligence and it allows each one to recognize its own. The puppy does not yet have teeth when he rejects from his throat what has harmed him. The calf does not yet have horns when he knows where his weapons will be implanted.

These points demonstrate that the natural properties of all animals are not taught [but innate], and that there is nothing in these animals that is unordered or undefined, but all bear the traces of the wisdom that made them, showing in themselves that they were produced already prepared to guard themselves.

The dog's logic and memory

The dog does not share in reason, but he has senses as powerful as reason. For what the wise of the world barely discovered with much effort in life-long meditation, I mean the combinations of syllogisms, the dog shows these forth, instructed by nature. Following the track of a beast, when he finds that it goes in various directions he examines the tracks that go each way and practically works the syllogistic reasoning through what he does. The beast, he says, turned this way or that or on this other side. Then it did not go this way or that. What is left is that it went on the other side; thus by eliminating the false statements he finds the truth.[84] What more is achieved by those who, solemnly seated before geometrical figures, trace lines in the dust and by eliminating two out of three propositions discover the truth?

Moral exegesis

As for the animal's memory of a favor received, does it not put to shame anyone ungrateful to benefactors? For many dogs are remembered that let themselves die in deserts beside their assassinated masters. Some, indeed, led searchers for the murderers while the track was still warm and brought the malefactors to justice. What will men say who not only do not love the Lord who made and nourished them but have as friends those who "speak iniquity against God" (Ps. 74:6), and share in the same table with them, and while taking their food from it endure blasphemies against the one who feeds them?

Fertility, feeding, and form

9.5 (154,13) But let us return to contemplate the creation. The animals easiest to capture are the most fertile. This is why hares and wild goats are prolific and wild sheep bear twins so that the species may not disappear, consumed by carnivores. Those that destroy others are less fertile. The lioness becomes a mother only once, for the young lion comes forth after destroying the mother's womb with its claws.[85] Vipers eat up the womb and come forth, paying suitable rewards to the one who bore them. There is nothing among these beings that was not foreseen, nor anything excluded from the care they deserve. And if you consider the members of the animals you will find that the Creator added nothing superfluous and did not take away anything necessary. He provided carnivorous animals with sharp teeth, for they needed such for their kind of food. For those armed with a half-circle of teeth he prepared many and various receptacles for the food. Because the food was not sufficiently thinned out in the first receptacle, he gave what was swallowed to pass anew so that ground down by chewing the cud it would be assimilated to the eater. Stomachs, third stomachs (echinoi), second stomachs (kekruphaloi), and fourth stomachs (enustra) are not useless for the [ruminant] animals that have them, but each fulfills a necessary function.[86]

The camel's neck is long so that it may be as long as its feet and reach the plant off which it lives. The neck of the bear is short and pressed into its shoulders, like that of the lion, the tiger, and all of this kind. They do not feed on grass and it is not necessary for them to bend down to the ground. They are carnivorous and live by hunting animals.

Why does the elephant have a trunk? Because the animal is large, the largest of land animals, and, made to inspire fear in those who meet it, had to have a weighty and compact body. If its neck had been large in proportion to its feet, it would have been difficult to carry because of the excessive weight which would have bent it downward. But now the head is joined with the backbone by some cervical vertebrae, and it is the trunk that supplies the want of a neck and through which the elephant draws in food and draws up drink.[87] To hold up its weight it has feet without joints and made of a single block like columns. If it rested on porous and watery members, its joints would constantly be dislocated; when the animal bent its knee or stood up they would not suffice to hold it up. But in fact the foot of the elephant ends at the ankle joint, and has no joints with either the ankle or the knee. For movable joints would not support the great weight, diffused and quivering, of the animal's flesh. Hence there was need for that nose descending to the feet. Do you not see them in battles, how they lead the phalanx like animated towers?[88] Or as hills of flesh cutting through the ranks of the enemy with an irresistible rush?

If their lower parts had not been in proportion to the rest, the animal would not have survived long. But in fact "some say that the elephant lives three hundred years"[89] and more; therefore it had to be compact, with disjointed members. As for its food, as we said, the trunk, serpentine and naturally flexible, raises it up from below. Thus the maxim is true that nothing can be found either superfluous or lacking in created things. However, God has made this animal, so large, subject to us, so that it is taught to understand and accepts being beaten; clearly teaching us that he subordinated everything to us because we were made after the image of the Creator.

One can see the fathomless wisdom (Eph. 3:9) not only in the large animals; in the smallest ones the marvel is no less. For as I have no more admiration for the highest peaks of the mountains, the ones that are near the clouds and from constant winds preserve winter weather, or for the hollow of the ravines that not only escape the bad storms of the heights but always have warm air; so also in the constitution of animals I am not moved more by the size of the elephant than by the mouse that is fearsome to the elephant, or by the most minute sting of the scorpion, how the Artisan hollowed it out like a flute so that through it the poison is implanted in the wounded.[90]

And let no one blame the Creator because of this, that he introduced venomous and destructive and hostile animals to our life; or else one might also blame an instructor who brings into order the facility of youth and makes license temperate by blows and whips.[91]

9. 6 (157,15) Beasts are demonstrations of faith. Have you believed in the Lord? "You will walk on the asp and the basilisk; you will tread on the tracks of snakes and scorpions" (Ps. 90:13). You have the power faith gives you to walk over snakes and scorpions. Do you not see that the viper, attaching itself to Paul's hand while he gathered firewood (Acts 28:3), did him no harm because it found the saint full of faith? But if you are faithless do not fear the beast more than your own disbelief, through which you have made yourself easily affected by all corruption.

[At this point (157,21) Basil, finally done with animals, turns to the creation of human beings and ends his homilies with them.]

6

THE LATIN FATHERS AND ISIDORE: PORTENTS

1 Earlier Latin authors. 2 Sulpicius Severus. 3 Ambrose and Jerome. 4 Augustine. 5 Verecundus of Junca. 6 Gregory the Great. 7 Isidore of Seville on portents.

1 Earlier Latin authors

In discussing animals the Latin Fathers stood close to the Greeks, though they very rarely used Greek sources. They preferred Cicero's *Nature of the Gods* (itself based on Greek) or Pliny's *Natural History*, with its employment of Aristotle. We have already discussed the early Latin Christian Tertullian, who says little about animals generally but defends them against Marcion as created by God. The slightly later Minucius Felix occasionally deals with philosophical topics that animals illustrate. He proves providential care from the fact that some are protected by horns, others by teeth, hooves, stings, speed, and flight,[1] while ideal monarchy is found among bees and cattle (18.7).[2] He also criticizes the false stories "believed by our ancestors" about monsters such as Scylla, Chimaera, Hydra, and centaurs, as well as transformations of human beings into birds and beasts or trees and flowers. "If they had happened, they would happen now; because they cannot happen, they did not happen then."[3] Neither Arnobius nor Lactantius was especially concerned with animals, though Arnobius denounced sacrifices to the gods by taking items from Pliny's *Natural History*.[4]

> If you suppose the gods are honored, and their souls are affected, by the blood of living beings, why don't you slaughter mules and elephants and asses for them? Why not also dogs, bears, wolves, camels, hyenas, and lions? And since you include birds among the animals, why not vultures, eagles, storks, *immusuli*, *buteones*, ravens, sparrow hawks, night owls, and with them salamanders, water snakes, vipers, poisonous ants? Do these lack blood when they are moved by a like cause, the vital spirit?

He passes over Pliny's notice on the phoenix and goes on to list, ironically, plants that the gods might eat.[5] Lactantius too offers little of interest, except for a quotation from Cicero's *Nature of the Gods* on the utility of harmful animals.[6]

2 Sulpicius Severus

Greater interest in animals and credulity about them arises among later Christians (and pagans). Sulpicius Severus was a friend of Martin, bishop of Tours in the late fourth century, and wrote not only his life but also dialogues on him and other ascetics.[7] He included a number of miracle stories about such animals as a lion that ate dates in a desert oasis in Egypt,[8] a thieving wolf that repented and exhibited its remorse in human fashion,[9] and a lioness that asked anchorites near Memphis to open the eyes of her cubs born blind. One did so by invoking God and touching their eyes, and five days later she brought him his reward, an animal skin, which he wore as a mantle.[10]

The same dialogue tells of an anchorite in the desert who lived on herbs and roots. Unable to recognize the poisonous ones, he was slowly dying when a wild ibex came by. The anchorite tossed it a bunch of freshly picked herbs, and the ibex threw away the bad ones. Thus "the holy man, learning from the ibex what he should eat and what reject, escaped the danger of dying from hunger."[11] Again, near Tours Martin saw hunters with dogs pursuing a hare and ordered them to stop and let it go. "You might have thought them bound or rather nailed to the ground as they stopped in their tracks. And the little hare, with its persecutors bound, escaped safely."[12] A dangerous snake was swimming across a river to attack Martin and his companions but stopped when Martin said, "In the name of the Lord I order you to go back." When it obeyed the saint complained, "Snakes hear me, but not men."[13]

3 Ambrose and Jerome

Ambrose, bishop of Milan, soon imitated Basil of Caesarea in his own nine homilies on the Hexaemeron, preached in Holy Week (30 March–4 April) 386,[14] though he made much more extensive use of allegory. He refers to Basil when he says that "more expert authors who have precedence over us, whether in time or in ability, have pointed out that night is a shadow of earth."[15] Some of his animal lore is strange. In an oration on the death of Satyrus he makes the odd claim that the Indian phoenix flies from Ethiopia to Lycaonia, and in his treatise *On Penance* confuses the phoenix with the eagle.[16] He did rely, however, on the exegetical method of Palaephatus to explain away the story of the sirens, deriving it from an underlying account about girls (*puellae*) who lived on a rockbound coast.[17]

Regrettably, Ambrose ventures into theory when he explains why wild animals and beasts have four legs while man has only two. Man shows his kinship to the two-legged birds and like them he aims at what is high.[18] The *Clementine Homilies* and *Recognitions* had asked the similar (though less theological) question as to why the elephant's bulk is carried on four legs, while the tiny mosquito or gnat has six, but "Clement" sagely replied that the time was not right for an answer.[19] Ambrose is not so reticent.

Ambrose is not responsible for the seventh-century claim in the *Decretum Gelasianum* that the *Physiologus* is an apocryphal treatise "composed by heretics and prefixed by the name of the blessed Ambrose."[20]

Ambrose was frequently attacked by the monk and scholar Jerome, who had come to deny Origen's orthodoxy but like Ambrose kept using his exegetical works in his own. Gribomont pointed out that "in 390 he translated the homilies on Luke, to discredit Ambrose's commentary (nourished on Origen); the same motive led him to translate Didymus on the Holy Spirit, 387–90, against Ambrose's analogous treatise [of 381]."[21] No fewer than twenty-two texts, compiled by Paredi, show that he detested Ambrose.[22] The most subtly virulent of them comes from Jerome's *Famous Men*. "Ambrose, bishop of Milan, is still writing. Since he is still alive, I shall refrain from giving my opinion on him, lest I should be accused either of toadying to or speaking the truth about him."[23] His notice of his own works is nearly ten times as long. He often insisted that Ambrose was a plagiarist, especially of Origen and even Philo.[24] In addition, there was something personal that may have arisen during Jerome's conflict with the Roman clergy.

Jerome himself used Palaephatus to interpret various myths in his additions to Eusebius' *Chronicle*. Phrixus was rescued not by a ram but a nurse. Pegasus was the ship, not the winged horse, of Bellerophon. Cadmus did not sow teeth that turned into men but met unexpected opponents. The "wings" Daedalus made for Icarus were the sails of a ship. "Sphinx" was the name of Cadmus' wife. Lapiths and centaurs were noble horsemen. Finally, the sirens were really prostitutes.[25] Augustine's friend Orosius would take two of these examples from the *Chronicle*.[26]

4 Augustine

Augustine was converted to Christianity in 386 partly through Ambrose's allegorical exegesis,[27] but later turned away from allegorization and in the commentary *Genesis to the Letter* upheld literal exegesis against the Donatist Tyconius.[28] He valued "natural history" as an aid to exegesis, and in his treatise *On Christian Doctrine* stressed the value of "geography," a demonstration-like narrative presenting not past events (= history) but present ones. Similarly his contemporary Vibius Sequester used geography for the exegesis of Latin poets, as Marrou noted. The main divisions of geography deal with the locations of sites and the natures of animals, trees, herbs, stones, and other bodies.[29] Such natural history includes mineralogy, or (as Marrou put it) "the elements of a *lapidary* in the medieval sense." Augustine sometimes relied on personal observations, and says that when he first saw the working of a magnet he was "utterly aghast," but most of his accounts come from the books of Pliny or Solinus.[30] He certainly used Basil on the Hexaemeron, and quotes him almost exactly on the "Syrian" exegete of Genesis we have mentioned.[31] He was more enthusiastic about Ambrose than Jerome had been, perhaps because Jerome had attacked both of them. In an unusual situation Augustine cited his own experience in order to argue that fish remember.[32] He recalled a pond at Bulla Regia in Africa where fish watched movements on the edge because at a fixed hour they generally received food from passersby. Marrou notes how Augustine's observations were "oriented toward curiosities, singular facts."[33]

Augustine's choices of animal lore reminded Marrou of bestiaries or the *Physiologus*, not more sober narratives. He has two kinds of animal stories. First, there are stories that are "exact but banal," a few based on observation, but mostly bookish and extraordinary, for example the eagle's breaking of its own curved beak.[34] Second, there are tales of various imaginary animals; he takes examples from "the learned" or from scripture.[35] As a trained rhetorician Augustine boldly questioned mythological stories such as the one about the pelican. He pointed out that since Psalm 101 says it dwells in solitude there is no reason to ask questions about its shape, members, voice, or habits. As for the parent that kills the young and laments for three days, then uses its blood to raise the dead, he says, "Perhaps this is true, perhaps it is false."[36] Similarly he rejected eagle fables when discussing Psalm 102.

Augustine continued to consider the authenticity of strange stories, especially on the monsters found in writings like Pliny's *Natural History*. In fact, he based his treatment in the *City of God* almost entirely on Pliny, though he claimed one source as "a mosaic on the esplanade at Carthage." He classified them in typical rhetorical fash-

Plate 16 Phoenix, woodcut from *Der Physiologus: Tiere und ihre Symbolik*, © Artemis Verlag AG, Zurich, 1995, p. 14.

ion as (1) non-existent or (2) non-human or (3) human.[37] Stories about such animals as the minotaur are "invented fables,"[38] though he referred to mares that conceive from the wind (so Pliny and Solinus), to the salamander as living in fire, to the peacock's meat (he knew) as not decaying; "but as my interest is in other matters I cannot take time to continue the subject."[39]

5 Verecundus of Junca in Africa

Another bishop in Africa was Verecundus of Junca, who wrote a commentary on the biblical canticles and died in 552.[40] He told the usual/unusual stories about the eagle's chicks and the sun, the activities of the deer, the rarity of Jonah's sea monster, and the origin of the mule from horse and ass.[41] He said that evidence for the sea monster came from "histories of experienced naturalists" such as Pliny's *Natural History*, Solinus, and the (lost) treatise of his own contemporary John of Constantinople *On the Nature of Animals*. These told of monsters of "three *jugera* and more . . . considered to be islands by the ignorant."[42] Such sources were to be prominent in the writings of Gregory the Great and Isidore of Seville.

6 Gregory the Great

In his *Moralia*, Gregory the Great (pope 590–604) used conventional ideas about animals especially in interpreting the Book of Job. Joan

111

Petersen speaks of "the special relationship with the animal creation" found not only in Jerome's lives of the miracle-workers but also in Gregory and "commonplace in Celtic Christianity."[43] This was not a basic concern for Gregory, however. Riché and Boglioni have briefly discussed his zoological information, probably derived "from some non-Christian treatise that anticipated bestiaries and lapidaries." Riché notes that "like all cultivated exegetes he uses what he knows about the behavior of animals."[44] Bits of the *Moralia* reappear in the *Etymologies* of Isidore for his accounts of four real animals (ibex, deer, rhinoceros, and fox), two imaginary (ant-lion and unicorn), and one bird, the ostrich. Gregory dedicated his work to Isidore's older brother and predecessor as bishop of Seville, Leander, who had converted Reccared, king of the Visigoths, to Catholic Christianity from Arianism.

7 Isidore of Seville on portents

More systematic study among Christians arose in the seventh century with the great encyclopedia, called *Etymologies*, by Isidore, bishop (600/1–636) of Seville. Isidore used the Christian *Physiologus*, Ambrose, Jerome, Augustine, and Gregory, but also turned back to the animal lore of the Latin commentators on Vergil and, behind them, to the studies by Pliny and Solinus. Like his predecessors, he did no original research, for he intended to follow "ancient writers and especially as they are recorded in the works of Catholics."[45] He mined the fathers for their classical sources and gave preference to patristic ideas.

Isidore had turned to the study of animals only gradually, and mentioned them only three times in his early treatise *On Ecclesiastical Offices*, written between 598 and 615. First, he reproved pagans and Christians who on the Kalends of January wore the skins of beasts, observed auspices, danced, sang, and drank, though their attire was less damaging than their behavior.[46] Again, when Paul said, "It is good not to eat meat and not to drink wine" (Rom. 14.21), he was prohibiting "luxury." "We can eat fish because the Lord accepted it after the resurrection. Neither the Savior nor the apostles forbade it."[47] Finally a mythical animal provided an example. There are church clerics, under episcopal control, but there are also those who lack a head (*acefali*), and resemble the hippocentaur, "like neither horses nor men but, as the poet says, 'a mixed kind and two-formed offspring.'"[48] We may add that he was already fond of the bizarre. When he describes vocal training he cites Pliny but changes Pliny's model from Nero, who wore a lead plate while singing, to "the ancients."[49]

Around 613 he wrote *On the Nature of Things*, dealing with celestial phenomena and the calendar, for Sisibut, king of Spain, who had sent him a poem presumably inspired by lunar and solar eclipses in 612.[50] Thus he referred to Ambrose nine times (once to the Hexaemeron), three times to Augustine, once to Jerome, once to Solinus, and tacitly to Gregory's *Moralia*. He was already using sources that recur in the *Etymologies*, such as the *Clementine Recognitions*, Lucan (named eight times), Lucretius (twice), Naevius, Varro, and Vergil, as well as unnamed sources that included Servius on Vergil. But Fontaine has shown that the basic structure of this book was due to five other works: the *Meteorologica* of Aristotle, the treatise *On the World* by Pseudo-Aristotle, the collection of philosophers' opinions by Aetius, and the *Natural History* of Pliny.[51] Following Ambrose and simplifying Gregory, however, he often derived allegorical meanings from his materials.[52]

This does not mean that he suddenly began looking into these works. During his education in rhetoric and the Latin fathers he had encountered most of them. It means only that to produce the *Etymologies* he could, and did, turn to readily available sources.

Isidore died before finishing his *Etymologies*, divided into twenty books by his friend Braulio, bishop of Saragossa.[53] The title reflects his basic literary interests, and his method often leads him into fanciful word-derivations which he considers scientific. He discusses animals at the end of Book XI and in the whole of Book XII, and is less credulous than the author of the *Physiologus*. He has avoided many legendary anecdotes because he has analyzed narratives in the manner of Greek rhetoric, dividing them into three classes defined as historical fact, fiction, and myth.[54] For Isidore historical "facts" really took place, and even if "argumenta" (fictitious accounts) did not occur they could have occurred. Fables (myths) did not occur and cannot occur, however, because they are contrary to nature. The *Physiologus*, of course, had paid no attention to such distinctions, but Isidore was better trained in rhetorical analysis and more concerned with it. Though he discussed many of the fabled creatures found in the *Physiologus*, he did not often classify them as "animals." Relying on Varro (through Augustine), he placed "monsters" and "fabulous portents" at the end of the eleventh book (or did his editor Braulio do this?), accepting the first group of portents as trustworthy (11.3.1–27), and even (like Pliny) citing Aristotle as an authority. These stories are placed under the heading "portents" and are different from the materials "on animals," but they are also different from a few fabulous and fictitious accounts which can be explained away (11.3.28–39). Isidore definitely believes that transformations of men into beasts, or vice versa, are possible, and it seems surprising that he accepts the existence of vampires (11.4).

Henkel notes Isidore's criticism, possibly after Augustine, of the tales about the weasel and the pelican and his references to the existence of hearsay.[55] Isidore's work is somewhat more "scientific" than the *Physiologus*, and Henkel rightly insists that medieval people did not regard the latter as a textbook of zoology. It is not what we should call scientific, however, for it is based on neither observation nor analysis but simply on rhetorical tradition.

Isidore's sources

On Isidore's sources Jacques Fontaine comments that

> the problem of the work's sources is unsolved and partly insoluble. These sources are biblical, patristic and classical but, in the latter case, often from various manuals, a good many of which are lost without trace. This plurality of sources, minutely followed and combined, also guarantees the relative originality of their Isidorian "rewriting."[56]

In our notes we have emphasized Isidore's known sources because they indicate the kind of materials he found meaningful. He follows the basic tradition of Latin zoological writing, which began with Pliny the Elder in the first century. One of Isidore's major sources was Pliny's *Natural History*. This work, dedicated to the emperor Titus, is a great collection of "facts," some ordinarily accepted, others rather unusual. Book VIII contains accounts of various animals, beginning with elephants; IX, aquatic animals from largest to smallest; and X, birds, with more general remarks on reproduction, senses, food and drink, affection, and sleep. Book XI is concerned with insects. Later on, Books XXVIII–XXX discuss drugs obtained from land animals and XXXI–XXXII those from aquatic animals. In his first book Pliny lists the contents of Books II–XXXVII along with the authorities consulted for the facts. He has found that "the most trustworthy and recent writers have transcribed the ancients word for word, without acknowledgment."[57] (Such was the case among later encyclopedists too.)

We learn from his nephew that Pliny spent most of the night reading, taking notes, and making extracts, and this even during meals, baths, and travel in town and country. Consequently he could leave 160 notebooks of selected passages copied in small writing on both sides of the page. He relied on assistants, and the day he died near Vesuvius he had assigned his nephew the task of excerpting

Livy.[58] He was proud that students had dealt with very few of his sources because of their lack of popular appeal.[59] Later encyclopedists used the same unavoidable method: scissors and paste.

Another important source for Isidore was the early third century *Polyhistor* or *Collection of Remarkable Things* by Gaius Julius Solinus. This author, unlike Pliny (source of three quarters of his materials[60]), arranged his materials geographicallly, moving from Rome to the islands before heading eastward, then doubling back to the north and west. He proceeded through Africa and Egypt, then east as far as India and Parthia, finally returning from Babylon to the Atlantic Ocean.

For etymologies in general Isidore could have used various treatises by Varro, but he certainly followed much later grammarians and antiquarians such as Servius on Vergil or Festus on the meaning of words, and for that matter Augustine *On the City of God*. Specifically, for the twelfth book on supposedly real animals he used two named sources, not only Pliny but also Lucan, who discussed African snakes in the ninth book of his *Civil War* (with scholia).[61] In addition he used two principal sources not named, Solinus[62] and the fourth-century Vergilian scholia of Servius.[63] He used a few patristic sources but named only Ambrose.[64] Like other encyclopedists he did not hesitate to use sources unknown to us and to edit his known sources.

Isidore restored the categories and general order of Pliny but used more of the language of Solinus. After discussing "prodigies" in Book 11 (3–4) he turned to more trustworthy, or at least ordinary, stories about animals (12) – domestic (1), wild (2), and minute (3); then snakes (4) and worms (5); and finally fishes (6), birds (7), and minute flying creatures (= insects, 8), for all this relying chiefly on the scholia on Vergil and Lucan as well as the works of Pliny, Solinus, Jerome, and Augustine. Schmekel claimed that the sources were too diverse for Isidore to have put them together himself, and that the classification of animals is not his either. If such combinations came from Isidore, says Schmekel, "he would be one of the chief systematicians of all time."[65] Why would this be so? Presumably Isidore used vast quantities of notes taken by monks and put them together like a mosaic.[66] He was indeed a "systematician." Besides, most of his work is based on literature without regard for any historical assessment.

No encyclopedist aims at originality, and all rely on assistants when they compile selections of secondary materials. They do not need to look for the earliest sources. The fourth-century alphabetized catalogue of Vibius Sequester provides a good parallel. He begins his treatise *On rivers, springs, lakes, groves, marshes, mountains, and peoples* with items mentioned in scholia to Vergil, then turns to the fourteenth book of Silius Italicus for Sicily in the second Punic war, next to Lucan, mostly for the Illyrian coast, and finally to Ovid's *Metamorphoses* for the marvelous powers and transformations of rivers, springs, lakes, and marshes.[67] Isidore is more systematic.

In spite of his devotion to scholarship, he did not strongly criticize the fabulous narratives of the *Physiologus*. He had no doubts about the unicorn and the virgin, a story Gregory the Great had approved as based on sound zoological research.[68] Isidore, indeed, used the descriptions of about eighteen animals found in the *Physiologus* even though he systematized and mildly criticized them. After all, he believed in portents, monsters, and transformations,[69] though he rejected stories that could be explained etymologically.[70] Thus, after following Augustine, he had doubts about the pelican's self-sacrifice and denied the weasel's odd form of mating. He found it incredible that ships should move more slowly when the right foot of a tortoise is on board, but the scepticism was first Pliny's.[71] Predictions based on birds seemed theologically unsound.[72]

Well after Isidore's time an anonymous compiler imitated his manner in a work entitled *On Beasts and Other Subjects*,[73] of which Carmody says, "*De Bestiis* is one of the more authentic and complete collections of chapters from the Latin Physiologus" because later editors added numerous passages from Solinus and Isidore.[74] The *Physiologus* remained a field for art in its depiction of the fanciful, while Isidore was viewed as a work of encyclopedic literature in the great tradition.[75]

Plate 17 Hoopoe, woodcut from *Der Physiologus: Tiere und ihre Symbolik*, © Artemis Verlag AG, Zurich, 1995, p. 16.

We begin our translation of Isidore with his discussion of portents and credibility (11.3–4) because so many animals are mentioned in his treatment.

Isidore Etymologies *Book 11* on man and portents

Chapter 3: Portents

1 "Varro" says "that portents are born apparently against nature; but they are not against nature, for they occur by the divine will, since the will of the Creator is the nature of each created thing."[76] Hence the gentiles themselves call God sometimes nature, sometimes God.[77]

2 "Therefore a portent takes place not against nature but against what is known of nature.[78] Portents or Ostents, Monsters, and Prodigies are so called because they seem to portend and show and demonstrate and predict future events. 3 Portents are so called from portending, that is, showing in advance. Ostents, because they seem to show (*ostendere*) some future event. Prodigies, because they speak of the future (*porro dicant*), that is, predict future events. Monsters are so called from warning (*monitu*), because they show something by indicating it"[79] or because they immediately show what will appear. This is the true usage, but it is corrupted by the misuse of many authors.

4 Certain creations of portent seem provided to signify the future. For God sometimes wants to signify future events through some faults in those being born, as also through dreams and oracles, by which he forewarns and indicates to certain peoples or individuals that there will be disaster, as is proved by many examples.

5 To Xerxes a fox born of a mare portended that his kingdom would be destroyed.[80] For Alexander a monster created from a woman, with the upper parts of a man, but dead, the lower parts of various beasts, but alive, signified the sudden killing of the king: for the worse had survived the better.[81] These monsters given in signs do not live long but constantly die as they are born.[82]

6 There is a difference between a portent and something portentous. For portents are what are transformed, as it is said that in Umbria a woman bore a snake. Hence Lucan (1.563): "Her infant terrified the mother."[83] But the portentous undergoes only a slight transformation, for example being born with six fingers.[84]

PORTENTS IN INDIVIDUAL RACES

7 Therefore portents or portentous events take place from the size of the whole body beyond the usual measure of men, such as was Tityus

"lying on nine acres,"[85] as Homer notes (*Odyssey* 11.577), or from the smallness of the whole body, such as dwarves or those whom the Greeks call Pygmies because they are a "cubit" in stature. Others from the size of the parts, such as a shapeless head or superfluous parts of members, such as two-headed and three-handed, or "dog-toothed, two of whose teeth protrude."[86]

8 Others are so called from the lack of parts, in which one part is much smaller than the other, as hand from hand or foot from foot. Others from diminution, such as being generated without hand or head, whom the Greeks call "deprived." Others are abortive, when only a head or a leg is born. There are others partly transformed, like those who have the face of a lion or a dog, or a bull's head and body, as they record the Minotaur was born of Pasiphae; which the Greeks call another shape. 9 Others, in every part transformed into a portent of an alien creature, as the story tells of a vine generated from a woman.[87] Others have a change of location without transformation, such as eyes in the chest or in the forehead, ears above the temples; or, as Aristotle reported, someone had the liver on the left, the spleen on the right.[88] 10 Others in accordance with "connaturation," as when in one hand more fingers are of similar nature and fewer in the other, or in the feet. Others because of an early and untimely creation, such as those who are born with teeth or bearded or gray-haired. Others by the combination of many differences, like the manifold portent for Alexander which we mentioned earlier (11.3.5). 11 Others are from mixture of sex, such as what are called androgynes and hermaphrodites. Hermaphrodites are so called because both sexes appear in them. Hermes among the Greeks is masculine, Aphrodite feminine. These have the right breast male, the left breast female, and by uniting beget and give birth in turn.

MONSTERS IN THE WHOLE HUMAN RACE

12 As in individual races there are certain monsters of men, so in the whole human race there are monster races such as giants, baboons, Cyclopes, etc. 13 Giants are called after the etymology of the Greek word. Greeks consider them *gēgeneis*, that is, earthborn, because in fable the earth bore them with immense weight and like itself. For earth is *Gē* and *genos* is kind; hence the crowd calls them "sons of earth"; their kind is uncertain. 14 Some unskilled exegetes of the holy scriptures falsely suppose that "the apostate angels lay with the daughters of men" before the deluge and "thence the whole earth was then filled with giants, that is, men excessively large and strong."[89]

15 Baboons (*cynocephali*) are so called because they have dog-heads,

and "their bark proves they are beasts rather than men." These are born in India.[90]

16 The same India generates the Round-Eyed, and they are called Cyclopes because they are said to have one eye in the middle of the forehead. They are also called *agriophagitai* because they eat only the flesh of wild animals.[91]

17 "People believe that the Blemmyae in Libya are born without a head, and have mouth and eyes in their chest. Others are born without necks, having eyes in their shoulders."[92]

18 "Monstrous beings are ascribed to the remote Orient: some with no noses, with a flat face and shapeless countenance"; others with the lower lip so prominent that when they sleep in the sun's heat it covers the whole face; "others with hardened mouth, ingesting food by a small hole through a reed pipe. Some are said to be without tongues, using a nod or motion in place of a word."[93]

19 They say there are *Panotii* ("all ears") in Scythia; the ears are so spread out that that they cover the whole body with them. For *pan* in Greek means "all" and *ōta* are "ears."[94] 20 The Artabatitae in Ethiopia are said to walk lying down, like quadrupeds. None lives beyond the fortieth year.[95]

21 Satyrs are dwarves with hooked noses, a horn on the face and feet like those of goats, such as Saint Antony saw in the desert. Interrogated by the servant of God it is said to have replied, "I am mortal, an inhabitant of the desert whom the gentile world, deluded by various errors, worships as fauns and satyrs."[96] 22 There are also said to be men of the woods whom some call fig-related fauns.

FEET AND HEIGHT

23 The race of Sciopodae is reported in Ethiopia, with single thighs and remarkable speed. The Greeks call them *skiopodai* because they lie on the ground in the summer and are shaded by the size of their feet.[97] 24 Antipodes in Libya have feet behind their legs and eight toes on the feet.[98]

25 Horse feet (*hippopodes*) are in Scythia, "with human form and horses' feet."[99]

26 They say that in India there is a people called *Makrobioi*, with a stature of twelve feet. There is also a people there with a stature of one cubit, whom the Greeks call Pygmies from "cubit" [*pugmē*]. We have spoken of them before. They live in the mountains of India, near the Ocean.[100]

27 They say that in the same India there is a race of women who conceive five times a year and do not live beyond the eighth year.[101]

Fictitious animals

FABULOUS THREES

28 Other fabulous portents of men are non-existent but are explained as intentional fictions, such as "Geryon king of Spain, endowed with a triple form."[102] For there were three brothers, of such concord that in three bodies there was as if one soul.

29 The Gorgons were prostitutes with snakes for hair; those who looked at them changed into stones. "They had one eye which they used in turn. But there were three sisters with one beauty, as if with one eye, who so stupefied those who saw them that they were thought to turn them into stones."[103]

30 They imagine that "there were three Sirens, part virgins, part birds," with wings and claws. "One of them sang, another played the flute, the third the lyre. They drew sailors, decoyed by song, to shipwreck. 31 According to the truth, however, they were prostitutes who led travelers down to poverty and were said to impose shipwreck on them."[104] They had wings and claws because Love flies and wounds. They are said to have stayed in the waves because a wave created Venus.

32 They also say that Scylla was a woman provided with dog-heads and loud barking, because of the strait of the Sicilian sea, in which those who navigate, terrified by the crests of the waves running together, suppose that the waves are barking, dashed together in the abyss of swallowing spray.[105]

33 They also invent monstrous irrational animals such as Cerberus, dog of the underworld, with three heads, signifying that there are three ages at which death devours man, that is, infancy, youth, and old age. Some think that "Cerberus was named from *kreoboros*, that is, carnivorous."[106]

34 And they say that the hydra was a snake with nine heads, "in Latin *excetra* because when one head was cut off three grew back (*excrescebant*). But it is a fact that Hydra was a place pouring forth waters and devastating a nearby city, in which when one passage was closed many burst forth. 35 For *hydra* is so called [in Greek] from water."[107] Ambrose mentions it as being like heresies, saying, "For heresy grew from its wounds like a hydra of fables; and while it is often cut off it has put forth what is destined for fire and to perish in a blaze."[108]

36 They also invent the tripartite Chimaera, "in face a lion, in after parts a dragon, a she-goat between" (*Iliad* 6.181). Certain naturalists (*physiologi*) say that this is no animal[109] but "a mountain in Cilicia," nourishing "lions" and "goats" in some locations, burning for some

120

Plate 18 Elephant, woodcut from *Der Physiologus: Tiere und ihre Symbolik*,
© Artemis Verlag AG, Zurich, 1995, p. 63.

and "full of snakes" for others. "Bellerophon made it habitable and is therefore said to have killed Chimaera."[110]

CENTAURS, ETC.

37 The species – man mixed with horse – gave a name to centaurs. Some say these were horsemen of the Thessalians, because when rushing in battle they seemed to be one body of horses and men, and they declared the centaurs were invented from this.[111]

38 The minotaur took its name from bull (*taurus*) and man. This is the beast which according to fable was shut up in the Labyrinth. Of it, Ovid (*Art of Love* 2.24) says: "A man half bull and a bull half man."[112]

39 The onocentaur is so called because it is said to have the appearance of half man and half ass, like the Hippocentaurs because it is thought that the nature of horses and men were joined in them.[113]

Chapter 4: Animals transformed

1 Certain monstrous transformations and changes into beasts are described, as in the case of "that notorious witch Circe, who" is

said to have "changed the companions of Ulysses into animals, and about the Arcadians who, chosen by lot, swam across a certain lake and there were changed into wolves."[114] 2 For "they also confirm with historical attestation, not fabulous falsehood, that the companions of Diomedes were changed into birds."[115] And some assert that vampires (*strigae*) originate from human beings.[116] For in many crimes the appearances of criminals are changed and either by magical incantations or with the aid of drugs they change with their whole bodies into wild animals.[117]

3 Indeed through nature many things accept mutation and in decay are transformed into various species, as bees from the putrid flesh of calves, beetles from horses, locusts from mules, scorpions from crabs. Ovid: "If you cut off the hollow claws of a sea-crab a scorpion will come forth and threaten with hooked tail" (*Metamorphoses* 15.369, 371).

ISIDORE OF SEVILLE, BOOK 12 *ON ANIMALS*

1 Cattle and beasts of burden. 2 Beasts. 3 Minute animals.
4 Snakes. 5 Worms. 6 Fish. 7 Birds. 8 Smaller flying animals.

Chapter 1: Cattle and beasts of burden

"To all animate beings Adam first gave names, calling each by a name
from its present situation according to the condition of nature it
serves."[1]

2 The gentiles gave each animal a name in their own language; for
Adam did not impose those names in Latin or Greek or the language
of any barbarian nations, but in that language which was one for all
before the deluge, called Hebrew.[2]

3 In Latin animals or animates are so called because they are
animated by life and moved by spirit.

4 Quadrupeds[3] are so called because they walk on four feet, though
while they are like tame animals they are not under human care, such
as deer, does, wild asses, et cetera. They are not beasts like lions, nor
domestic animals whose use can help mankind.

5 "We call *pecus* everything that lacks human voice and appearance."[4] Properly the name *pecus* is used of those animals fit for eating,
such as sheep and pigs; or useful to mankind, such as horses and oxen.
There is a difference between *pecora* and *pecudes*, for "the ancients
commonly called all animals *pecora*,"[5] but *pecudes* only those animals
that are eaten, as if *pecu-edes*. But in general every animal is called *pecus*
from feeding (*pascendo*).

7 Beasts of burden (*iumenta*) derive their name because they help
(*iuvent*) our labor either in bearing a load by their aid or in plowing.
For the ox pulls a wagon and with the plowshare turns the hardest
clods of earth. Horse and ass carry loads and reduce the labor of men
in walking. Hence they are called *iumenta* because they help men, for
they are animals of great strength.[6] 8 Similarly a herd (*armenta*),
either "because they are suited for arms," that is, for war, or because

we use them in arms. Others understand *armenta* as only oxen, from plowing (*arando*), as if *aramenta*, "or because they are armed (*armata*) with horns." There is a difference between herds and flocks (*greges*): "herds are of horses and oxen, but flocks of goats and sheep."[7]

9 The sheep (*ovis*) is an animal with soft wool, weak in body, placid in spirit, so called from offering (*oblatio*) because originally with the ancients not bulls but "sheep were slaughtered. They call some of them two-toothed (*bidentes*) because among eight teeth they have two longer ones,"[8] which the gentiles chiefly offered in sacrifice.

10 The wether (*vervex*) is so called either from strength (*vires*) because it is stronger than the other sheep, or because it is "man" (*vir*), that is, male, or because it has a worm (*vermis*) in its head; when aroused by an itch they strike one another and smite with great force.[9]

11 The ram (*aries*) is so called either *apo tou Areos*, that is, from Mars – hence, among us, males in flocks are called *mares* – or because this animal is the first to be sacrificed on altars and called *aries* because placed on altars (*aris*). Hence comes that saying: "The ram is slain at the altar."[10]

12 The lamb (*agnus*) the Greeks name *apo tou hagnou*, as if "pious," but the Latins think it has this name because more than other animals it knows (*agnoscat*) its mother, so that even if it is lost in a large flock it immediately recognizes the voice of its parent from its bleat.[11]

13 Young goats (*haedi*) are so called from eating (*edendo*), for the young are very fat, with a pleasant taste; hence "to eat" and also "edible."

14 The goat (*hircus*) is a "lascivious animal," fond of butting and always eager to mate. Because of lust it is slant-eyed and thence it draws its name. For "*hirqui* are the corners of the eyes according to Suetonius" (*Miscellany* 171).[12] Its nature is so hot that its blood alone dissolves the adamant stone, over which neither fire nor the substance of iron prevails.[13] The larger goats are called *cinyphii* from the river Cinyphe in Libya, where the large ones are born.

15 Some say that goats male and female (*capri et caprae*) are so called from "plucking (*carpendis*) shrubs." Others, because they pursue difficult things (*captent aspera*). Some, "from the noise of their legs (*crepitu crurum*)," whence "she-goats are called *crepae*."[14] These are wild goats which the Greeks called *dorkai* because of their sharper sight, that is, *oxuderkesteron*.[15] "They live in high mountains and even from afar they see all who come."[16]

16 The same goes for *capreae*; also the ibexes (*ibices*), as if they were *avices*, because like birds they hold difficult and lofty places and live on high, and because of the height they are barely visible to human sight. 17 Hence the South calls ibexes birds which dwell by the Nile.

These animals, as we have said, live in the highest rocks, and if they sense the presence of wild animals or men, they dive down from the highest peaks of the rocks and attack with their horns.[17]

18 Deer (*cervi*) are so called *apo ton keratōn*, that is from horns; for in Greek horns are called *kerata*.[18] These enemies of snakes, when they sense that they are oppressed by weakness, "extract them by the breath of their nostrils from caverns, and overcoming the ravages of their poison use them for food. They provide dittany as a medicine for themselves, for by eating it they drive out arrows that have struck them."[19] 19 "They admire the whistling of pipes. With ears erect their hearing is sharp but if down, not at all. When they swim across" huge "rivers" or "seas, they lay their heads on the rumps of those ahead," and when following one another they do not feel the burden of the weight.[20]

20 Goat-stags (*tragelaphi*) are so called by the Greeks. While they are of the same kind as deer they have shaggy shoulders, like goats, and hairy chins with long beards. They live only around Phasis.[21]

21 Small mules (*hinnuli*) are the male offspring of deer, from *innuere* because they hide at their mother's nod.[22]

22 The doe (*dammula*) is so called because it escapes from the hand (*de manu*). It is a timid and unwarlike animal, of which Martial says: "For his tusk the boar is feared; horns defend the deer. What are we, unwarlike does, but prey?"[23]

23 The hare (*lepus*) is from *levipes* (light foot), because it runs fast.[24] Among the Greeks it is called *lagos* for its speed, for it is a fast animal, rather timid.

24 Rabbits (*cuniculi*),[25] a kind of rural animal, named from *caniculi* (small dogs) because they are caught when tracked by dogs or are kept out of their caves.

25 The pig (*sus*) because it digs up (*subigat*) pasture, that is, searches for food by digging in the ground. Boar (*verres*) because it has great strength (*vires*). Porker (*porcus*), as if hoggish (*spurcus*). For it plunges into mud and mire and smears itself with slime. Horace (*Epistles* 1.2.26): "And the pig, friend of mud." And hence come "filth" (*spurcitia*) and "spurious" (*spurius*).

The swine[26] (*suillus*) is called after its bristles (*saeti*). Of it Dracontius says: "The swine foretells the force of each poison."[27] It attacks snakes and when it fights the asp it raises its tail and as the asp begins to observe it as a threat and attacks it, it is deceived and caught.

26 We call the hairs of pigs bristles (*setae*), and *setae* are named from *sus*: by whom they are called shoemakers (*sutores*), because they sew (*suo*) from bristles, that is, sew skins together.

27 Boar (*aper*) is named after ferocity (*feritate*), with the letter F

removed and P supplied. Hence among the Greeks it is called *suagros*, that is, wild.

28 Heifer (*iuvencus*) is so called because it begins to assist (*iuvare*) in the service of men in tilling the ground,[28] or because with the gentiles a heifer is always and everywhere sacrificed to Jupiter, never a bull.[29] For age is a consideration in the victims.

29 Bull (*taurus*) is a Greek name, as is ox (*bous*). "The color of Indian bulls is golden, their agility as of a bird, their hair turned backward. They turn their head flexibly as they wish. By the hardness of their back they expel every weapon with harsh wildness."[30]

30 The Greeks call the ox *bous*. The Latins call it plow-ox (*trio*) because it beats the earth (*terram terat*), as if *terio*. Naevius: "This peasant driver of plow-oxen."[31] The breadth of skin from chin to legs is called *palearia*, from pelt, as if *pellearia*; which is a sign of generosity in an ox. There is a remarkable loyalty of oxen toward their associates; for one looks after another and with frequent lowing attests its loyal affection if it happens to fail.[32]

31 *Vacca* is cow, like *bacca*. It has the property of changeable names, like *leo leaena, draco dracaena*.[33]

32 Calves of both sexes (*vitulus et vitula*) are so called from freshness (*viriditas*), that is, of a green age, like *virgo*. For when born it is a bullock or heifer.[34]

33 Buffaloes (*bubali*) are so called because they are like oxen (*bos*), but "so ungovernable that for their wildness they do not take the yoke on their necks." Africa produces them.[35]

34 Aurochs (*uri*) [now extinct] are wild oxen in Germany, with horns extended so far that at royal tables cup-bearers use them for their capacity.[36]

35 The situation of the camel gives it its name, either because when they are loaded they lie down in order to be shorter and low, for in Greek *chamai* means low and short; or because there is a hump on their back (*dorsum*), for the Greek word *camur* means hump.[37] "Other regions send these forth, but Arabia sends the most. There is a difference: the Arabians have two humps on their backs, the camels of other regions have one."[38]

36 Dromedary is a kind of camel, of lesser height but greater speed. Hence comes its name, for *dromos* in Greek means course and velocity. It goes a hundred miles a day and more.[39] It is an animal that chews its cud like the ox and the sheep.

37 "Chewing the cud (*ruminatio*) is so called from (*ruma*), the protruding part of the gullet, through which food discharged by certain animals is called back."[40]

38 Ass (*asinus*) and little ass (*asellus*) are so called from sitting (*sedendo*) as if *a-sedus*. But this name, which suits horses better, this

animal took on because before men caught horses they began to control this one. It is a slow animal and resisting for no reason, but man immediately took charge of it as he wished. 39 *Onager* means wild ass, for the Greeks call the ass *onos* and *agrion* means wild. Africa has large ones, wild and wandering in the desert. "Single males preside over flocks of females. They are jealous of the newborn males and cut off their testicles with one bite. Fearing this, their mothers hide them in secret places."[41] 40 Arcadian asses are so called because the large and tall ones were first brought thence. "A small ass is more necessary for the field because it endures work and almost rejects idleness."[42]

Horses

41 Horses (*equi*) are so called because when yoked to quadrigas they were made equal (*aequabantur*) in form and linked, and similar in course.

42 The nag (*caballus* = *cheval*) was formerly called *cabo* because in walking it hollows out (*concavet*) the ground with its hoof, which other animals do not have. It is also called *sonipes* because it sounds with its feet (*pedibus sonat*).[43]

43 There is much liveliness among horses, for they exult in fields, smell a war, are roused to battle by the sound of a trumpet, are provoked to race by voice, grieve when they are defeated, exult when they win. Some sense "enemies in war so that they seek out the adversaries with biting; some recognize their own masters and forget tameness if they are changed."[44] Others receive on their back none but their master. Many pour forth tears for slain or dying masters. Only the horse weeps for man and feels the emotion of grief.[45] Hence also in centaurs the nature of horses and men is mixed.[46]

44 Those who race are accustomed to reckon a future event from the grief or speed of horses. The long life of Persian, Hunnish, Epirotic, and Sicilian horses extends beyond fifty years, though it is commonly supposed to be shorter among those from Spain, Numidia, and Gaul.

45 In noble horses, as the ancients say, "four things are observed: form, beauty, merit, and color. Form, so that there is a strong and solid body, a height becoming to its strength, a long flank, a narrow belly, large and rounded buttocks, a chest broadly extended, a body knotty with the thickness of muscles, a foot dry and made firm with hollow horn. 46 Beauty, so that there is a small and dry head, skin sticking close to the bones, ears short and perceptive, large eyes, broad nostrils, an erect neck, thick mane and tail, roundness with the fixed solidity of the hooves."[47] 47 Its merit is that it is bold in spirit, fast on its feet, with shaking members, an indication of

bravery. Some are easily aroused from deep rest, or held back from increased speed. The motion of a horse is indicated by its ears,[48] its power in the shaking members.[49]

48 "This color is especially notable: chestnut (*badius*), golden (*aureus*), rosy (*roseus*), brown (*myrteus*), deer-colored (*cervinus*), pale yellow (*gilvus*), bluish (*glaucus*), checkered (*scutulatus*), gray (*canus*), shining (*candidus*), white (*albus*), dappled (*guttatus*), black (*niger*)."[50] In sequential order, varicolored from black; distinct, from chestnut, the rest varicolored or, the worst, ash-color. 49 The ancients called *badius* (chestnut) *vadius* because it walks (*vadit*) more strongly than other animals. It is the same as "palm branch (*spadix*), which they call *phoenicatus*," and it is called *spadix* from the color of the palm, which the Sicilians call *spadica*. 50 "Blueish (*glaucus*) is like having painted eyes, moistened with a certain brightness"; for the ancients called the white of the eye *album*. "Pale yellow (*gilvus*) is Melian," sub-white. Dappled (*guttatus*) is white with scattered black dots. 51 "Shining (*candidus*) is different from white (*albus*). For *albus* has a certain paleness, while *candidus* is snowy, infused with pure light."[51] Gray (*canus*) is so-called because it comes from "shining" and black. "Checkered" (*scutulatus*) is so called because of the eyes; it has shining among purple. 52 Varied (*varius*) because it has stripes of different colors. Those who have only their feet white are called white-nailed (*petili*); only the forehead, hard-skinned (*callidi*).53 Deer color (*cervinus*) is what is ordinarily called *guaranes*. Ordinary people call it airy (*aeranes*) because its color is like air. Brown (*myrteus*) is "pressed into purple." 54 *Dosina* is so called because its color is from the ass (*de asina*); it is the same as ash-colored (*cinereus*). These originate from the country and we call them horses that are wild and hence unable to move to city rank. 55 *Mauron* is black; for the Greeks call black *mauron*. *Mannus* is a smaller horse, ordinarily called *brunicus*. "The ancients spoke of *veredi* (courier's horses) because they carried, that is, pulled (*veherent*), carriages (*redae*)";[52] or because they ran on the public streets through which carriages ordinarily went.

Hybrid horses

56 There are three kinds of horses: one noble, fit for wars and work; another ordinary and common, fit for carrying, not for riding; a third originating from the mixture of two kinds, called hybrid because born of different parents, like the mule.

57 The mule (*mulus*) has a name taken from Greek; or because when brought under the millers' yoke it pulls slow mill wheels (*molas*) around for grinding (*molendo*).

Plate 19 (*a*) Panotius, (*b*) one of the *Blemmyae*, (*c*) sciapod. Taken from Hartmann Schedel, 'Monstrous races from the edges of the Earth', in *Liber Chronicarum*, Nuremburg, 1493.

"The Jews assert that Ana the grandson of Esau first made herds of horses mounted by asses in the desert so that mules, new animals contrary to nature, might be born thence. He also admitted wild asses (*onagros*) to the female asses and invented their copulation so that the swiftest asses might be born of them."[53] 58 Human industry indeed has forced the conception of a different animal and thus discovered a different kind by adulterous union; as Jacob obtained the likenesses of unnatural colors. "For his sheep conceived such foetuses as they contemplated in the mirror of the waters the shadows of goats mounting from above."[54] 59 And this is said to take place in herds of horses, that they offer noble horses to the sight of those which conceive, by which they can conceive and create ones like them. For fanciers of doves too place portraits of the most beautiful painted doves in those places where they live, so that they may generate others like the sight they catch.

60 Therefore some order pregnant women not to look at the ugly faces of animals such as baboons and monkeys lest by happening on these sights they bring forth similar offspring. "It is the nature of females that what they see or have in mind during the last rages of pleasure, when they conceive they bring forth such an offspring."[55] For an animal in the act of Venus transmits forms inside from outside, and when satiated by their appearance seizes their appearance for its own property. 61 In animals those are called double-genus, born of different species, such as mule from mare and ass, a different mule from horse and female ass,[56] "hybrids" from boar and pigs;[57] *tityrus*[58] from sheep and goat; *musmo* from goat and ram. He is the leader of the flock.[59]

Chapter 2: Beasts

1 "The term 'beasts' properly suits lions, pards, tigers, wolves, and foxes, dogs and monkeys, etc., which attack with either mouth or claws, except for snakes."[60] They are called "beasts" from the force (*vis*) with which they rage.

2 Wild beasts or "*ferae* are so called because they use their natural freedom and are moved by their desire."[61] For their wills are free and they wander hither and thither and go wherever their heart (*animus*) leads them.

3 The word "lion" (*leo*), of Greek origin, is inflected in Latin. In Greek it is called *leon* and is a bastard word because partly corrupt. "*Leaena* is all Greek as is she-dragon (*dracaena*). To call the lioness *lea* is poetic license."[62] *Leo* in Greek means "king" in Latin, because it is the first among all beasts. 4 "Its genus is tripartite. Among them the small ones with curly mane are weak; the larger ones with

straight hair are violent."[63] "Front and tail indicate their courage. Their strength is in the chest, their endurance in the head."[64] "When surrounded by hunters they look at the ground so as not to be frightened by the spears. They fear the sound of wheels, but fires more."[65] 5 "When they sleep, their eyes watch; when they walk, their tail covers over their tracks so that no hunter may find them. When they generate a cub, the cub is said to sleep for three days and three nights; then, when the sleeping place is shaken as if by the growl or roar of the father, it is said to raise the sleeping cub."[66] Of them Lucretius (5.1036–37) says: "Lions' cubs already fight with claws and feet and bite."[67] 6 In relation to man "the nature of lions is so gentle that they cannot be angered unless struck."[68] "Their mercifulness is obvious from many instances. For they spare the prostrate; they allow the repatriation of their captives; they kill a man only when extremely hungry."[69]

7 The tiger (*tigris*) is so called because of its rapid flight, for so the Persians and Medes name the arrow.[70] It is a beast marked by various spots, admirable for power and speed, after whose name the river Tigris is called, because it is the fastest of all rivers. Hyrcania [on the Caspian Sea] generates most of them.[71]

8 Panther, so called either because it is the friend of all animals except the dragon or because it delights in the society of its own kind and turns whatever it receives to the same likeness. For in Greek *pan* means "all." The beast "is painted over with minute eyes so that with eye-shaped circles black or white may be differentiated from tawny."[72] 9 This animal gives birth just once, and the reason is obvious. For when the cubs grow in the uterus of their mother they have power with mature strength for being born, for they hate the delay; and therefore with their claws they tear the womb burdened with fetuses as impeding birth, and it pours out the offspring, or rather sends it out, driven by the pain. Thereafter the genital semen infused does not stick firmly to the damaged and scarred areas but rebounds without effect. For "Pliny says that animals with sharp claws often cannot bring forth, for they are injured by the cubs moving within."[73]

10 Pard, second after the panther, is of many colors, very swift and inclined to blood. With a leap it rushes to death.[74]

11 The leopard is born of the adultery of the lioness and the pard, and thus has a third origin, as Pliny in the *Natural History* says the lion lies down with the female pard, or the pard with the lioness, and from either mating degenerate offspring are created, like the offspring of an ass and a mare or of a horse and a she-ass.[75]

12 Rhinoceros, so called by the Greeks, is translated into Latin as "with horn in nose." It is "the same as *monoceros*," that is, unicorn,

because "it has one horn in the middle of its forehead and four feet; it is so acute and strong that it tosses or perforates whatever it attacks."[76] For it often contends with elephants and kills them by wounding them in the belly.[77] 13 It has such strength that it can be caught by no power of hunters,[78] but, "as authors on the nature of animals assert, a virgin girl is set before it and she uncovers her bosom to the approaching animal,"[79] and with all its fierceness laid aside, it lays his head in it, and thus quieted it is captured as if defenseless.[80]

14 The Greeks think the elephant was named after the size of its body, which surpasses a mountain in size, for Greeks call a mountain *lophos*. Among the Indians, however, its name comes from its voice, *barrus*; hence its cry is called *barritus* and the teeth *ebur* (ivory).[81] 15 The ancient Romans called them Lucanian oxen: oxen, because they saw no animal larger; Lucanian, because in Lucania Pyrrhus first used them in battle with Romans.[82] For this kind of animal is well suited to military affairs. For with them the Persians and Indians, with wooden turrets set on them, fight with arrows as from a wall. They are very strong "in intellect and memory."[83] 16 "They walk in herds," they greet <the sun> with what movement they can make, they flee from a mouse, they mate in secret,[84] but when they give birth they send away the offspring to waters or islands because the dragons are their enemies, and when bound by them they are killed.[85] "For two years they carry the fetus, not more, which they generate one at a time, not more, but only one. They live three hundred years."[86] Earlier, elephants were born only in Africa and India, now only in India.[87]

17 Griffin (*grypes*) is so called because it is a feathered animal and a quadruped. "This kind of beast is born in the Hyperborean mountains. They are lions in every part of the body, with wings and face like an eagle, and most hostile to horses."[88] They rend the men they see.

18 "The chameleon does not have one color"[89] but is sprinkled variously like a pard. It is so called [because it has the likeness of a camel and a lion]. The body of the chameleon easily changes to the colors it sees, but the bodily appearance of other animals is not so easy to change.[90]

19 The giraffe (*camelopardus*) is so called because while it is covered with white spots like a pard, it is like a horse in neck, with feet like those of cattle, with head like a camel. Ethiopia generates it.[91]

20 The lynx is so called because counted among wolves. Its back has distinct spots, like a pard, but it resembles a wolf. Hence in Greek *lukos*, in Latin *lynx*. They say "its urine becomes as hard as a precious stone called lynx-water. The lynxes themselves sense it, as is

proved by this evidence: they cover the digested liquid with sand as much as they can, by a certain natural jealousy so that such a voiding will not pass into human use."[92] "Pliny says that lynxes admit only one mate."[93]

21 Beavers (*castores*) are so called from being castrated, for "their testicles are well suited for medicines and when they feel a hunter is near they castrate themselves"[94] and amputate their strength by bites. "Of this Cicero said in the Scaurian oration (Frag. 2.7): 'They ransom themselves from hunters by that part of the body for which they are chiefly hunted.' Juvenal (12:34–36): 'Who makes himself a eunuch, desiring to escape with the loss of a testicle.' They are also called *fibri* and Pontic dogs."[95]

22 The bear (*ursus*) is said to be so called because it shapes its offspring with its mouth, as if begun (*orsus*). For they say that "they generate shapeless offspring and that a bit of flesh is born which the mother by licking forms into members."[96] Hence comes that saying: "Thus the tongue shapes the foetus when the bear brings forth." But unripeness makes the births, and "it gives birth on the thirtieth day. Hence it happens that the headlong fertility creates shapeless ones. The bear's head is weak; its greatest strength is in its arms and legs; hence they sometimes stand erect."[97]

23 Wolf (*lupus*), of Greek origin, is transferred into our language; for they call wolves *lukoi*: but *lukos* in Greek comes from its morals, because mad with rapacity it kills whatever it encounters. Others say they are called wolves as if *leo-pos* because like the lion their strength is in their feet, and whatever it presses with its foot does not live. 24 "It is a rapacious beast desirous of blood; country folk say that a man loses his voice if a wolf sees him first. Hence it is said to anyone who falls silent abruptly: 'It is the wolf of the fable.' Certainly if it senses itself being watched it puts off the boldness of ferocity." Wolves mate no more than twelve days a year, they endure hunger for a long time, and after long fasting eat a lot.[98] "Ethiopia produces wolves crested on the neck, and so varied that, they say, it lacks no color."[99]

25 Dog in Latin (*canis*) seems to have a Greek etymology, for in Greek it is called *kuōn*. Some think it is so called from the sound of its barking because it makes a noise; hence also *canere*.[100] Nothing is more sagacious than dogs, for they have more sense than other animals. 26 "They alone recognize their names" and "love their masters";[101] they defend their masters' houses; they offer themselves to death for their masters; they willingly run to the hunt with their master; they do not leave the dead body of their master.[102] Lastly, it is their nature not to be separate from men. In dogs there are two qualities: bravery or speed.

27 *Catuli* is a term of abuse for the cubs of beasts; properly *catuli* are from dogs (*canes*), so called by a diminutive.[103]

28 "Wolf-dogs (*lycisci*), as Pliny says, are dogs born from wolves and dogs when they happen to unite."[104] In India female dogs are bound in the woods by night and admitted to wild tigers, who leap upon them. The dogs born of the same brood are fierce and strong and overthrow lions in combat.[105]

29 Foxes (*vulpes*) are named as if pleasurable (*volupes*), for the fox flies with its feet (*volat pedibus*)[106] and never runs on direct routes but on winding curves, a defrauding animal with deceptive schemes.[107] For when it does not have food it feigns death and thus when birds come down as to a cadaver, it grabs and devours them.[108]

Monkeys

30 "Monkeys (*simiae*) is a Greek name meaning with pushed-in noses. Hence we say *simiae*"[109] because they have pushed-in noses and are ugly to look at, disgusting with baggy wrinkles, though goats too have a compressed nose. Others think *simiae* are called by the Latin word because much simi-litude to human reason is sensed in them; but this is false. 31 They understand the planets and "rejoice in the new moon but are sad when it becomes horned and concave. They love their offspring and carry them before them; when neglected they cling to the mother." There are five species, of which "the *cercopitheci* are tailed";[110] for when a monkey has a tail some call it an ape.

32 "Sphinxes, with shaggy hair, prominent breasts, so gentle as to forget wildness. Baboons (*cynocephali*) are like monkeys," with dog-like face, hence called Dogheads. 33 "*Satyrs* have a rather pleasant face and are restless, making gesticulations. Maiden-hairs (*callitriches*) differ from the others in almost their whole appearance."[111]

34 The "lion-killer (*leontophonos*) is a small animal, so called because it urinates when captured; meat sprinkled with its ashes and set at crossroads kills lions if they eat any of it."[112]

35 The porcupine (*histrix*), an animal in Africa like the hedgehog, is named after the scraping of the thorns it looses from its back and sends forth to wound pursuing dogs.[113]

36 The skink (*enhydros*) is a little beast, so called because it lives in water, especially the Nile. If it finds a sleeping crocodile it first rolls in the mud and enters through its mouth into its belly, and devouring all its inner parts it goes out alive from the viscera of the crocodile, leaving it dead.[114]

37 The ichneumon has a Greek name because from its smell are produced what is both healthful and poisonous in foods.[115]

38 The cat (*musio*) is so called becase it attacks mice. People

generally call it *cattus* (cat), from capture. Others say that it *cattat*, that is, sees. For it sees so sharply (*acute*) that it overcomes the darkness of night by the shining of light.[116] "Hence *catus* comes from Greek *kaiesthai*, that is, brilliant."[117]

39 Ferret (*furo*) is named from *furvus* (dark), the root of *fur* (thief).[118]

40 *Melo*, either because it has very round members or because it looks for honeycombs and assiduously gets honey (*mella*).

Chapter 3: Minute animals

1 The mouse (*mus*) is a very small animal. Its name is Greek, and the derivative is Latin. Others say that mice are born from the moisture of the earth; for *mus* is earth, whence *humus* (ground).[119] Their liver grows in the full moon, just as certain marine animals grow and shrink when the moon wanes.

2 The shrew-mouse (*sorex*) is Latin; because it gnaws and cuts like a saw (*serra*). The ancients called *sorex saurix*, like *claudus* for *clodus*.[120]

3 The weasel (*mustella*) is so called as a "long mouse," for it is called *telum* from its length.[121] Being subtle of mind it transfers and changes its abode to houses, where it feeds its cubs. It attacks snakes and mice. There are two kinds of weasels, one in the woods, outstanding for size, which the Greeks call *iktidas*; the other wandering about in houses. Some wrongly suppose that "the weasel conceives orally and gives birth through the ear."[122]

4 Spider mouse (*mus araneum*), from its spider's bite. "In Sardinia there is a very small spider-shaped animal called *solifuga* ("sun-fleeing") because it avoids the day. It is most common in silver mines, creeping in darkness, and it poisons those who imprudently sit on it."[123]

5 The mole (*talpa*) is so called because it is condemned to perpetual blindness and darkness. It has no eyes and always digs the ground and takes out soil, and eats roots under fruits. The Greeks call it *asphalaka*.[124]

6 Dormice (*glires*) are "so called because sleep makes them fat. For *gliscere* means grow (*crescere*)."[125] For they sleep the whole winter and lie motionless as if dead, but revive in the summer.[126]

7 The hedgehog (*ericius*) is an animal equipped with quills, named after its stiffening when it is covered by its quills, by which it is protected against harm from all sides. For as soon as it senses any harm it immediately stiffens and turns into a ball, pulling its arms into itself. It has a certain forethought, for when it cuts a bunch of grapes from a vine it rolls itself over it and thus shows the grapes to its offspring.[127]

8 The cricket (*grillus*) has its name from the sound of its voice. "It walks backward, bores into the earth, and chirps at night. It is hunted with an ant tied to a hair and put in its hole, the hunter first blowing the dust away lest it hide, and so it is pulled out with the embraces of the ant."[128]

9 "The ant (*formica*) is so called because it carries bits (*ferat micas*) of grain."[129] There are many examples of its ingenuity, for it anticipates the future and in summer prepares what it eats in winter. "At harvest it picks the wheat but does not touch the barley."[130] When rain falls on its grain it puts all of it out [to dry]. There are said to be "ants in Ethiopia shaped like a dog; they dig up grains of gold with their feet and guard them so no one will take them away, and seizing them they persevere till death."[131]

10 The ant-lion (*formicoleon*) is either the lion of ants or indeed equally ant and lion. It is a small animal rather hostile to ants because it hides in sand and kills the ants carrying grain. Accordingly it is called lion and ant because to other animals it is like an ant, but to ants like a lion.[132]

Chapter 4: Snakes[133]

1 The term *anguis* applies to the genus of all snakes, which can be coiled and twisted. Hence *anguis*, because it is angular and never straight. Among the gentiles "*angues* were always regarded as *Genii* of particular places; hence Persius says: "Paint two snakes, boys, the place is holy" (1.113)."[134]

2 *Coluber* is named because it cultivates shade or because it slides in slippery tracks with sinuous twists.[135] "For 'slippery' applies to whatever slides while being held, like a fish and a snake."[136]

3 The snake (*serpens*) takes its name from its crawling with hidden steps, for it does not creep with definite steps but with the most minute exertions of its scales. But those that go on four feet, like various lizards and newts, are not called snakes but reptiles. Snakes are reptiles because they creep on belly and chest. There are as many poisons (*venena*) as there are kinds (*genera*); as many deaths (*pernicies*) as species; as many griefs (*dolores*) as *colores*.[137]

Plate 20 (opposite) Adam names the animals. This scene illustrates the text from Isidore of Seville's Etymologies XXI.II.1–8; XII.VII.1–9, in which the animals are named and classified. Fol 5r. Reproduced with permission, from the *Bestiary*. Copyright © Aberdeen University Library.

Land snakes

4 The dragon (cf. Pliny 29.67) is the largest of all serpents, or of all animals on earth. The Greeks call it *drakon*, hence its derived name in Latin is *draco*. Often when it is extracted from caves it is borne in the air,[138] and the air is stirred up because of it. "It is crested, with a small mouth and narrow windpipes through which it draws breath and sticks out its tongue. It has its strength not in its teeth but in its tail and harms by beating rather than by jaws."[139] 5 "It is free from poisons"[140] and needs no poisons to kill; for it kills whatever it entangles. Not even the elephant is safe, for all its size.[141] For lurking in the accustomed paths of the elephant, it shackles their legs with its folds and kills them by suffocation.[142] It grows in Ethiopia and India, in the very burning of perennial heat.

6 *Basilisk* in Greek is kinglet (*regulus*) in Latin, because it is the king of snakes, so that those who see it flee, because "it kills them by its smell, for it kills even a man if it looks at him."[143] Indeed, at sight of it no bird in flight passes unharmed, but however distant it is, it is devoured, burned up by its mouth.[144] 7 Yet "it is overcome by weasels which men insert in the holes in which it lurks."[145] Therefore it flees from things seen which pursue and kill it. It is half a foot in length, lined with white spots.[146]

8 Kinglets (*reguli*), like scorpions, follow dry ground and after coming to water they make men hydrophobic and frenzied.[147]

9 The hissing snake (*sibilus*) is the same as *regulus*. It kills with a hiss before it bites or burns.[148]

10 The viper is so-called because it "*vi-pariat*, gives birth by force." For when her womb groans toward birth, the young do not wait for the mature loosing of nature but "gnawing her sides they burst forth by force and with the mother's death. Lucan (6.490): 'Knotted vipers split apart and unite again.'"[149] 11 But it is said that the male, inserted into the mouth of the viper, spits out semen, and she, turned to madness by the pleasure of lust, bites off the male head inserted in her mouth.[150] So it happens that both parents die, the male in intercourse, the female in parturition. From the viper come tablets called "antidotes"[151] by the Greeks.

Asps

12 The asp is so called because with a bite it emits and scatters poisons; for the Greeks call poison *ios* and thence comes *aspis*, because it kills with a venomous bite. It has diverse kinds and species and unequal harmful effects. It is said that when an asp begins to suffer from an enchanter who calls it forth by certain appropriate incanta-

tions to bring it out of its cave when it does not want to go, it presses one ear to the ground and strikes and covers the other with its tail; and thus by not hearing the magical words it does not go out to the enchanter.[152]

13 *Dipsas* is a kind of asp, in Latin *situla* because the one bitten dies of thirst.[153]

14 *Hypnalis* is a kind of asp, so called because it kills in sleep: Cleopatra placed it on herself and thus was freed by death as if by sleep.[154]

15 *Haemorrhois* is called "asp" because the one bitten by it sweats blood, so that "with distended veins it calls forth whatever life there is through the blood."[155] For in Greek blood is *haima*.

16 The *praester* is an asp which runs with mouth always open and steaming. The poet mentions it thus: "The greedy *prester*, that opens wide its foaming mouth" (Lucan 9.722). "The one whom it strikes is distended and killed by its enormous weight; for rot follows the swollen victim."[156]

17 The deadly *seps*, which when it devours a man consumes him at once so that he liquefies in the mouth of the snake.[157]

18 The horned snake (*cerastes*) is so called because on its head it has horns like a ram's; for the Greeks call horns *kerata*. "It has four horns, and by displaying them as bait it instantly kills the animals it provokes. It covers its whole body with sand and offers no indication of itself except of that part by which it catches allured birds or animals."[158] It is more flexible than other snakes, so that it seems not to have a spine.

19 "The roller snake (*scytale*) is so called because its skin shines with so much variety that by its marks it slows down those who see it. And because it is rather slow in creeping, it overcomes those it cannot pursue by stupefying them with its marvelous appearance. It has so much heat that even in winter it sheds the skin of its hot body."[159] On this Lucan (9.717–18) writes: "And the *scytale* which alone can shed its skin while hoar-frost is still scattered on the ground."

20 The *amphisbaena* is so called because it has two heads, one in its proper place, the other in its tail.[160] It moves from either head with a circular movement of the body. This alone among snakes commits itself to cold, going out first of all. On which the same Lucan (9.710) says: "the dread *amphisbaena*, which moves toward its twin heads." Its eyes shine like lamps.

Water snakes

21 The *enhydris* is a snake living in water,[161] for the Greeks call water *hudōr*.

22 The *hydros* is a water snake that makes those bitten swell up; some call its disease *boa*[162] because it is cured by ox dung.

23 The *hydra* is a dragon with many heads, such as lived in the swamp of Lerna in the province of Arcadia and "in Latin was called *exceber*, which, when one head was cut off, three grew" – but this is fable. For "it is clear that *hydra* was a place spewing forth waters that devastated a nearby city, in which when one channel was closed, many burst forth. When Hercules saw it he burned the region and thus closed the water channels. For *hydra* is named after water."[163]

24 The "*chelydros* is a snake, also called *chersydros*, which lives both in water and on land. For the Greeks "call land *cherson* and water *hudōr*."[164] It makes smoke the land through which it slips. Macer described it thus: "Whether the backs breathe out froth of venom, or the lands smoke, by which the dread serpent slips."[165] And Lucan (9.711): "The *chelydrus*, whose track smokes as it glides along."

25 The *natrix* is a snake that infects water with poison; for in whatever spring it is, it mixes it with poison.[166]

26 The *cenchris* is an inflexible snake which always takes a direct route. Of it, the same Lucan (9.712): "And always moves in a straight line." For it always moves directly, for if it twisted while it runs it would creep.

27 The *parias* is a snake which always walks on its tail and seems to make a furrow. Of it the same Lucan says (9.721): "Content to plow a track with its tail."

28 The *boas*, "a snake of Italy immense in size; it pursues herds of cattle and oxen, and mostly it attaches to udders full of milk, and kills them by sucking, thus called *boas* from the depopulation of oxen (*boa*)."[167]

Miscellaneous snakes

29 The *iaculus* is a flying snake of which Lucan says (9.720): "And the *iaculi* birds."[168] They leap forth from trees when some animal goes by, and dart upon it, and hence are called darters (*iaculi*). In Arabia, however, "there are snakes with wings, called sirens, whose strength is so great that a bite is followed by death before pain."[169]

30 The *ammodytes* is so called because it has the color of sand. On which the poet says (Lucan 9.714–16): "Its belly is more painted with little checks than Theban serpentine; of the same color as the sand and indistinguishable from it, the *ammodytes*."[170]

31 The *seps*[171] is a rare snake, which consumes not only body but bones with poison. On it the poet says (Lucan 9.723): "The deadly *seps*, which destroys the bones with the body."

32 The *dipsas*[172] is said to be a snake of such rarity that when it is trampled it is not seen. It emits its poison before it is felt, so that its appearance anticipates death and does not cause grief to the one who will die. On which the poet (Lucan 9.737–39): "Aulus, a young standard-bearer of Etruscan blood, trod on a *dipsas*, and it drew back its head and bit him. He had hardly any pain or feeling of the tooth."

33 The *solpunga* is a serpent which is not seen.[173] The *caecula* is so called because it is small and has no eyes.[174]

Other reptiles

The centipede (*centupes*) is named for the multitude of its feet.[175]

34 The lizard (*lacertus*) is a reptile so called because it has arms. There are many kinds of lizards, such as *botrax* (35), *salamandra* (36), *saura* (37), *stellio* (38).

35 *Botrax* has the face of a frog, for the Greeks call the frog *batrachos*.[176]

36 The salamander is so called because it prevails against fire.[177] "Among all the venomous its strength is greatest. For others strike individuals, but this one kills many at once. For if it crawls into a tree it infects all the fruits with poison, and it kills those who eat; or if it falls into a well the power of its poison kills those who drink."[178] When it fights against fires it alone among animals puts them out. For it lives in the midst of the flames without pain or diminution; not only is it not burned but it puts out the fire.[179]

37 When the lizard (*saura*) ages its eyes go blind and it enters an opening in a wall that looks toward the east, looks at the risen sun, and gets light.[180]

38 The newt (*stellio*) takes its name from its color, for its back is painted with lucent drops like stars. On it, Ovid: "He has a name suited to his color, since his body is spangled with various spots" (*Metamorphoses* 5.460–61). It is said to be such a foe of scorpions that its appearance brings fear and numbness to them.

Snakes in general

39 There are other kinds of snakes, such as *ammodytae*,[181] *elephantiae*, *chamaedracontes*. In sum, "so many names of snakes, so many dead people."[182] All snakes are by nature cold and do not strike except when they warm up; for when they are cold they touch nothing. 40 Hence their poisons harm more by day than by night. For they are drowsy in the cold of night, and rightly, for they are cold with the

night dew. 41 Hence when anyone is struck by the poison of serpents he is first made numb; and afterward where the poison becomes hot and burns it immediately kills the man. "Poison (*venenum*) is so called because it goes through the veins."[183] Its destructiveness runs through the veins by the increased quickening of the body and finishes off the soul. 42 Hence poison cannot harm unless it touches the blood of a man. Lucan (9.614): "The poison of snakes is deadly only when mixed with blood." Every poison is cold, and therefore the soul, which is fiery, escapes from the cold poison. Among natural goods, which we see common to us and the irrational animals, the snake excels by a certain sharpness of sense. 43 Hence it is read in Genesis (3:1): "The snake was wiser than all the beasts of the earth." "And Pliny says" (if it is credible) "that the snake's head, even if it escapes by two fingers' breadth, nevertheless lives."[184] Hence it throws its whole body ahead toward those who strike it. 44 "Snakes universally have feeble vision. They rarely look ahead, and reasonably, since they have eyes not in the forehead but in the temples, so that they hear faster than they see."[185] "No animal moves its tongue with such speed as the snake, so that it seems to have a triple tongue though it is one."[186] 45 "The bodies of snakes are wet, so that wherever they go they indicate the path by moisture."[187] The trails of snakes are such that though they seem to lack feet they creep with their ribs and the push of their scales, which run parallel from the top of the throat to the bottom of the belly. They move with the scales, like nails, and ribs, like thighs. 46 Hence if it is struck by a blow in any part of the body from belly to head, it is weakened and cannot take a straight course, because wherever that blow strikes it loosens the spine, through which the base of the ribs and the movement of the body are directed. Snakes are said to live a long time so that when their old tunic has been cast off they also cast off old age and are said to return to youth. 47 The snakes' tunics are called *exuviae* because when they age they put them off (*exuunt*) and thus return to youth. They are called *ex-uviae* and *ind-uviae* because they are put off and put on.[188] 48 "Pythagoras says that the snake is created from the spinal marrow of a dead man, and Ovid mentions it in his *Metamorphoses* (15.389–90), saying: 'There are those who believe that when the spine putrifies in the closed coffin the human marrow is changed into a snake.'"[189] If this is credible, it rightly happens that as the death of man came about through the snake, so through the death of man the snake comes to be.[190] It is said that the snake does not dare touch a naked man.[191]

Chapter 5: Worms

Earth, water, air, mud, leaf, wood, and clothing worms

1 The worm (*vermis*) is an animal which is born mostly from flesh or wood or from any earthly thing without any intercourse,[192] though sometimes it is born from an egg, like the scorpion. There are worms of the earth, water, air, flesh, leaves, wood, or clothing.

2 The spider (*aranea*), an air-worm, named from its food the air. From its tiny body it lets forth a long thread and always intent on its goal it never stops working, always keeping hanging by its art.

3 The leech (*sanguisaga*), a water-worm, so called because it sucks blood. It plots against drinkers and when it slips between the jaws, or wherever it sticks, it draws out blood; and when it is drenched with blood it vomits forth what it drank so that it may suck afresh.

4 *Scorpio*, an earth-worm, "should be classified with worms, not snakes,"[193] an animal armed with a sting, and from that bears a Greek name because it attacks with its tail and pours poisons into the opened wound. It is a trait of the scorpion that it does not strike the palm of the hand.

5 The beetle (*cantharis*) is an earth-worm which when applied to the human body fills bladders with liquid by its inflammation.[194]

6 The multipede (*multipes*), an earth-worm, so called from the multitude of its feet. If touched it rolls up into a ball. It is born under a rock from liquid and earth.[195]

7 The slug or snail (*limax*), called a mud-worm because born in mud or from mud, and therefore always considered dirty and unclean.[196]

8 The silkworm (*bombyx*), a leaf-worm from whose web silk is made. It is called by the name of what it evacuates when it produces a thread and only air remains in it.[197] 9 The caterpillar (*eruca*) is a leaf-worm that twists in vegetables or vine-leaves, named from gnawing (*erodendo*). Plautus (*Cistellaria* 728–29) mentions it: "He imitates a mischievous and pernicious beast, involved in vine-leaves." For it entangles itself and "does not fly like the locust, and moving here and there it emits a sort of paste; but it stays on as the fruits die and with slow leap and sluggish bites consumes everything."[198]

10 The Greeks call wood-worms *teredones* because they eat by gnawing (*terendo*). We call them termites. Among the Latins they are called "wood-worms, which felled trees generate at an inopportune time."[199]

11 The moth (*tinea*), clothing-worm, called from its holding (*teneat*) and adhering to what it consumes. Hence also the *pertinax*, because it does the same thing in the same way.

143

Flesh worms

12 Flesh-worms (*vermes carnium*): hemicranius (13a), *lumbricus* (13b), ascaridae (14a), *costi* (14b), *pediculi* (14c), *pulices* (15a), *lendes* (15b), *tarmus* (15c), *ricinus* (15d), *usia* (16), *cimex* (17).

13a *Hemicranius*, worm of the head [lost].[200]

13b The intestinal worm (*lumbricus*), worm of the intestines, so called as if serpent (*lubricus*) because it slides (*labitur*) or because it is in the intestines (*lumbi*).

14a *Ascaridae* [lost].[201]

14b *Costi* [lost].

14c Skin-worms are named after their feet (*pedes*). They are called *pediculi*.

15a Fleas (*pulices*) are so called because nourished mostly from dust.

15b Nits (*lendes*) [lost].[202]

15c The lard-worm (*tarmus*) [lost].[203]

15d The dog-worm (*ricinus*) is so called because it adheres to the ears of dogs; for dog in Greek is *kuōn*.[204]

16 The pig-worm (*usia*) is so called because it burns, for where it bites, there the place burns and blisters occur.

17 The bedbug (*cimex*) is named after the resemblance to some herb, whose stench it has.[205]

Worms in general

18 The worm (*vermis*) properly so called is born in putrid flesh, moth in clothing, caterpillar in vegetables, wood-worm in wood, lard-worm in lard. 19 The worm like the snake does not move with distinct steps but with motions of its scales, because like the snake it has no hardness of the spine but the parts of its body are gradually stretched and contracted in the direction of its body, and by contracting the outstretched parts it develops its movement, and thus set in motion it slides along.

Chapter 6: Fish

Fish and reptiles in general

1 Fishes (*pisces*) are so called, like cattle (*pecus*), from feeding (*pascendo*).[206]

2 Reptiles (*reptilia*) are those that swim, because they have the appearance and nature of creeping; though they dive into the deep, in swimming they crawl. Thus David: "This sea is great and spacious: there are the reptiles, of which there is no number" (Psalm 104:25).

144

3 Certain kinds of fish are amphibious, so called because they are accustomed to walk on land and swim in water. For in Greek *amphi* means "both," that is, because they live in water and on land: such as seals, crocodiles, and hippopotami, i. e. river horses.[207]

4 Men gave names to cattle and beasts and birds (Gen. 2:20) before fishes, because they were seen and known earlier than fishes. Later the names of fishes were gradually established, when the kinds were known, either from similarities to land animals or to suit the proper species or behavior [or color or shape or sex].[208] 5 From similarity to land animals: like frogs and calves and lions and black sea-carp and peacocks of diverse colors, painted on back and neck, and various thrushes with white, and the other details that justify the names of the species of land animals. From behavior of land animals: as dogs in the sea from dogs on land, because they bite; and wolves, which with reprobate voracity attack others. 6 From color: such as graylings (*umbrae*) because they have a gray color; and gilt-breams (*auratae*),[209] because their head has the color of gold; and various (*varii*) from their variety, popularly called trout (*tructae*).[210] From shape: such as orb because spherical and all head; and such as sole because like the soles of shoes.[211] From sex: such as sea-mouse (*musculus*), the masculine of whale (*balena*), for this monster conceives by coition with it.[212] Hence also the shellfish mussels, from whose milk the oysters conceive.[213]

Large marine animals

7 Whales (*ballenae*) are beasts of immense size, so called from emitting and pouring water. They raise waves higher than the other beasts of the sea, for *ballein* in Greek means emit. 8 Monsters (*cete, to kētos, ta kētē*),[214] that is, because of horribleness. They are huge kinds of beasts, with bodies equal to mountains,[215] like the monster that took in Jonah, whose belly was of such size that it resembled hell and hence the prophet said (Jonah 2:2), "He heard me from the belly of hell."

Names from land animals

9 "Sea horses (*equi marini*), because in the fore part they are horses but behind they end as a fish." "Seals (*phocae*)," they say, "are sea calves,"[216] as if *bo-acae*.

10 Dark blue (*caerulei*) are so called from their color, for caerulean is green with black, like the sea.

11 Dolphins (*delphini*) have a definite name, because they follow human voices or because they come together in a crowd to sing

together. "Nothing in the sea is swifter, for they fly over most ships that attack them. When they sport in the waves and jump headlong in strong waves, they seem to indicate storms; these are properly called Simones."[217] There is also a kind of dolphin in the Nile with a saw-shaped back, which kills crocodiles, cutting the soft parts of the belly.[218]

12 Sea pigs (*porci marini*), commonly called *suilli* (swine), while they seek food dig up the ground under water like pigs. Around their gullet they have the function of a mouth, and unless they submerge the snout in the sand they do not collect food.[219]

13 "Sea crows" (*corvi*) are named from the "voice of the heart" (*cordis voce*) because they grunt from the chest and are caught because betrayed by their sound.[220]

14 Tunny (*thynni*) have a Greek name. "They appear in springtime, and come in on the right side and go out on the left. They are supposed to do this because they see more keenly with the right eye than with the left."[221]

15 The swordfish (*gladius*) is so called because it "has a pointed beak by which it pierces and sinks ships."[222]

16 The sawfish (*serra*) is so called because it has a saw-toothed crest and cuts a ship by swimming under it.

17 The scorpion is so called because it stings when lifted by hand. They "say that when ten crabs are tied with a handful of basil (*ocimum*) all the scorpions in the vicinity will gather in that place."[223]

18 The spiderfish (*aranea*) is a kind of fish so called because it stings in the air, for it has goads by which it strikes.[224]

Nile beasts

19 The crocodile, so called from its golden color, born in the Nile, "a quadruped on land and vigorous in the water, mostly twenty cubits in length, armed with fierce teeth" and claws, with such hardness of skin that it does not feel the blows of heavy stones on its back. 20 At night in the water, by day it rests on the land; it drops its eggs on the land; male and female watch by turns. Certain fishes with saw-backs cut the soft parts of the belly and kill them. Alone among animals it is said to move the upper jawbone."[225]

21 The hippopotamus is "like a horse in back, mane, and whinny, with a turned-back beak, teeth like a wild boar, and a twisted tail." In daytime it stays in the water; "at night it feeds on wheat";[226] and the Nile generates it.

22 The *pagrum* (unknown), which the Greeks call *phagron*[227] because it has hard teeth so that it eats oysters in the sea.

Plate 21 An ibis regurgitates food to its young and holds a snake in its claw. Fol 47r. Reproduced with permission, from the *Bestiary*. Copyright © Aberdeen University Library.

23 The tooth-fish (*dentix*) is so called from the number and size of its teeth. The hare (*lepus*) is so called from the similarity of its head.

24 The bass (*lupus*) is named after its intensity. It is an ingenious fish when captured. "When encircled by a net it plows a hole in the sand with its tail and thus concealed escapes from the net."[228]

25 The mullet (*mullus*) is so called because it is soft (*mollis*) and tender. They say that eating it inhibits lust and dulls eyesight, but men who often eat it smell of fish. "If a mullet is killed in wine those who drink it have a distaste for wine."[229] 26 Another mullet (*mugilis*) bears its name because it is very agile (*multum agilis*). For where it senses the traps of fishermen have been set, it immediately turns back and leaps across the nets so that you see the fish fly.[230]

27 The black-tail (*melanurus*), because it has a black tail and black wings; for the Greeks call black *melan*.[231]

147

28 The dogfish (?) (*glaucus*) is named from the color, which is whiteish; for the Greeks call whiteish *glaukon*. This rarely appears in summer except in cloudy weather.

29 *Thymallus* takes its name from the flower called thyme, but as it is pleasant in appearance and agreeable in taste, it smells like a flower and infuses odors with its body.[232]

30 The spearfish (*escarus*) is so called because it alone is said to chew its food (*esca*); other fishes do not chew the cud. They say "it is ingenious; for when caught in a weel it does not burst out to the front or thrust its head through the twigs imprisoning it, but turns round, widens the gaps by repeated blows of its tail, and thus goes backward. If by chance another *scarus* outside sees it, it seizes its tail with its teeth and helps the first to break out."[233]

31 The spearfish (*sparus*) takes its name from the lance, which has the same shape; for terrestrial names were discovered before marine ones. For *sparus* is a spear, named from *spargendum* (hurl).[234]

32 The southern (*australis*) fish, either because "it takes water from the waves by mouth" or because "the fish is born when the Pleiades begin to set."[235]

33 The angle fish (*hamio*), found among rocks, is marked by unbroken stripes of purple and other colors on its right and left sides. It is called *hamio* because it is caught by a hook (*hamus*).

34 The sucker (*echenais*), "a small fish," "half a foot long," takes its name because by clinging to a ship it holds it fast (*echei-naus*). "Gales may blow, storms may rage," but the ship is seen to stand still as if rooted in the sea and not be moved, "not by resistance but only by adhesion." Latins called this fish delay (*mora*) "because it forces ships to stand still."[236]

35 "Star-gazer (*uranoscopos*), from the eye it has in its head,"[237] out of which it always looks up.

36 *Millago*[238] is so called because "it flies over the water," and "whenever it is seen flying over the water it means the weather is changing."

37 The small shark (*squatus*) is so called because its scales (*squamae*) are sharp; hence wood is polished with its skin.[239]

38 The city of Syria "now called Tyre was formerly named Sarra from a certain fish that abounds there, which in their language they call *sar*," from which come the names of the similar little fish *sardae* and *sardinae*.[240] 39 The *allec* is a little fish suited for the moistening of salted fish and named hence. 40 Whitebait (*aphorus*) is a little fish which because of its small size cannot be caught with a hook.[241]

41 The likeness to a snake (*anguis*) gave the eel (*anguilla*) its name. Its origin is from mud, and when taken thence it is so soft that the harder you press it the faster it slips away. "They say that the Oriental

river Ganges generates eels of three hundred feet."[242] Eels are killed with wine and those who drink of it have disgust for wine.[243]

42 The weever fish "(*draco marinus*) has prickles on its gills pointing toward its tail."[244] When anyone strikes them, wherever it moves it pours forth poison, and is named hence.

43 The Greeks call the lamprey *muraena* because it winds itself in coils. They say "it is only of the female sex and conceives from a snake; therefore it is summoned by fishermen with hissing as of a serpent and is captured. It is hard to kill with a club, but easy to catch with a rod. It is certain that its life is in its tail, for if the head is struck it can scarcely be killed, but when its tail is struck it dies at once."[245]

44 The conger-eel (*congrus*) [lost].

The polypus, that is, many-footed; for it has many entwinings. It ingeniously "attacks a fish-hook with its tentacles, not teeth, and does not let go until it has nibbled round the bait."[246]

45 The electric ray (*torpedo*) is so called because it makes its body become stiff (*torpescere*) if anyone touches it while it is alive. Pliny tells that "in the Indian Ocean[247] the electric ray, even at a long distance, or touched with a spear or rod, the strongest arms are numbed and feet swift in racing are paralyzed." So great is its strength that even "the breath from its body affects our limbs."

46 The cuttlefish (*sepia*) is so called because it is more easily caught when enclosed in weels (*sepibus*). It is an obscene kind when it mates, for it conceives by mouth like a viper. "Its ink has such strength that, some say, when poured into a lamp the former light vanishes and people appear as black as Ethiopians."[248]

47 *Lulligo*. They say that "in the Ocean off Mauretania, not far from the Lixus river, such a throng of lulligos flies from the water that they can even sink ships."[249]

Shellfish

48 Shellfish (*conchae*) and snails (*cochleae*) are so called because as the moon wanes they get thin, that is, become empty. "The members of all animals enclosed in the sea and shellfish swell as the moon waxes"[250] and shrink as it wanes. For when the moon waxes it increases moisture, but when it is waning the moisture decreases. The philosophers of nature (*physici*) say this. Shellfish (*conchae*) is the name from the first ending, but *cochleae* as a diminutive, as if little shellfish (*conchleae*).

49 There are many kinds of shellfish. Among them are the pearl-bearing, called *oceloe*, in whose flesh the precious stone is made solid.[251] Those who have written on the nature of animals have

recorded that by night they approach the shore and conceive a pearl from the heavenly (*caelesti*) dew; hence they are called *oceloe*.[252]

50 The purple fish (*murex*) is a sea snail, named for its acumen and severity, also called *conchilium* (purple) because when cut with iron it emits tears that are purple in color, from which purple is dyed; and thence it is called *ostrum* (purple) because this tincture is drawn from the tears of the shellfish.[253]

51 Crabs (*cancri*) are so called because they are shellfish with legs (*crura*). They are animals hostile toward oysters, and live off their meat with wonderful ingenuity; for because their strong shell cannot be opened they watch for the oyster to open the closure of its shells; then the crab stealthily inserts a little stone and with the closure hindered it eats away the meat of the oyster.[254] "Some say that when ten crabs are tied to a handful of basil all the scorpions in the vicinity will gather in that place."[255] There are two kinds of crabs, river and sea.

52 The oyster (*ostrea*) is named for the shell by which the softness of the flesh inside is protected; for the Greeks call shell *ostra*. They say the oyster is neuter[256] but its flesh is feminine.

53 Mussels (*musculi*), as we said before (12.6.6), are snails from whose milk the oysters conceive, and they are called *musculi* as if the name were *masculi*.[257]

54 Clams (*pelorides*) are named from Pelorus, a promontory of Sicily, where they abound. "Behold the harsh north wind from the seat of Pelorus" (Vergil *Aeneid* 3.687).

55 Razor-fish (*ungues*) are "so called from their similarity to the nails of humans."[258]

56 The tortoise (*testudo*) is so called because it is covered by a shell like a roof. There are four kinds: land, sea, mud, that is, living in mire and marshes; the fourth kind is river, which live in water courses. Some say — which is incredible — that ships go more slowly when carrying the right foot of a tortoise.[259]

57 The sea-urchin (*echinus*) derives its name from the land-urchin, commonly called *iricium*; it has a double shell.[260]

58 Frogs (*ranae*) are named from their chattering, because they make noise around their native marshes, and "make vocal sounds with importunate shouts."[261]

59 Toads (*agredulae*) are small frogs that live on dry ground or in fields (*agris*) and hence are so called. Some say that "dogs do not bark if they are given live frogs in their mess."[262]

60 The sponge (*sfungia*), from *fingere* (fashion), that is, polish and cleanse. Afranius (415): "I come to you, that I may place my neck on the linen," that is, "wipe." Cicero (*For Sestius* 77): "Blood was wiped off with sponges." For it seems to be an animal clinging to rocks by blood.[263] Hence when it is cut away it loses blood.

Marine life in general

61 For some live in the water and move about, like fish; others are fixed, like oysters, sea-urchins, sponges. Of these some are called male because they have narrow and more compact gullets, others female, which have larger and continuous gullets; some are harder, which the Greeks call *"tragoi"* and we can call "goatish" because of their harshness.

62 The softest species is called paint-brushes (*penicilli*)[264] because they are suited for tumors of the eyes and useful for wiping off inflammations. Sponges become white on purpose, for in summer they are spread out toward the sun and like Punic wax drink up whiteness.

63 The names of all the animals living in the waters are a hundred and forty-four, says Pliny (32.142–54), divided into genera of beasts, and snakes common to land and water, crabs, shellfish, locusts, mussels, polyps, soles, lizards, cuttlefish and those like them, of which many, by a certain natural understanding, recognize the sequence of their times, and some range in their own areas without alteration. 64 Among female fish some reproduce by intercourse with the male and bear young; others lay eggs without masculine intercourse, though he subsequently pours out ejaculated semen; and those touched by this service become productive, but those not moistened remain sterile.

Chapter 7: Birds

1 There is one name for birds but it covers diverse kinds. For as they differ in appearance, so with diversity of nature. Some are sincere, like doves (Matt. 10:16), others astute, like the partridge. Some subject themselves to being touched, like the hawk, while others shrink back, like the Garamantian birds. Some delight in the life of mankind, like the swallow, while others love a secret life in the desert, like the turtle-dove. Some eat only the seed they find, like the goose, while others eat meat and are intent on plundering, like the kite. Some are native, always in the same places, like the sparrow, while others are temporary, returning at suitable times, like storks and swallows. Some congregate, that is, fly in flocks, like starlings and quail, while others are lone birds, that is, solitary because of plots to plunder them, like the eagle, the hawk, and the like. Some have strident voices, like the swallow, while others emit the sweetest songs, like the swan and the blackbird. Still others imitate human words and voices, like the parrot and the magpie.[265]

2 But as they differ in kind, so they are countless in customs; no

one can discover how many kinds of birds there are. For no one could penetrate the deserted areas of all India and Ethiopia or Scythia to know the kinds or differences.[266]

3 They are called aves (*a-ves*) because they do not have fixed routes (*viae*) but run about in byways (*avia*).

4 Birds are named *volucres* (winged) from *volando* (flying), for "when we say 'fly' we also say 'walk.' *Vola* is the middle part of the foot or hand,"[267] and in birds the middle part of the wings, by whose motion the feathers are agitated.

5 Chicks (*pulli*) is the name of the offspring of all birds, but also the offspring of quadrupeds are called *pulli*; and a small man is called *pullus*. The recently born are called *pulli* because they are "polluted"; hence black clothing is also called *pulla*.

6 Wings (*alae*), in which *pennae* (feathers), set in order, show the practise of flight. They are called *alae* because with them the birds feed (*alant*) their relations and look after their offspring.

7 Feather (*penna*) takes its name from being suspended (*pendendo*), that is, from flying, from which comes *pendere*; for birds are moved by the aid of wings when they entrust themselves to the air.

8 Plumage (*pluma*) is like *piluma*; for like *pili* (hair) on the body of quadrupeds, so is plumage on birds.

9 Many names of birds were composed from the sound of their cry, such as *grus* (stork), *corvus* (raven), *cygnus* (swan), *pavo* (peacock), *ulula* (screech owl), *cuculus* (cuckoo), *graculus* (jackdaw), etc. For the variety of their cry taught men what they should be named.

10 The eagle (*aquila*) is so called from the sharpness (*acumen*) of its eyes. "For it has such eyesight that when it is borne on motionless wing above the seas and does not suffer human observation, from so great a height it sees little fish swimming and dropping down like a missile drags its victim to shore with its wings."[268] 11 For it is said not to lower its gaze from the ray of the sun;[269] hence it presents its chicks, suspended from its claws, to the rays of the sun. It keeps as worthy of the stock those it sees hold their gaze without moving, but rejects any it sees blink as degenerate.[270]

12 The vulture (*vultur*) is thought to be named after its slow flight (*volatus*), because from the size of its body it does not have rapid flight. They say that the females do not engage in sexual intercourse, and conceive and generate without copulation; when born they live nearly a century.[271] Vultures like eagles sense cadavers across the seas; flying high they sight many that are hidden by the obscurity of mountains.

13 Slowfoot (*bradipes*) is the Greek name (*bradupous*) for our *tarda*, because held back by slow flight it is never lifted, like other birds, by the speed of its wings.[272]

14 Cranes (*grues*) took their name from their own voice, for they murmur with such a sound. While they are hurrying somewhere they follow the order of the letters of the alphabet. Of them Lucan says (5.716): "The letter is broken and disappears as the wings are scattered." They seek the highest altitudes so they may more easily see the lands they seek. 15 With its voice it sets right the line of birds it is driving; when it grows hoarse another bird takes its place. At night they divide the watches and take turns on guard, holding little stones suspended by their claws by which they betray sleep; their cry indicates what is to be feared.[273] Their color reveals their age, for they darken with old age.

16 Storks (*ciconiae*) are named from the sound that they croak, as if *cicaniae*; "it is a sound of the mouth, they say, rather than of the voice, because they make it by shaking their beaks." These heralds of spring, companions of society and enemies of snakes, fly across seas and arrive in line in Asia.[274] Two crows precede them, and they follow like an army.[275] 17 "They exhibit remarkable piety toward their offspring, for they watch their nests so zealously that they lose their feathers by constant brooding. As long as they spend in bringing up the young, so long in turn they are fed by their young."[276]

18 The swan (*olor*) is a bird which the Greeks call *kuknos*. The *olor* is so called because it is all white with feathers. No one mentions a black swan (*cygnus*),[277] for in Greek *holos* means "all." The *cygnus* is named from singing (*canendo*), because it pours forth the charm of song with modulated sounds. "It sings sweetly because it has a long curving neck, and the voice struggling out by a long and winding way necessarily emits various notes."[278] 19 They say that in the Hyperborean regions when people are playing the cithara, many swans (*olores*) fly there and quite closely sing together. *Olores* is the Latin name; in Greek they are called *kuknoi*.[279] "Sailors say that this makes a good prognosis for them, as Aemilius (Macer fr. 5) says: 'The swan is always most happy as an auspice; sailors ask for it because it does not submerge in the waves.'"[280]

20 The ostrich (*struthio*) is called by the Greek name because it is seen to have wings like a bird but is not raised high above the ground. It neglects to warm its eggs but when ejected they are animated by the warmth of the dust.[281]

21 The heron (*ardea*) "is called as if it were *ardua*, that is,"[282] in flight for others. Lucan (5.553–54): "The heron dares to fly aloft." For "it fears the lightning and flies above the clouds so that it cannot feel the gusts of the clouds."[283] "When it flies higher it signifies a storm."[284]

22 The phoenix, a bird of Arabia, is so called because it has a purple (*phoeniceus*) color, or because in the whole world it is singular

and unique. For the Arabs call singular and unique *phoenix*, It lives 500 years and more and, when it senses it has grown old, it collects twigs of spices and constructs a pyre for itself and, turning toward the ray of the sun, by the clapping of its wings it feeds a fire it has set, and thus rises again from its ashes.[285]

23 "The *cinnamolgus*, also a bird of Arabia, is so called because in high groves it weaves nests from cinnamon bushes, and since men cannot climb up because of the height and fragility of the branches they attack the nests with leaded arrows and thus bring down those cinnamons and sell them at high prices because merchants favor that cinnamon more than other kinds."[286]

24 The parrot (*psittacus*), born on the coasts of "India, with green color, purple collar . . . a tongue broader than other birds. Hence it expresses articulated words"[287] so that if you did not see it you would think a man was speaking. By nature it greets people by saying *Ave* or *Chaire*. Hence comes that expression: "I a parrot will learn the names of others from you; I learned on my own to say 'Hail Caesar.'"[288]

25 *Halcyon*, a sea-bird, as if it were *alcyanea* (sea foam),[289] because it makes its nest in winter in the calms of Ocean and hatches its chicks. While it is keeping watch it is said that the sea grows mild with extended calm and winds silent in continuous tranquility for seven days, and the very nature of things complies with its bringing forth young.[290]

26 The pelican, an Egyptian bird, dwelling in the solitude of the river Nile, whence it takes its name; for Egypt is called Canopus. She is said, if it is true, to kill her offspring and lament over them for three days, then wound herself and by shedding her blood revive her sons.[291]

Birds named after places or persons

27 *Stymphalidae* are birds named after the Stymphadic islands, where they abound. Hercules used arrows against them; they are sea-birds dwelling on islands.[292]

28 *Diomedean birds*, so called from the companions of Diomedes, who the myths say were changed into these birds, like "coots in shape,"[293] swans in size, with a bright color and hard and large beaks. They live around Apulia in the Diomedean island [in the Adriatic] among the cliffs on the shore, and flying over the rocks they differentiate their own from strangers. 29 For if he is Greek they come closer and flatter, but if foreign they fight by biting, as if with tearful voices lamenting either their own transformation or the death of the king. For Diomedes was killed by the Illyrians. These birds are called Diomedean, and the Greeks call them *erōdioi*.[294]

Plate 22 Pelicans: three scenes showing babies attacking their parent, parents killing babies and the mother piercing her side to resurrect her offspring. Fol 35r. Reproduced with permission, from the *Bestiary*. Copyright © Aberdeen University Library.

30 *Memnonides*, birds of Egypt, are called after the place where Memnon perished; for they say that in companies they fly from Egypt to Ilium near the tomb of Memnon, and therefore the Ilians call them Memnonian. In the fifth year they come to Ilium and, after flying about for two days, on the third they begin to fight, tearing one another with claws and beaks.[295]

31 *Hercynian* birds are called after Hercynium, a forest of Germany where they are born. Their wings shine in the dark so brightly that although it is dark night and thick darkness they shine to guard the route ahead, and the course of the way appears by the indication of the flashing feathers.[296]

32 The pelican (*onocrotalos*) the Greeks name after its long beak. "There are two kinds, aquatic and solitary."[297]

33 The ibis, a bird of the river Nile, which purges itself by pouring water into its anus with its beak. "It eats the eggs of snakes, carrying most welcome food from them to its nests."[298]

Other birds

34 The bee-eater (*merops*), the same as *gauli*, said to conceal their parents and feed them.[299]

35 The jackdaw (*monedula*), as if *monetula* (money-guard), which when it finds gold takes it away and hides it, Cicero *For Valerius Flaccus*: "No more gold for you than would be bestowed on a jackdaw."[300]

Day and night birds

36 The bat (*vespertilio*) takes its name from the time because in flight from the light at the evening twilight it flies about driven by precipitate motion and hangs on the most fragile of branches. The animal resembles mice, making a sound not with voice but a squeak. It is a flying quadruped, unlike other birds.[301]

37 The nightingale (*luscinia*), a bird that takes its name from its marking the beginning of the rising day with its song, as if *lucinia*.[302] It is the same as *acredula*, of which Cicero says in the *Prognostica*: "And the *acredula* exercises its morning songs."[303]

38 The *ulula* bird *apo tou ololuzein*, that is, from lamentation[304] and mourning, for when it cries it imitates either weeping or sighing. "Hence the augurs say that if it laments it signifies grief, if silent, prosperity."[305]

39 The screech owl (*bubo*) has a name composed from the sound of its voice, a deadly bird, burdened with feathers but always held down by heavy laziness. It wanders in tombs day and night and always stays

in caves. On it Ovid: "He has become a loathsome bird, prophet of woe, the slothful screech owl (*bubo*), a dire omen to men" (*Metamorphoses* 5.549–50).[306]

40 The owl (*noctua*) is so called because it flies about at night and cannot see by day. For its vision is dulled by the splendor of the rising sun.[307] The island of Crete does not possess this bird, and if it comes there from elsewhere it dies at once.[308] The *noctua* is not the *bubo*, for the *bubo* is larger.

41 The night raven (*nycticorax*) is a night bird because it loves the night. It is a bird that avoids light and cannot bear seeing the sun.[309]

42 The screech owl (*strix*) with a name from the sound of its voice; for when it cries it is strident (*stridet*). On which Lucan (6.689): "The restless owl (*bubo*) and the night-flying screech owl (*strix*) lament." This bird is commonly called *amma* (Greek for "nurse"), from loving (*amando*) infants; hence it is said to offer milk to the newborn.

Raven and crow

43 The raven (*corvus*) or *corax* takes its name from the sound of its gullet because it caws (*coracinet*).

44 The crow (*cornix*), an old bird, is called by a Greek name among the Latins,[310] and augurs say that it increases human anxieties by the indications it gives, reveals ambushes, and foretells the future. [But] it is great wickedness to believe that God entrusts his counsels to crows. They say that among many other auspices it "portends rain" by its sounds; hence comes that expression (Vergil *Georgics* 1.388): "Then the plump crow summons the rain with its impudent voice."[311]

45 The jackdaw (*graculus*) named for garrulity – not as some claim, that it flies in a swarm (*gregatim*) – since they are obviously called after their voice. It is a most loquacious kind of bird and rude in sound.

46 Magpies (*picae*) as if poetic, because the magpie expresses words with distinct sounds, like a man. For hanging in the branches of trees they sound forth with inopportune garrulity, and if they cannot explain their language in speech, they nevertheless imitate the sound of the human voice. Of which someone appropriately says: "I, the chattering magpie, salute you, my master, with intelligible voice; if you did not see me you would deny I am a bird."[312]

47 The woodpecker (*picus*), is named from Picus, son of Saturn, because it was used in auguries. For they say this bird has something divine, proved because in whatever tree it nests a nail or whatever else

is affixed cannot adhere for long but immediately falls out where inserted.[313] "This is the Picus Martius and a *pica* is different."[314]

48 The peacock (*pavo*) takes its name from the sound of its voice. Its flesh is so hard that it barely feels decay and is not easily cooked.[315] Of which someone speaks thus (Martial 13.70): "Do you admire it whenever it spreads its spangled wings, and yet, hard one, can deliver it to the cruel cook?"

49 The pheasant (*phasianus*), named after Phasis, a Greek island, from which it was first transported. That old couplet (Martial 13.72) attests this: "I was transported first by Argo's keel; before that nothing but Phasis was known to me."

50 The cock (*gallus*), so called from castration, for the testicles are removed from this alone among birds. For the ancients called the castrated *galli*. As from lion comes *leaena* and from dragon *dracaena*, so from *gallus gallina*. "Some say that if hens' limbs are stirred up in liquid gold they absorb it."[316]

51 The duck (*ans*) has a suitable name from its constancy (*assiduitate*) in swimming (*natandi*). Of its kind some are called *germanae* because they supply more food than others.

52 *Ans* gave its name to the goose (*anser*) by derivation or from likeness or because it too swims frequently (*natandi frequentia*). It testifies to the night watches by the constancy of its noise.[317] "No animal senses the human smell the way the goose does"; hence by its noise the ascent of the Gauls to the Capitol was discovered.[318]

53 The coot (*fulica*) is so called because its flesh has a pleasant taste. For [Greek] *lagōs* (hare) means *lepus* [as if *lepos*, charm], and hence among the Greeks it is called *lagōs*. It is a bird of stagnant waters, with a nest in the midst of the water or on the rocks surrounded by water, and it always takes pleasure in the deep. When it senses a storm it flees and plays on the sea.[319]

54 The cormorant (*mergis* = *mergus*) takes its name from constancy in diving. For often with head lowered into the deep they collect signs of the winds under the waves and foreseeing a storm on the surface they move toward the land with a loud cry. For "it is clear that there is a severe storm at sea when the cormorants flee to the shore."[320]

55 The hawk (*accipiter*) is a bird armed more with spirit than claws, and bears the greater strength in a smaller body. It derives its name from accepting, that is, from taking (*capiendo*). It is a bird eager to rob other birds and is therefore called *accipiter*, that is, robber; hence Paul the Apostle (2 Cor. 11:20): "You bear it, if anyone strikes you," for in order to say "if anyone strikes you," he said "if anyone robs you" (*accipit*). 56 Hawks are said to be impious toward their chicks, for when they see them able to attempt flight they offer them no food,

but strike them with their wings, toss them from the nest, and compel them to hunt from infancy, so that they will not be fat as adults.

57 The falcon (*capus*) is so called in the Italian language from *capiendo* (take). Our people call this bird falcon,[321] because it has curved claws.

58 The kite (*milvus*) is soft in strength and flight and is so called as a soft bird; but it is most rapacious and always hostile toward domestic birds.[322]

59 The bonebreaker (*ossifragus*) is a bird popularly so called because it drops bones from the air and breaks them. Hence it takes its name from breaking bones.

60 The turtle-dove (*turtur*) takes its name from the word. "It is a modest bird, always staying on the summits" of mountains and in deserted solitudes.[323]

61 Doves (*columbae*) because their necks change into different colors; they are tame birds, living with crowds of men, and without gall; which the ancients called "of Venus" because they frequent their nests and make love with a kiss.[324]

62 Ring doves (*palumbes*), because they are stuffed with food; commonly called *tetae*.[325] It is a chaste bird, so called from its habits, because it is a companion of chastity; for it is said that if it loses its corporeal consort it lives alone and does not look for any more copulation.

63 The partridge (*perdix*) takes its name from the word *perdesthai* (to break wind), a crafty and impure bird. For male mounts male and headlong lust forgets sex. It is so deceitful that it steals and warms the eggs of another; but its fraud has no result: when the chicks hear the voice of their own mother, by a natural instinct they leave the one who warmed them and return to their mother.[326]

64 Quail (*coturnices*) are named after the sound of their voice. The Greeks call them *ortugai* because they were first sighted on the island of Ortygia. Their arrival has fixed times; for in summer they cross the hindering seas.

65 The landrail (*ortygometra*) is so called because it leads the flock. When the hawk sees it approaching land it seizes it, and therefore all take care to get an escort of a different kind, through which they may avoid the first dangers. Their favorite food is poison seed, and therefore the ancients forbade eating them.[327]

66 The Greeks name the hoopoe (*upupa*) because it inspects human excretion and feeds on stinking ordure: a most disgusting bird, with a helmet of upstanding crests, always lingering in tombs and human excrement.[328]

67 Cuckoos (*ciculi*), which the Spanish call *tuci*,[329] are so called

from the sound. They have a fixed time for coming, perched on the shoulders of kites (*milvi*) because of their short and slight flights, so that they will not fail, weary in the long spaces of the air. Their saliva generates grasshoppers.

68 Sparrows (*passeres*) are small birds, so called from their smallness (*parvitas*), hence *pusilli* are *parvi*.

69 The blackbird (*merula*) in ancient times was called *medula*, because it dances. Others say it is called *merula* because it flies alone, as flying *mera*. Though everywhere else it is black, in Achaea it is white.

70 The swallow (*erundo* = *hirundo*) is so called because it does not take food while sitting but catches and eats its food in the air. It is a noisy bird, flying through winding circles and twisting routes, most constant in building nests and bringing up the young. It possesses a certain foresight because it goes out to fall and does not seek the heights. It is not attacked by ill-omened birds and it is the prey of none. It crosses the seas and stays there in winter.

71 Thrushes (*turdi*) are named for their lateness (*tardi*), for at the end of winter they fly away. A *turdela* is a larger *turdus*, whose excrement is thought to generate birdlime. Hence there was a proverb among the ancients, "It is bad for a bird to defecate on itself."

72 The branbird (*furfurio*) is so called because it feeds before meal is reduced to flour.[330]

73 Fig-pickers (*ficedulae*) are so called because they eat figs. It is expressed in that ancient verse (Martial 13.49): "Since figs nourish me and I feed on sweet grapes, why did not the grape give me my name?"

74 Thistle-finch is called *carduelus* because it feeds on thorns and thistles (*carduus*); hence "among the Greeks it is called *acalanthis*, from *akanthai*, that is, thorns, which it eats."[331]

Augury from birds

75 Augurs say that signs are created in the gesture, motion, flight, and voice of birds. 76 They call birds "divining" which give an auspice by mouth and song, such as raven, crow, woodpecker; 77 "high"[332] which by flight seem to show forth future events. If unfavorable they are called "preventative" (*inebrae*); if favorable, "prophetic" (*praepetes*);[333] for all birds seek what is ahead (*priora petunt*) when they fly. 78 They count as the third kind of augury in birds, called "common," a form combined of the two, that is, when birds give auguries by mouth and flight.[334] But this is not trustworthy.

Eggs of birds

79 All kinds of birds are born twice. For first the eggs are generated, and then they are shaped and animated by the warmth of the mother's body.

80 Eggs (*ova*) are so called because they are uvid. Hence also the *uva* (grape), because it is filled inside with a *humor* (liquid). For humid is what has liquid outside; uvid, what has it inside.[335]

81 Certain eggs are conceived by the empty wind; but they are not generative unless they are conceived with masculine intercourse and penetrated by seminal spirit. They say the eggs are so strong that wood bathed with them does not burn, nor does clothing. Mixed with lime they are said to glue fragments of glass together.

Chapter 8: Smaller flying animals

Bees, wasps, hornets, etc.

1 Bees (*apes*) are so called either "because they bind themselves together with their feet or because they are born without feet (*a-pes*) . . . For later they get both feet and wings."[336] Vigilant in producing honey, they dwell in fixed abodes, put together their domiciles with ineffable skill, store the honeycomb out of various flowers, and with woven wax fill their quarters with countless offspring, have an army and kings, wage war, escape from smoke, are irritated by noise. 2 Many witnesses say they are born out of the cadavers of oxen. For to create them "the flesh of the slaughtered calves is flogged, so that worms are created from the putrified blood and these later become bees. It is said correctly that bees are sprung from oxen, like hornets from horses, drone-bees from mules, wasps from asses."[337] 3 "The Greeks call *oestri* the larger bees in the farthest parts of the honeycomb; some think these are kings"[338] – so called because they pitch camps (*castra*). "The drone (*fucus*) is larger than a bee but smaller than a hornet."[339] "It is called *fucus* because it eats the works of others, as if *fagus* [= *phagos*]; for it feeds on what it did not work for."[340] Vergil (*Georgics* 4.168) says of it, "Drive the drones, a lazy herd, from the cribs."

4 Wasps (*vespae*) [lost]. Hornets (*crabrones*) are so called from *cabus*, that is, *caballus* (pack-horse), because they originate from them. For as hornets are born from the putrid flesh of horses, so beetles too are often born from them; hence their name.

5 "Land beetles like a tick are called bulls (*tauri*)."[341]

"The *buprestis* is a small animal in Italy very much like a long-legged beetle. It especially deceives the ox at pasture, and hence derives its name. When it is swallowed it causes inflammation on reaching the gall and bursts the animal."[342]

6 The glow-worm (*cicendela*) is of the genus of beetles; so named because it shines when walking or flying.[343] 7 Cockroaches (*blattae*) are named after the color which they dye the hand if caught, and hence they call the color *blatteum* (purple). This animal does not endure seeing light, unlike flies; for the fly seeks light and the cockroach flees from it and walks abroad only at night.[344]

8 Butterflies (*papiliones*) are tiny birds which abound especially in flowering mallows and make small worms born from their excrement.

9 The locust (*locusta*), because it has long feet like a spear, hence the Greeks call it, both marine and land, *astakos* (crayfish).[345]

10 Crickets (*cicadae*) are born from the spit of the cuckoo. They are mute in Italy at Rhegium but not elsewhere.[346]

Irritating insects

11 The fly (*musca*), from Greek, like *mus*. These like bees when killed in water sometimes revive after an hour.[347]

12 The dogfly in Greek is *cynomya*, for *kuōn* in Greek means dog.[348]

13 The mosquito (*culex*) is so called after the sting which sucks blood; for it has in its mouth a tube like a goad by which it bores through the flesh in order to drink the blood.[349]

14 Midges (*sciniphes*) are flies that are "very minute" but harmful with their stings; "by the third plague the proud people of the Egyptians was slain" (Exodus 8:16).[350]

15 The horsefly (*oestrus*) is an animal of herds (Exodus 8.29), very irritating with its sting. "*Oestrus* is Greek, in Latin *asilus*, commonly called *tabanus* (gadfly)."[351]

16 Gnats (*bibiones*) are insects born in wine, commonly called *mustiones* from *mustum* (new wine). Hence Afranius: "When you look at me and begin to speak, *bibiones* fly from your mouth into your eyes."[352]

17 Weevil (*gurgulio*) is so called because it is "practically nothing but a gullet."[353]

NOTES

1 BIBLICAL ANIMALS

1 Phoenician myth similarly described a primeval snake as "most spiritual" (Philo of Byblos in Eusebius *Preparation for the Gospel* 1.10.46).
2 *Iliad* 19.404–17; Hesiod *Works and Days* 204–12; Aelian 4.54, with references to Homer and Euripides Fr. 920 Nauck.
3 *Acts of Thomas* 30–33 (AAA 2.2.147–50); ibid. 39–41 (AAA 156–59).
4 A. van den Hoek, *Clement of Alexandria and his Use of Philo in the Stromateis* (Leiden: Brill, 1988); *Origen Against Celsus* 6.21.
5 Plato *Statesman* 271E.
6 Philo *Questions on Genesis* 1.31, 32, 48.
7 *Creation* 156–57.
8 E. Stein, *Alttestamentliche Bibelkritik in der späthellenistischen Literatur* (Lvov, 1935), 18; Origen *Celsus* 4.36, cf. 39.
9 Philo *Creation* 158, 160.
10 *Allegory* 2.72, 75.
11 1 Timothy 2:14 insists that Eve was deceived but does not mention the serpent.
12 *Dialogue* 103.5.
13 Eusebius 4.26.2.
14 Melito Fragment 5 Hall.
15 Theophilus 2.23; compare Philo *Questions on Genesis* 1.48.
16 Ibid. 2.28.
17 *Heresies* 3.23.2.
18 Hippolytus *Refutation* 5 praef.; 5.9.12.
19 Ibid. 5.26.22–23, 31.
20 Context and references in R. M. Grant, *Heresy and Criticism* (Louisville: Westminster/John Knox, 1993), 83–85. Philo had already resolved such problems, as we have seen.
21 *Odyssey* 10.390; allegorized by "Heraclitus" *Incredibles* 16 (p. 79, 8 Festa).
22 Sextus Empiricus *Outlines of Pyrrhonism* 1.63. On the other hand, Pliny considers the goat the *foedissimum animalium* (37.60).
23 Oxyrhynchus Papyrus 840.
24 Mark 5:1–20 and parallels. For evidence of demons cf. Lucian *Lover of Lies* 16 (black and smoky); Josephus *Antiquities* 8.48 (overturns cup or basin of water); Philostratus *Life of Apollonius* 4.20 (overturns statue; similarly *Acts of Peter with Simon* 11 [AAA 1.59]); M. Dibelius, *Die Formgeschichte des Evangeliums* (2nd edn, Tübingen: Mohr, 1933), 86.

25 Heraclitus (*FVS* 22 B 13; references); 2 Pet. 2:22; Clement *Exhortation* 92.4; *Miscellanies* 1.2.2; 2.68.3.

26 Firmicus Maternus *On the Error of Profane Religions* 9.2–3 (CSEL 2.91); commentary by A. Pastorino (Florence: "La Nuova Italia," 1956), 119–20.

27 Examples of gluttony, Musonius Rufus 18B; Clement *Tutor* 2.11.4 (from Musonius).

28 Irenaeus 5.8.2–3.

29 Epiphanius 24.5.2.

30 Hippolytus 5.8.33.

31 Especially *Acharnians* 768–87 (cf. W. Richter, "Schwein," *KP* 5 [1975], 47); similarly "dog" in *Greek Anthology* 5.105.

32 Hippolytus 9.17.1.

33 Justin *Dialogue* 10.1; Athenagoras *Embassy* 3.1 (p. 26, 2 Marcovich, with full references). Origen says the slander is less common than it was (*Celsus* 6.27), while Eusebius (4.7.14) claims it is passé.

34 Clement *Miscellanies* 3.10.1. For dogs and goats as shameless cf. Aelian 7.19.

35 Herodotus 2.47.

36 Philo *Special Laws* 4.101; *Agriculture* 144.

37 Barnabas 10.1. Aesop says it cries out because aware it will be slaughtered (Clement *Miscellanies* 7.33.3).

38 Plutarch *Isis and Osiris* 353F; cf. *Table-Talk* 4.5, 670F (also 670A: ugly and dirty).

39 Clement *Miscellanies* 5.51.3, akin to Plutarch *Table-Talk* 4.5, 671A.

40 Clement *Miscellanies* 7.33.1–4.

41 Cf. A. S. Pease, *M. Tulli Ciceronis De Natura Deorum* 1 (Cambridge, MA: Harvard University Press, 1955), 289–91.

42 Cf. J. Geffcken, *Zwei griechische Apologeten* (Leipzig and Berlin: Teubner, 1907), xxvii.

43 Cf. Philo *Creation* 45: men believe in phenomena rather than God.

44 Nock, "The Vocabulary of the New Testament," *JBL* 52 (1933), 139; reprinted in *Essays on Religion in the Ancient World*, ed. Z. Stewart (Oxford: Clarendon, 1972), 347.

45 Aristides *Apology* 12.7; Justin *Apology* 24, 1; Athenagoras 1.1; Clement *Exhortation* 41.4; *Tutor* 3.4.4.

46 Cf. Lev. 19:19: "You shall not allow two different kinds of beast to mate together."

47 Philo *Special Laws* 3.46; 4.204–5; cf. *Virtues* 146; Josephus *Antiquities* 4.228–29.

48 Cf. Philo *Special Laws* 1.260 ("the law does not prescribe for irrational creatures but for those that have mind and reason"); *Dreams* 1.101 (against literalists); *Epistle of Aristeas* 144.

49 Compare 1 Cor. 3:5–9 on Paul and Apollos as co-workers with or under God.

50 Aristeas 128–65 (birds 145–50, animals 163–66).

51 Ibid. 144, p. 41, 10–11 Wendland.

52 H. Usener, *Epicurea* (Leipzig: Teubner, 1887), 78, 10 (*Kyriai Doxai* 32); for Stoics cf. *SVF* III 367–76.

53 *SVF* 2.1152–67 (1153, Cicero *Nature of the Gods* 2.37, mentions the ox).

54 *Special Laws* 1.260.

55 A. Terian, *Philonis Alexandrini De Animalibus* (Chico CA: Scholars Press, 1981), especially 187–89, 198–99.

56 Philo *Virtues* 140, 145–46.

57 Hesiod *Works and Days* 604–8 (nine-year-old bulls are "best for work," 436–38; in midwinter they should not have much fodder, 559).

58 Diogenes Laertius 8.20.
59 Josephus *Antiquities* 4.233.
60 Pliny 8.180.
61 Plutarch *Eating Meat* 998B.
62 Aelian 2.57; 4.25; 12.34; *Miscellany* 5.14.
63 Plutarch *Cleverness* 970A–B.
64 Aelian 6.49; Aristotle *Hist* 577b30 (Pliny 8.175).
65 Plutarch *Marcus Cato* 5.5.
66 Discussion in R. K. French, *Ancient Natural History: Histories of Nature* (London: Routledge, 1994), 178–82.
67 The basic study of the question is R. Sorabji, *Animal Minds and Human Morals* (Ithaca: Cornell University Press, 1993).
68 Varro *Latin Language* 6.56; Seneca *Anger* 1.3.3–8; cf. Sorabji, *Animal Minds and Human Morals* 60–61, 81. Also Justin *Apology* 1.43.8.
69 Galen *Protrepticus* 1 (p. 1 Kaibel). Webs and honeycombs from "nature," Seneca *Epistles* 121.22–23.
70 Sextus Empiricus *Outlines of Pyrrhonism* 1.62–77; Porphyry *Abstinence* 3.2–17.
71 Plutarch *Cleverness of Animals*; dog as example, 963D.
72 Philo *On Animals* 38–39 (p. 85 Terian).
73 Lion/monkey: monkeys' blood as aperitif, Pliny 8.52; medicine for aging lion, Aelian 15.17; Philostratus *Life of Apollonius of Tyana* 3.4; monkey as laxative, Aelian 5.39; J. H. Waszink, *Tertulliani De Anima* (Amsterdam: Meulenhoff, 1947), 312.
74 Tatian 18 (p. 38, 16 Marcovich); 17 (p. 35, 1).
75 W. Gemoll, *Nepualii fragmentum* (Striegau: Tschörner, 1884), p. 1, nos. 1–4. Gemoll wrongly emended *echinon* to *karkinon* rather than *echidnan* (p. 6, note). For dogs and grass, Aelian 5.46; 8.9; dogs and grass, pigs and river-crabs, Plutarch *Natural Phenomena* 918B–C, with parallels by F. H. Sandbach (LCL 11), 204–5 (cf. Plutarch *Cleverness* 974B–C); Philo *Animals* 38, p. 85 Terian, gives other examples.
76 Cicero *Nature of the Gods* 3.21, with Pease's note, 2.1009; defense of ant rationality by Aelian 6.50.
77 W. Kroll, "Nepualios," *RE* 16 (1935), 2535–37; J.-R. Vieillefond, *Les "Cestes" de Julius Africanus* (Florence: Sansoni/Paris: Didier, 1970), 203–4 (II 4), 352 (n. 165); Sabbath, Nepualius p. 2, no. 53.
78 Aelian 1.22, noted by Gemoll.
79 Origen *Celsus* 4.74–87, with the notes of Chadwick, 242–53.
80 H. Conzelmann on Acts (85) compares Lev. 17–18; Philo *Special Laws* 4.122–232; Origen *Celsus* 8.30 (perhaps demons eat things strangled).
81 Epiphanius *Heresies* 30.22.4 (altering Luke 22:15 to "I did *not* desire to eat this paschal meal *of meat* with you"); H. J. Schoeps, *Theologie und Geschichte des Judenchristentums* (Tübingen: Mohr, 1949), 194.
82 Matt. 3:4. Epiphanius notes the change (*Heresies* 30.13.4–5); cf. Schoeps, *Theologie*, 188–96.
83 James, Hegesippus in Eusebius 2.23.5; Matthew, Clement *Tutor* 2.15.1–2; 16.1; cf. *Martyrdom of Matthew* (AAA 2.1.218, 8): eats what falls off trees.
84 E.g., Alexander of Lycopolis *Against the Doctrines of Mani* 4 (p. 7, 20–21 Brinkmann). Marcionites in A. v.Harnack, *Marcion: Das Evangelium vom fremden Gott* (*TU* 45, 2nd edn, 1924), 149–50.
85 Ambrose *On Noah* 26.94 (CSEL 32.1.480–81). I owe this reference to Henry Chadwick.
86 Augustine *On the Customs of the Catholic Church* 2.17.54 (CSEL 90.136–37);

Chrysippus in Cicero *On Ends* 3.20.67 (*SVF* III 371); cf. Sorabji, *Animal Minds and Human Morals*, 195–205, comparing *CD* 1.20. At p. 199 n. 32 and 202 n. 59 the reference to "Basil *Liturgy*" seems wrong; not found in F. E. Brightman, *Liturgies Eastern and Western* I *Eastern* (Oxford: Clarendon Press, 1896), 309–44; 400–11; perhaps the Armenian Liturgy, p. 413 line 2, the rhetorical "all creatures are renewed"?

87 Cf. "Tierschonung und Vegetarismus" in U. Dierauer, *Tier und Mensch im Denken der Antike* (Amsterdam: Grüner, 1977), 285–93; O. Kern, *Orphicorum fragmenta* (Berlin: Weidmann, 1922), 61–62; Plato *Laws* 782C; Euripides *Hippolytus* 952–53; Plutarch *Seven Wise Men* 159C.

88 Diogenes Laertius 8.33, 37–38; Philostratus *Life of Apollonius* 1.8 and 32; 6.11; Iamblichus *Pythagorean Life* 24, p. 62, 7 Deubner.

89 Tatian 19.10 (p. 40, 35–37 Marcovich).

90 *Against Marcion*, Harnack 270*.

91 An example in Justin *Apology* 2.2.7.

92 Theophilus 2.17–18; Is. 11:6–9 (cf. 65:25).

93 Irenaeus 5.33.4; R. M. Grant, *Irenaeus of Lyons* (London: Routledge, 1997), 179–80.

94 Clement *Tutor* 2.11.1; cf. J. Haussleiter, *Der Vegetarismus in der Antike*, Religionsgeschichtliche Versuche und Vorarbeiten 24 (1935), 269. Clement transfers "does not sin" from 1 Cor. 7:28, 36. His "Pythagoreans" amount to the Stoic Musonius Rufus (18A, pp. 112–13 Lutz).

95 Clement *Tutor* 2.15.1–2; Plato *Republic* 372C; cf. Plutarch *Table Talk* 664A.

96 Clement *Miscellanies* 7.32.8–9; 33.7. Plutarch presents Androcydes anonymously (*Tranquillity* 472B; *Eating of Meat* 995E); Clement's quotations appear in the anthology of Stobaeus.

97 H. Chadwick, *The Sentences of Sextus* (Cambridge: Cambridge University Press, 1959), 24 (no. 109); cf. 107, citing Clement (*Miscellanies* 7.32.8) and Origen (*Celsus* 8.30).

98 R. M. Grant, "Dietary Laws Among Pythagoreans, Jews and Christians," *HTR* 73 (1980), 300–1.

99 Fragment in the rhetorician Tryphon *Tropes* 2 (III 193, 31 Spengel); cf. Clement *Miscellanies* 5.45.2–3 (calls him a Pythagorean); 7.33.7 (also cited, but anonymously, in Plutarch *Tranquillity* 472B, *Eating Meat* 995E).

100 Iamblichus 24, p. 63, 10–13 Deubner.

101 Philo *Special Laws* 4.100–5, 106–18.

102 Justin *Dialogue* 20.3.

103 Origen *Celsus* 4.93. Cf. M. Douglas, "The Abominations of Leviticus," in W. A. Lessa and E. Z. Vogt (eds), *Reader in Comparative Religion. An Anthropological Approach* (4th edn, New York: Harper & Row, 1979), 149–52.

104 Eusebius 5.13.4; Dio 56.16.3.2; Suetonius *Tiberius* 32.2; Plutarch *Solon* 30.2.

2 UNUSUAL ANIMALS

1 Cf. Joel 3:16, Jer. 25:30.

2 The discussion of this lion is based on my forthcoming chapter in *Essays presented to Everett Ferguson*, edited by A.J. Malherbe, F.W. Norris, and J.W. Thompson.

3 Ignatius *Smyrn.* 4.2.

4 F. X. Funk and F. Diekamp, *Patres Apostolici* 2 (Tübingen, Laupp, 1913), 382.

5 Seneca *Epistles* 41.6 (I owe the reference to Patricia Miller); also 7.4. Sulla was the first to loose lions, *Dialogues* 10.13.6.

6 Pliny 6.195.
7 Galen *Faculties of Foods* 3.2 (6.664 Kühn); cf. *Temperaments and Force of Simple Drugs* 5.9 (11.734).
8 *Faculties of Foods* 2.6 (6.567 Kühn); spleen in *Black Bile* 7 (5.134). On all this cf. Steier, "Löwe," *RE* 13 (1926), 981–82 (Tierhetze).
9 John Moschus *Spiritual Meadow* 2 (PG 87.3.2853C); *Life of Mary Aegyptiaca* 26–27 (PL 73.688D–90A).
10 Hippolytus *Daniel Commentary* 3.29.4.
11 Tertullian *On Baptism* 17.5.
12 Jerome *Famous Men* 7.
13 Just as he cannot remember people he baptized in Corinth (1 Cor. 1:16).
14 Pliny 8.56–58; other stories in 8.59–61. A. Marx, *Griechische Märchen von dankbaren Tieren und Verwandtes* (Stuttgart: Kohlhammer, 1889), 55–70, remains basic.
15 Sextus Empiricus *Outlines of Pyrrhonism* 1.70.
16 Seneca *Benefits* 2.19.1.
17 Josephus *Antiquities* 18.257.
18 W. Dittenberger, *Orientis Graeci Inscriptiones Selectae*, 662; cf. A. Bernand and E. Bernand, *Les Inscriptions grecques et latines du Colosse de Memnon* (Cairo: Mémoires de l'Institut Française d'archéologie orientale, vol. 31, 1960), 164–65 (no. 71). J. Schwartz suggested that an ancient forger wrote it (*Bulletin de l'Institut français d'archéologie orientale du Caire* 49, 1950, 50 n. 2). The Bernands insist that the author could be an unknown Apion, partly because he "modestly" calls himself "winner of many victories."
19 Pliny 30.18 (F 15 Jacoby); cf. Josephus *Against Apion* 2.14 (F 22).
20 Pliny 31.22 (F 29), 37.75 (F 16).
21 Aelian 11.40 (F 13), also from Aelian in Aristophanes, *Epitome of Aristotle On Animals*, p. 130, 5–6 Lambros; cf. M. Wellmann, "Aelianus," *RE* 1 (1891), 486; A. L. Scholfield, *Aelian* 1 (LCL, 1958), xii n. 2.
22 Philostratus *Lives of the Sophists* 2.31, 625. He calls himself a Roman (Aelian 12.25; cf. 14.45).
23 Aelian 10.29 (F 12).
24 Aulus Gellius 6.8.4–7 (F 6); also in Pliny 9.25 with Roman authorities. The younger Pliny insists (too much?) on the truth of a similar tale from Hippo in Africa (*Epistles* 9.33), without mentioning his uncle's use of it (9.26).
25 Aulus Gellius 5.14 (F 5 Jacoby).
26 Aelian 7.48; 7.23. Another version of the story appears among the Latin fables of Aesop. A shepherd takes the thorn out and later, falsely accused of a crime, is recognized by the lion "at the next circus." Cf. L. W. Daly, *Aesop without Morals* (New York and London: Yoseloff, 1961), 256, no. 563; B. E. Perry, *Babrius and Phaedrus* (LCL 1965), 526.
27 W. Schneemelcher (ed.), *Hennecke New Testament Apocrypha* 2 (Philadelphia: Westminster, 1965), 388–89. On the papyrus and its contents, R. Kasser, "Acta Pauli 1959," *Revue d'histoire et de philosophie religieuses* 40 (1960), 45–57.
28 The location at Ephesus may be an inference from 1 Corinthians 15:32 with its ambiguous reference to fighting beasts in that city. Another text was 2 Timothy 4:17, with a reference to Paul as saved from the lion's jaws.
29 *Acts of Paul* in C. Schmidt, *PRAXEIS PAULOU* (Hamburg: Augustin, 1936), 38–43, p. 5 of the Hamburg papyrus; first English translation by B. M. Metzger, "St. Paul and the Baptized Lion," *Princeton Seminary Bulletin* 39 (1945), 11–21. I am grateful to him for an offprint.
30 *Acts of Peter with Simon* 9–12 (AAA 1.56–60).

31 Commodian *Carmen Apologeticum* 618–22; Filastrius, *Haer.* 88.6 (CCL 9.256).

32 *Acts of Paul and Thecla* 28, 33 (AAA 1.255, 259).

33 H. Thurston and D. Attwater, *Butler's Lives of the Saints* (New York: Kenedy, 1956), 1.486–87; 3.692. For Gerasimus, John Moschus *Spiritual Meadow* 107 (PG 87.3.2965D–2968A); *Acta Apocrypha S. Eleutherii* in AASS 10 (Aprilis II), 532B (cf. 531F).

34 Josephus *Antiquities* 9.213–14. The Euxine (Black) Sea is his own addition.

35 Irenaeus *Heresies* 5.5.2.

36 Jerome *On Jonah* (CCL 76.394–95).

37 Pliny 9.11.

38 Ibid. 32.10. We do not know the dimensions ascribed to Jonah's fish.

39 Chapter 4, *Phys* 17.

40 Herodotus 3.40–42. A "parallel" not quite relevant comes from Augustine's large collection of wonders. He tells how an ailing Carthaginian noblewoman was persuaded by a Jew to wear a hair girdle with a magic ring (containing a stone found in an ox's kidney) under her clothes. Though it somehow slipped off, she found it and threw girdle and ring away into a river, knowing she would be healed. Augustine insists that the tale is true (*CD* 22.8).

41 *CD* 22.7.

42 A. P. Forbes, *Lives of S. Ninian and S. Kentigern.* The Historians of Scotland, 5 (Edinburgh: Edmonston and Douglas, 1874), 222–26. D'Arcy Thompson (*Fishes*, 224) points out that there are only two references to the salmon, neither of them Greek, in classical literature. Pliny 9.68 says that in Aquitaine "it is preferred to all sea-fish," while Ausonius (*Moselle* 97–105) notes salmon's pink flesh and renown as a delicacy.

43 M.-J. Lagrange, *Évangile selon Saint Matthieu* (Paris: Gabalda, 1923), 342.

44 Hesiod *Works and Days* 276–78 (no justice); Aristotle *Hist* 610b18–19 (cf. 591b17); Polybius 15.20.3 (proverbial); Varro *Menippean Satires* 289 (proverbial); Plutarch 964B (citing Hesiod); 970B (no justice); Oppian *Fishing* 2.43–55 (no justice; eating); Aelian 6.50 (same); Sextus Empiricus *Against Professors* 2.32 (same). Cf. M. Marcovich, *Athenagoras Legatio* (Berlin and New York: De Gruyter, 1990), 107.

45 Athenagoras *Embassy* 34.2; Theophilus 2.16; cf. Irenaeus 5.24.2; Clement *Miscellanies* 1.181.6; also Basil *Hex* 7.3; W. Parsons, "Lest Men Like Fishes . . .," *Traditio* 3 (1945), 380–88.

46 Aelian 5.20; Athenaeus 315E (cf. Thompson, *Fishes*, 182). Clement replaces "fish" by "animal."

47 Fish, unlike serpents, are generally good, at least for eating (Matt. 7:10 = Luke 11:11).

48 *Testament of Zebulon* 6.5–6.

49 Jerome *On Ezekiel Commentary* 14.47.6 (CCL 75.715); P. Courcelle, *Late Latin Writers and their Greek Sources* (Cambridge MA: Harvard University Press, 1969), 88. Jerome goes on to list a few that could not live in the Dead Sea, little snails, worms and snakes, "whose bodies we can know better than their names." Why, or how, should one count?

50 See my note, "One Hundred Fifty-Three Large Fish," *HTR* 42 (1949), 273–75.

51 A. W. Mair, *Oppian Colluthus Tryphiodorus* (LCL, 1928), 519–22.

52 Oppian *Fishing* 1.80; Pliny 9.43; 32.142.

53 Apuleius *Apology* 39; Ambrose *Hex* 5.2.5; Josephus *War* 3.508.

54 Aristotle *Hist* 533a26, b1–534b5. They sleep, 537a2.

55 Pliny 9.16–19. In his view there is a "life-giving breath" that "penetrates into water" and also into earth (9.17). Similarly the Christian Theophilus claims

that the life-giving spirit was given "so that the spirit might nourish the water and the water with the spirit might nourish the creation by penetrating it from all sides" (2.13, p. 59, 17–19 Marcovich). This is what fish breathe, according to Clement of Alexandria (*Miscellanies* 7.34.1); cf. Basil *Hex* 7.1.

56 Galen *Use of Parts* 6.2 (3.411 Kühn, 1.300, 9 Helmreich); 6.9 (3.443, 1.323, 18); 8.1 (3.610, 2.442.10–15); 14.6 (4.161; 2.298, 19).

57 Basil *Hex* 7.1; Aristotle *Resp* 479b8.

58 Philo *Creation* 65–66 (*SVF* II 722); 68. Cf. A. Terian, *Philonis Alexandrini De Animalibus* (Chico CA: Scholars Press, 1981), 39.

59 A. S. Pease, *M. Tulli Ciceronis De Natura Deorum* 2 (Cambridge MA: Harvard University Press, 1958), 960; *SVF* II 723.

60 A. van den Hoek, *Clement of Alexandria and his Use of Philo in the Stromateis* (Leiden: Brill, 1988), 185.

61 Clement *Miscellanies* 2.105.1–3 (2); 7.33.3 (Cleanthes).

62 Plato *Timaeus* 92B.

63 Aristotle *Hist* 622a3; Athenaeus 310F.

64 Plutarch *Cleverness of Animals* 970B, 975B.

65 Ibid. 976D–E, 977C–985C. Didymus simply notes that men catch very large fish with nets (*Genesis*, p. 152 Nautin).

66 Basil *Hex* 7.4.

67 J. Levie, "Les Sources de la 7e et de la 8e homélies de saint Basile sur l'Hexaéméron," *Musée Belge* 19–24 (1920), 142–45.

68 Compare Ambrose *Hex* 5.10.29: mute, deprived of reason.

69 Basil *Hex* 8.1.

70 *Baptism* 1.3. F. J. Dölger (*ICHTHYS. Das Fischsymbol in frühchristlicher Zeit* 1 [Rome: Herder, 1910]) argued for a sacramental-artistic origin of the equation, but J. Engemann (*RAC* 7.1084) prefers an origin in the acrostic itself.

71 Sulpicius Severus *Letter* 3.7–8 (CSEL 1.147; SC 133.338–39).

72 A rabbi commented on "everything on dry land died" (Gen. 7:22) that "this excludes fish," but another suggested that before being taken into the ark they escaped to the Ocean (*Midrash Rabbah* 32.11); cf. Augustine *CD* 15.27.

73 *Liber miraculorum, Analecta Franciscana* 3 (1897), 122–23.

74 Matt. 10:16. Supposedly it has no bile. Thompson, *Birds*, 140, cites some authors who agree: Clement *Tutor* 1.14.1, a glossing allusion to Matt. 10:16; Horapollo *Hieroglyphics* 1.57, p. 120, 4 Sbordone (contradicted in 2.48, p. 165, 8), and Tertullian *Baptism* 8.3. Thompson also cites Galen *Black Bile* 9 for the pigeon's having bile. What Galen says, however (5.147, 9–11 Kühn), is that there is no yellow bile in doves because as in some other animals their gall-bladder is not near the liver. Aristotle said the pigeon's gall-bladder was near its intestines (*Hist* 506b21; cf. *Parts* 676b17); so Pliny 11.194 (Sbordone 120).

75 He must give them the seed that falls by the road (Mark 4:4 and parallels).

76 The parallel in Luke 12:24 refers explicitly to ravens.

77 Aristotle *Hist* 613b17–614a35; Wellmann, *Der Physiologos*, Philologus Suppl. 22.1 (1930), 4 and n. 17.

78 Aelian 3.16; 4.1.

79 *Jeremiah Homilies* 17.1 (pp. 143–44 Klostermann). Ambrose copied Origen's "natural history" in *Epistle* 40(32).1–8 (CSEL 82.2.36–40).

80 Eusebius 6.29.2–4. For the similar portent of a woodpecker at Rome cf. Pliny 10.41.

81 *Evangelium Thomae Graece* A 2, pp. 140–42 Tischendorf.

82 Pliny 29.28; cf. 11.4.

83 Aristotle *Parts* 645a6–23, 28–31.

84 *Acts of John* 60–61 (AAA 2.180–81).

85 For a commentary see E. Junod and J. D. Kaestli, *Acta Iohannis* (CCA 2.527–41); cf. E. Plümacher, "Paignion und Biberfabel," *Apocrypha* 3 (1992), 69–109, especially for analogous stories about Pythagoras (Porphyry *Life of Pythagoras* 23–24 // Iamblichus *Pythagorean Life* 13.60–61).

86 On bedbugs in general, O. Keller, *Die antike Tierwelt* 2 (Leipzig: Engelmann, 1913), 399–400; M. Davies and J. Kathirithamby, *Greek Insects* (New York: Oxford University Press, 1986; my thanks to Matthew Dickie for this reference), 46–47; cf. Aristophanes *Clouds* 634, 699, 710, 725; *Frogs* 115 (in hotels).

87 For hotels, T. Kleberg, *Hôtels, restaurants et cabarets dans l'antiquité romaine* (Uppsala: Almqvist & Wiksells, 1957), 93, 113.

88 Translation by D. Magie (LCL).

89 Petronius *Satyricon* 98. His word *sciniphes* comes from Greek *sknipes*. For *sknipes* in a tree cf. Plutarch *Table-Talk* 2.3, 636D ("bark-beetles," LCL [1969], not what Petronius has in mind).

90 Artemidorus *Oneirocritica* 3.8, cited by P. C. Miller, *Dreams in Late Antiquity* (Princeton: Princeton University Press, 1994), 86–87.

91 Pausanias 5.14.1; Aelian 5.17, cf. 11.8; Junod and Kaestli on *Acts of John* 60–61. Add that according to Pliny 10.79 "neither flies nor dogs enter the temple of Hercules in the Cattle-market at Rome," nor do they come close to Mount Carina on Crete (21.79).

92 Pliny 10.75; briefly in Clement *Exhortation* 38.4; Keller, *Antike Tierwelt*, 2.449.

93 Theodoret *Church History* 2.30.13–14.

94 E. C. Brewer, *Dictionary of Miracles* (Philadelphia: Lippincott, 1885), 364. The text is printed in B. Krusch and W. Levison, *Passiones vitaeque sanctorum* (Monumenta Germaniae historica, Scriptores rerum Merovingiorum 7, Hanover and Leipzig: Hahn, 1919), 1–18 (c.18, pp. 15, 18–24).

95 LCL 1.81.

96 Jerome *Life of Malchus* 7 (PL 23.59C–60A).

97 Clement *Exhortation* 39.6; Arnobius 4.26.

98 Ovid *Metamorphoses* 7.624–60; Apollodorus *Library* 3.12.6.6; Hyginus *Myths* 52.3, p. 44 Rose; Servius *Aen* 4.402.

99 Strabo 9.6.16, 375.

100 Cf. S. O. Dickerman, "Some Stock Illustrations of Animal Intelligence in Greek Psychology," *Transactions and Proceedings of the American Philological Association* 42 (1911), 123–30 (usually ant, bee, spider). With the Septuagint, Clement adds the bee (*Miscellanies* 1.33.6). In general, W. Robert-Tornow, *De apium mellisque apud veteres significatione et symbolica et mythologica* (Berlin: Weidmann, 1893).

101 *Phaedo* 82B.

102 11.11–70; R. K. French, *Ancient Natural History* (London and New York: Routledge, 1994), 250–52.

103 Terian, *Philonis Alexandrini De Animalibus*: pro (and con) spider 17–19 (77–78), bee 20–21, 61, 65 (77–78), ant 42 (91–92). See Dickerman's article cited in n. 100, as well as Terian's excellent commentary. Spiders among insects, Aristotle *Hist* 622b19; Pliny 11.79.

104 *Miscellanies* 1.11.2; Varro *Farming* 3.16.14; W. Telfer, "'Bees' in Clement of Alexandria," *JTS* 28 (1926–27), 167–78 (170).

105 *New York Times*, September 24, 1958 (I owe the clipping to my father, who took it to illustrate Vergil *Georgics* 3.219–20).

106 Origen *Isaiah Homilies* 2.2 (p. 252 Baehrens). Celsus drew attention to the leader bee (Origen *Celsus* 4.81).

107 Aristotle *Gen* 759a18, 759b33.

108 Xenophon *Estate Management* 7.34; Robert-Tornow, *De Apium*, 31–32.

109 Augustine *CD* 15.27.

110 Plutarch *Marital Precepts* 144D; *Geoponica* 15.2.19, p. 440 Beckh; Aelian 5.11; 1.58. It is Pliny (11.44) who adds that they hate menstrual blood (Robert-Tornow, *De Apium*, 13–15).

111 *SVF* II 1163 = Plutarch *Stoic Self-Contradictions* 1044D (Aristeas however is unenthusiastic about mice, 163–64).

112 *SVF* III 705 = Plutarch *Stoic Self-Contradictions* 1049A (LCL, 1976, 538–39 with notes by H. Cherniss).

113 Thurston and Attwater, *Butler's Lives of the Saints* 4.218; cf. R. Van de Weyer, *Celtic Fire* (New York: Doubleday, 1990), 122–23.

114 AASS 59 (Octobris XII), 881–82.

115 1 Clement 20.10; cf. Cicero *Nature of the Gods* 2.123: partnerships among small animals in search of food (cf. Pease, *M. Tulli Ciceronis De Natura Deorum Libri III* 2.862–63). J. J. Thierry (*VC* 14 [1960], 235–44) notes that the subject is food and rightly criticizes those who find sex in *suneleuseis* here.

116 J. H. Waszink, *Tertulliani De Anima* (Amsterdam: Muelenhoff, 1947), 188–89.

117 *Genesis Rabbah* I, tr. J. Neusner (Atlanta: Scholars, 1985), 104, from Parashah 10.

118 Basil *Hex* 8.7. Giet refers to Aristotle *Parts* 661b23.

119 Cf. Aelian 4.51 = 6.37.

120 Origen *Exodus Homilies* 4.6 (p. 178 Baehrens).

121 Gnats are viewed unsympathetically in Matt. 23:24.

122 Porphyry *Abstinence* 3.20 (p. 210, 10–15); based on Plutarch; J. S. Reid, *M. Tulli Ciceronis Academica* (London: Macmillan, 1885), 318.

123 Tertullian *Against Marcion* 1.14.1; cf. *Soul* 10.5, translated by Waszink, *Tertullian De Anima*, 187; A. von Harnack, *Marcion: Das Evangelium vom fremden Gott* (*TU* 45, 1924) 270*.

124 *Aus frühchristlicher Zeit* (Tübingen: Mohr, 1950), 257 n. 2.

125 Frogs do not often appear in the earliest Christian writings, but some later saints were able to stop their croaking during sermons or prayer. The idea had appeared earlier in Suetonius' life of Augustus, c. 94.

126 According to Origen (*Exodus Homilies* 4.6 [p. 178 Baehrens]) these are minute winged insects.

127 Origen relies on Proverbs 30:27 to state that locusts have no king (4.7 [p. 179]).

128 Augustine *GL* 3.14 (CSEL 28.1.80); for spontaneous generation cf. Origen *Homilies on Luke* 14 (p. 101 Rauer); *Celsus* 4.57. On Augustine, P. De Vooght, "La notion philosophique du miracle chez saint Augustin dans le 'De Trinitate' et le 'De Genesi ad litteram'," *Recherches de théologie ancienne et médiévale* 10 (1938), 317–43; also 11 (1939), 5–16; 197–222.

129 Augustine *On Genesis against the Manichees* 1.16.26 (PL 34.185C–D). The classification is Stoic; cf. *SVF* III 117–26.

3 UNREAL ANIMALS

1 *Progymnasmata* 6, *Rhetores Graeci* 2.96, 6 Spengel.

2 See Chapter 6, p. 109.

3 Cf. H. Diels and W. Kranz, *Die Fragmente der Vorsokratiker* (ed. 6, Berlin: Weidmann, 1951), 1.276 (30 [Melissos] B 11 and 1). Diels supposed the two were imaginary.
4 Palaephatus, preface (pp. 1–2 Festa).
5 Justin *Dialogue* 3.6.
6 Lucian *Hermotimus* 31 (LCL 6.316).
7 Lucian *True Story* 1.4 (LCL 1.252).
8 Pliny 7.6.
9 Palaephatus 4–5 (pp. 12–15 Festa).
10 Palaephatus 1 (pp. 2–5).
11 Lucretius 5.878–91 (also Scylla and Chimaera, 892–906).
12 Galen *Use of Parts* 3.1 (3.169–75 Kühn; 1.123, 22—128, 5 Helmreich).
13 Aelian 17.9; cf. R. K. French, *Ancient Natural History: Histories of Nature* (London and New York: Routledge, 1994), 267.
14 Clement *Miscellanies* 4.9.4.
15 *Phys* 13 (pp. 51–52 Sbordone).
16 Jerome *Life of Paul* 8 (PL 23.23A); cf. P. C. Miller, "Jerome's Centaur," *Journal of Early Christian Studies* 4 (1996), 216–21.
17 J. M. Petersen, *The Dialogues of Gregory the Great in their Late Antique Cultural Background* (Toronto: Pontifical Institute, 1984), 98, for Gregory cf. 179.
18 *John Commentary* 6.48 (p. 157, 13–14 Preuschen).
19 Philostratus *Life of Apollonius of Tyana* 3.6–8.
20 Sozomen 7.26 (PG 67, 1497B–1500A).
21 AASS 11 (Aprilis III), 766F.
22 G. Morin, "Le Dragon du forum romain: Sa légende et son histoire," *Revue Bénédictine* 31 (1914), 321–26.
23 *To his Wife* 1.6.3.
24 Antonius in *Carmina* by Paulinus of Nola (CSEL 30.329–38).
25 *Life of Saint Sylvester* in B. Mombritius, *Sanctuarium sive Vitae Sanctorum* (Paris: Fontemoing, 1910), 2.529–30.
26 Pseudo-Prosper *On the Promises and Predictions of God* (PL 51.834C–835A).
27 H. Thurston and D. Attwater, *Butler's Lives of the Saints* (New York: Kenedy, 1956), 2.148–50; J. B. Aufhauser, *Miracula S. Georgii* (Leipzig: Teubner, 1913), 113–29.
28 AASS 31 (Julii V), 31C–D.
29 On dragons, H. Delehaye, *Les Légendes hagiographiques* (2nd edn, Brussels: Bollandistes, 1906), 32.
30 The interval was 215 years (Manilius in Pliny 10.5).
31 1 Clement 25–26; Thompson, *Birds*, 182–84; "mythical creatures," D. S. Wallace-Hadrill, *The Greek Patristic View of Nature* (Manchester: Manchester University Press, 1968), 31–32.
32 Ovid *Metamorphoses* 15.361–410.
33 Seneca *Epistles* 42.1.
34 Tacitus *Annals* 6.28.
35 Pliny 10.3–5; story not *certum* but *fabulosum* (29.29).
36 Aelian 6.58.
37 Ezekiel in Eusebius *Gospel Preparation* 9.29.16.
38 Theophilus 1.13.
39 Irenaeus 2.28.2; but Aelian (3.13) says that in winter cranes go to Egypt, Libya, and Ethiopia, while Jeremiah 8:7 says that "the stork in the sky knows the time to migrate, the dove and the swift and the wryneck know the season of return, " though he does not say where they go.

40 Clement *Miscellanies* 4.105.1–119.2; cf. 4.135.1–3.
41 Ibid. 6.35.4.
42 Celsus and Origen *Celsus* 4.98 (p. 262 Chadwick).
43 References in J. B. Lightfoot, *The Apostolic Fathers* I.ii (London: Macmillan, 1890), 84–86.
44 Origen *First Principles* 4.3.2; cf. H. Crouzel and M. Simonetti, *Origène Traité des Principes* IV, commentary (Paris: Cerf, 1980), 196–97. Philo raised no questions about the goat-stag (*Special Laws* 4.105), though like Aristeas he did not name the griffin. The list of animals in Barnabas is based on Leviticus, not Deuteronomy.
45 Plato *Republic* 488A.
46 Herodotus 3.102 (on marmots cf. D. Warsh in *Chicago Tribune*, January 6, 1997, and *Aramco World*, September–October 1997); Pliny 11.111; Aelian 4.27.
47 Clement *Tutor* 2.120 (cf. 3.26); cf. Pliny 33.66 (Indian gold from ants, Scythian gold dug up by griffins, though the bird is fabulous, 10.136); Lucian *Saturnalia* 24 (Indian ants mine); Philostratus *Apollonius* 3.48 (Indian griffins take gold from rocks); Aelian 3.4 (Indian ants guard).
48 Origen *Celsus* 4.24.
49 *Phys*, secunda redactio 6 (pp. 182–83 Sbordone).
50 *Iliad* 6.179–83.
51 *Republic* 588C; cf. *Phaedrus* 229D: hippocentaurs, chimaera, gorgons, pegasuses, inconceivable, and absurd.
52 In J. M. Robinson, *The Nag Hammadi Library in English* (3rd edn, San Francisco: Harper & Row, 1988), 318–20. The Coptic leaves out "Scylla." Clement of Alexandria mentions none of the forms.
53 Methodius *Banquet* 8.12 (p. 97, 7–11 Bonwetsch).
54 Palaephatus 38 (pp. 37–39 Festa); cf. Strabo 14.3.5, 665; also Isidore 11.3.36 (p. 120); Sybille Haynes, *Land of the Chimaera* (New York: St. Martin's Press, 1974).
55 *Hist* 499b18–19: Indian ass (= rhinoceros) and oryx; cf. A. L. Peck, *Aristotle History of Animals* 1 (LCL, 1965), 237–38; both animals in *Parts* 663a22.
56 Justin *Dialogue* 91.2. "Irenaeus ii.42" [= 2.24.4], cited by O. Shepard, *The Lore of the Unicorn* (New York: Barnes & Noble, 1967), 284 n. 29, refers to the cross, not the unicorn, while Shepard's mention of "the disordered African fancy of Tertullian" (p. 81) neglects the fact that Tertullian is following the apologist Justin, no African.
57 Clement *Tutor* 1.17.1; Origen *Numbers Homilies* 16.6 (p. 144, 22 Baehrens); 17.6 (p. 165, 12); Eusebius *Proof of the Gospel* 10.8.
58 Tertullian *Against Marcion* 3.18.3 (*Against Jews* 10.7); cf. W. Richter, "Nashorn," *KP* 3 (1969), 1579–80.
59 Philostorgius *Church History* 3.11 (pp. 39–42 Bidez).
60 Ambrose *On the Blessings of the Patriarchs* 11 (55) (PL 14.725 [B]).
61 W. Wolska-Conus, *Cosmas Indicopleustès Topographie chrétienne* 3 (Paris: Cerf, 1973), 326–29 (314–33).
62 G. M. A. Hanfmann and J. R. T. Pollard, "Satyrs and Sileni," *Oxford Classical Dictionary* (2nd edn, Oxford: Clarendon, 1970), 956; F. Stoessl, "Silenos-Satyros," *KP* 5 (1975), 191–93; Pausanias 1.23.5–6 (behavior); Strabo 10.3.19, c.471 (Hesiod); Plutarch *Sulla* 27.2; summary, [Heraclitus] *Incredibles* 35 (p. 82 Festa).
63 Pliny 7.24.
64 Jerome *Life of Paul* 8 (PL 23.23A–B).
65 Jerome *On Habakkuk* 1.13–14 (CCL 76A.593).

4 ALEXANDRIANS AND THE *PHYSIOLOGUS*

1 Philo *On Animals* 38–39 (p. 85 Terian).

2 Philo *Special Laws* 4.100–5, 106–18.

3 Philo *Animals* 45 and 73. Quintilian agrees too (1.9.2).

4 Aristotle *Rhetoric* 2.20.6; Theon *Progymnasmata* 3; Hermogenes 1; Aphthonius 1; Sopater, fragment in Rabe's edition of Aphthonius, pp. 59–60; Nicolaus, pp. 6–8 Felten.

5 Quintilian 1.9.2.

6 Even though Lucian (*Death of Peregrinus* 16) refers to foods forbidden to Christians. Biblis of Lyons insisted that Christians could not taste blood (Eusebius 5.1.26; cf. Acts 15:29).

7 Barnabas 10:1–8.

8 Aelian 11.37 calls fish without scales *selakia*, but names only the moray; he classifies the octopus and cuttlefish as "cephalopod mollusca" (*malakia*). Nicander in Athenaeus 92D refers to shellfish that feed on the bottom.

9 *Dasupous* (rough-footed) means *lagōs* (hare). Oppian ends the third book of his *Hunting* by denouncing the female hare; further references by A. W. Mair, *Oppian* (LCL, 1928), 158–59.

10 On these and others, R. Kraft, *The Didache and Barnabas* (New York: Nelson, 1965), 109–13.

11 Pliny (8.218) cites Archelaus: "The hare is as many years old as it has passages for excrement." (He adds that the female reproduces without a male.) Clement accepts this story (*Tutor* 2.83.5), while Philostratus says the male hare bears young, "contrary to nature" (*Imagines* 1.6).

12 So Ovid *Metamorphoses* 15.409–10; Aelian 1.25; cf. Aesop 405–6 Halm. Pliny (8.105) points out that Aristotle rejected the notion (*Gen* 757a9; *Hist* 579b15). It appears in two Latin fables of Aesop; cf. L. W. Daly, *Aesop without Morals* (New York and London: Yoseloff, 1961), 194 (nos. 242–43); B. E. Perry, *Babrius and Phaedrus* (LCL, 1965), 470.

13 Anaxagoras (*FVS* 59 A 114) held this view.

14 Clement *Exhortation* 41.4; *Tutor* 3.4.4.

15 Clement *Miscellanies* 5.20.3–21.3.

16 Plutarch *Isis and Osiris* 363F. Diospolis is near Thebes, while Sais is in the Delta.

17 Ibid. 5.41–43, with the notes of A. Le Boulluec, *Clément d'Alexandrie, Les Stromates: Stromate* V, 2 (Paris: Cerf, 1981), 166–72; cf. A. Deiber, *Clément d'Alexandrie et l'Égypte*. Mémoires de l'Institut français du Caire 10 (1904).

18 Ed. F. Sbordone, Naples: Loffredo, [1940].

19 *Resp* 471b23; 475a29; W. S. Hett, *Aristotle On the Soul, Parva Naturalia, On Breath* (LCL, 1957), 436, 454.

20 *Hist* 605b20 (cf. Clement *Tutor* 2.66.1 on vultures and beetles) but wasps, bees and other insects do not take in air, *Hist* 487a32; Pliny holds that insects breathe (11.5–8) and are killed by oil (11.279).

21 His contemporary Marcus Aurelius noted (*Meditations* 6.16) that plants ventilate internally (*diapneitai: anapnein* is for animals).

22 Clement *Miscellanies* 7.31.4–5, 32.1–2.

23 The comparison is to the passage of air through the arteries: F. J. A. Hort and J. B. Mayor, *Clement of Alexandria Miscellanies Book VII* (London: Macmillan, 1902), 244, citing Michael Psellus (= PG 122.841) on the breathing of demons, as well as (p. 243) Marcus Aurelius on life as *anathumiasis* from blood and *diapneusis* from air (*Meditations* 6.15).

24 According to Aristotle, fish do not breathe (*Respiration* 479b13, followed by

NOTES

Basil *Hex* 7.1), but Anaxagoras and Democritus (cited by Aristotle) and Pliny insist that they do (2.18).

25 Aristotle explains buzzing in this way (*Respiration* 475a1).

26 The word occurs in Galen *Distinction of Pulses* 4.16 (8.760 Kühn).

27 Clement *Miscellanies* 7.34.1 = *SVF* II 721. Infused: Theophilus 2.13.

28 Clement *Tutor* 2.11.1; cf. J. Haussleiter, *Der Vegetarismus in der Antike*, Religionsgeschichtliche Versuche und Vorarbeiten 24 (1935), 269. Clement transfers "does not sin" from 1 Cor. 7:28, 36.

29 Clement *Tutor* 2.15.1–2; Plato *Republic* 372C; Plutarch *Table Talk* 664A.

30 Clement *Miscellanies* 7.32.8–9; 33.7. Plutarch presents Androcydes anonymously (*Tranquillity* 472B; *Eating of Meat* 995E); Clement's quotations appear in the anthology of Stobaeus.

31 H. Chadwick, *The Sentences of Sextus* (Cambridge: Cambridge University Press, 1959), 24 (no. 109); cf. 107, citing Clement (*Miscellanies* 7.32.8) and Origen (*Celsus* 8.30).

32 Clement *Miscellanies* 7.33.8. Herodotus 2.37 mentions the priests' avoidance of fish.

33 Clement *Exhortation* 39.5; cf. Plutarch *Isis and Osiris* 353C–D (Oxyrhynchus, Syene); Aelian 10.19 (Syene, Elephantine); 10.46 (Oxyrhynchus). On the identity of these Nile fishes cf. Thompson, *Fishes*, 155, 184, 274–75; all in a discussion of Nile fish in Athenaeus 312A–B.

34 Clement *Exhortation* 39.9; Porphyry *Abstinence* 2.60; 4.15–16; Athenagoras 30.1 (Lucian *Syrian Goddess* 14).

35 *Exhortation* 7.5–6; *Tutor* 2.7.4; *Miscellanies* 4.100.3; cf. also the anonymous address *To Diognetus* 12.

36 Fragment 10b Walzer–Rose.

37 Clement *Miscellanies* 4.105.1–119.2; cf. 4.135.1–3. The letter is 1 Clement, certainly not by an apostle.

38 Clement *Miscellanies* 6.35.4.

39 Clement *Miscellanies* 2.31.2, 35.5; later just called Barnabas, 5 times) or "the apostolic Barnabas, fellow-worker with Paul" (2.116.3). In the *Outlines* he called him one of the seventy disciples of Jesus (Eusebius 1.12.1; 2.1.4).

40 Clement *Tutor* 2.84.1.

41 Ibid. 2.88.1–2.

42 Aristeas 163–67; Plutarch *Isis and Osiris* 381B.

43 *Homily* 1.3.19 (CCL 22.28).

44 As I pointed out in *JTS* 27 (1976), 224.

45 *Clementine Recognitions* 8.25.4–5, pp. 231–32 Rehm.

46 *Phys* 24.

47 Ibid. 21.

48 Aristeas 165.

49 *First Principles* 4.3.1.

50 C. P. Bammel, "Adam in Origen," in R. Williams (ed.), *The Making of Orthodoxy . . . in Honour of Henry Chadwick* (Cambridge: Cambridge University Press 1989), 62–93.

51 Origen *Celsus* 1.37; cf. Thompson, *Birds*, 48.

52 Aristotle *Hist* 563a5; *Gen* 741b2.

53 Pliny 10.19 (from Aristotle); cf. Job 39:27–30, ending "where the slain are, there the vulture is" (eagle in verse 27 LXX); cf. Matt. 24:28, Luke 17:37.

54 Plutarch *Roman Questions* 286C; Aelian 2.46.

55 Basil *Hex* 8.6.

56 Cf. A. v. Harnack, *Der kirchengeschichtliche Ertrag der exegetischen Arbeiten des Origines*, 2 (*TU* 42.4, 1919), 100–2 (Naturkunde).

57 Origen *Jeremiah Homilies* 17.1, p. 143, 11 Klostermann: *kakoethestaton, dolion, panourgon* (Aristotle *Hist* 613b24: *kakoethes, panourgon*; cf. Aelian 4.1: *akolastotatoi*).

58 Origen *Jeremiah Homilies* 17.1 (p. 144, 1–3); Aristotle *Hist* 613b26 (*aphrodisiastikoi*); cf. Athenaeus 389A–F, quoting Aristotle and Clearchus, also Pliny 10.102: "In no other animal is there an equal working of lust."

59 *Jeremiah Homilies* fr. 3 (p. 200 Klostermann); Aristotle *Hist* 629b22, 27; Polybius in Pliny 8.47.

60 Aelian 4.34.

61 Sbordone 126 gives references to Gregory of Nyssa, Theodoret, and [Pseudo-]Athanasius.

62 Origen *Canticles Homilies* 2.11 (p. 56 Baehrens); also *Jeremiah Homilies* 18.9 (p. 163 Klostermann); *Matthew Commentary* 11.18 (p. 166); also Pliny 8.118 = 28.149; Aelian 2.9 ("a marvelous gift of nature"); Aristotle *Hist* 629b22, 27. Full references in H.-C. Puech, "Le Cerf et le serpent," *Cahiers archéologiques* 4 (1949), 17–60.

63 Origen *Canticles Commentary* 3 (p. 215, 4 Baehrens).

64 *Canticles Homilies* 2.11 (p. 56 Baehrens). Compare Jerome on *physiologi* (*Against Jovinian* 1.30 [PL 23.268C]).

65 *Canticles Homilies* 2, p. 155, 16; *Phys* 28.

66 Eusebius *Gospel Preparation* 14.25.4; Aristotle *Longevity* (especially 466a–467b); Theophrastus *Enquiry into Plants* 4.13. In the second century Phlegon of Tralles wrote *On the Long-Lived* – human beings, not animals or plants. Cf. C. L. Feltoe, *The Letters and Other Remains of Dionysius of Alexandria* (Cambridge: Cambridge University Press, 1904), 138–40.

67 *Celsus* 4.24.

68 For Theophrastus the *persea* is an Egyptian evergreen (*Plants* 4.2.5); he lists twenty-six evergreens (1.9.3).

69 P. Nautin in *Encyclopedia of the Early Church* (ed. Di Berardino), 235. Jerome *Famous Men* 109 said he was still alive aged 83 (in 393).

70 SC 233 (1976), 244 (1978).

71 SC 233.22–26; 110/11–138/39.

72 Didymus *On Genesis*, p. 84, 13–19 (1.196–97 Nautin); p. 94, 20–21 (220–21); p. 95, 20 (222–23).

73 Ibid. p. 96, 6–19 (224–25); p. 99, 2 (232–33).

74 F. Sbordone, *Physiologus* (Milan: "Dante Alighieri", 1936); cf. B. E. Perry, "Physiologos," *RE* 20 (1941), 1074–1129 (commentary, 1078–96); Cf. U. Treu, "Zur Datierung des Physiologus," *ZNW* 57 (1966), 101–4; R. Riedinger, "Der Physiologus in Klemens von Alexandreia," *BZ* 66 (1973), 273–307 (using a fragment from Pseudo-Caesarius); id., "Seid klug wie die Schlange und einfältig wie die Taube," *Byzantina* 7 (1975, 11–33 (23–25 lists parallels to Tertullian). For the symbolism see G. B. Ladner, *God, Cosmos, and Humankind. The World of Early Christian Symbolism* (Berkeley: University of California Press, 1995), 121–31.

75 D. Offermanns, *Der Physiologus nach den Handschriften G und M* (Beiträge zur klassischen Philologie 22). Cf. O. Hiltbrunner, "Physiologus," *KP* 4 (1972), 840. Our footnotes illustrate the kinds of sources the *Physiologus* must have used, as well as echoes even in Isidore of Seville.

76 Aelian 9.30 (keeps hunters from following); cf. 6.47 (hare conceals tracks).

77 Cf. *Ascension of Isaiah* 10 (2.659–61 Hennecke–Schneemelcher–Wilson); *Epistle of the Apostles* 13 (1.198–99).

78 Aelian 5.39 (born with eyes open; always awake); Horapollo 1.19, pp. 52–53 Sbordone. Cf. Isidore 12.2.5.

79 Aristotle *Gen* 742a9, 774b16 (cubs blind); *Hist* 579b8 (very small); Aelian 4.34 (cubs small and blind); but this has become a Christian allegory. Isidore 12.2.5 says the cub sleeps for three days.

80 Used by Isidore 12.4.37. A Christian allegory; cf. c. 11 (Sbordone) on the snake.

81 Cf. Theophilus 1.7.

82 According to Tobit 2:10 bird droppings cause blindness.

83 As in cc. 22, 23, 45 (Sbordone).

84 Cf. Plutarch *Convivial Questions* 5, 681C–D; Pliny 30.94; Aelian 17.13. Sbordone 12–13 lists possible sources for this compilation. Cf. Thompson, *Birds*, 185–86.

85 Pure allegory. N. Henkel, *Studien zum Physiologus im Mittelalter* (Tübingen: Niemeyer, 1976), 140–46, notes that like Augustine (*On Psalm* 101:7–8 [CCL 40.1430–31]) Isidore (12.7.26) expressed doubts (*si verum est*) about it. Aelian has heard that pelicans disgorge food to feed the young (3.23).

86 This second trait appears in M (Ambrosianus graec. A 45 sup.; cf. Offermanns, *Physiologus*, 31.

87 Aelian (6.45) mentions mutual hatred of pelican and quail, not snake.

88 Cf. Aristotle *Hist* 619b18.

89 The eagle looks at the sun (Aelian 2.26; Isidore 12.7.11), but the pure allegory is based on the Psalm verse.

90 A Christianized synthesis, with some Jewish and Egyptian traces in the names of months: Herodotus 2.73; Aelian 6.58; Pliny 10.2; Seneca *Epistles* 42; Tacitus *Histories* 6.28; 1 Clement 25. Isidore mentions the phoenix only in passing (17.7.1).

91 Aelian 10.16 (hoopoes' reverence for parents).

92 Aristotle *Marvels* 831a23; Pliny 8.108; Oppian *Hunting* 3.197 (the principal source); Aelian 6.39.

93 Hesiod *Theogony* 297–99, Herodotus 4.9.

94 Herodotus 3.109; Pliny 10.169; [Galen] *Theriacon to Piso* 9 (14.238–39 Kühn), with a quotation from Nicander *Theriaca* 128–34; cf. Horapollo 2.59–60. According to Irenaeus (4.41.3) they "walk in a different way and harm others"; allusion in Clement *Miscellanies* 4.100.3.

95 Isidore 12.4.48 ("it is said").

96 Aelian 9.16, sight and age; Aristotle *Parts* 691b32, turn heads backwards.

97 Isidore 12.3.9.

98 The LXX really reads: "Sirens will rest there and demons will dance there and ass-centaurs will dwell there, and hedgehogs will nest in their houses." (Aelian 17.9 is ambivalent about the existence of the ass-centaur.) Isidore considers sirens (11.3.30) and centaurs (11.3.37) fictitious. M. J. Curley notes a reference to this passage about sirens in Chaucer, *The Nun's Priest's Tale* 4457–62 (*Physiologus* [Austin: University of Texas Press, 1979], 77). For Fulgentius (2.9, pp. 49–50 Helm), it is self-evidently an allegory. Cf. P. Courcelle, "L'Interprétation evhémériste des Sirènes-courtisanes jusqu'au xiie siècle," Monographien zur Geschichte des Mittelalters 11 (Beiträge Luitpold Wallach), ed. K. Basl (Stuttgart: Hiersemann, 1975), 35–48.

99 This section is obviously based on Is. 13:22 LXX and continues *Physiologus* 13.

100 From Plutarch *Cleverness of Animals* 971F; more briefly in Isidore 12.3.7.

101 Like Oppian *Fishing* 2.107–19.

102 Astute and crafty, according to Irenaeus 4.41.3.

103 Other animals hostile to the snake: ichneumon (26), deer (30), elephant (43) (Sbordone 60).

104 Cf. Mark 15:34 and parallels. Obviously this is an allegory, unlike Isidore's notice (12.2.10).

105 Sweet smell from the leopard's mouth, Aelian 5.40; from the *aspidocelonē, Phys* 17.

106 Not listed among the *kētea* by Aelian 9.49 or Oppian *Fishing* 1.360–73 (Thompson, *Fishes*, 114). A *chelōn* is a gray mullet, but since the largest species grows "to two feet or a little more" (ibid. 288), this cannot be intended.

107 Cf. the aromatic panther of c. 16.

108 Paul saved Thecla from marriage with Thamyris according to the apocryphal *Acts of Paul and Thecla*.

109 There is a similar account in Didymus of Alexandria *On Genesis* (p. 112 Nautin). Basil (*Hex* 7.4) says there are sea monsters like very high mountains, and they are taken for islands (7.6).

110 The mooring story recurs in Milton's *Paradise Lost* (1.204–7). Cf. S. Elledge (ed.), *John Milton Paradise Lost* (New York: Norton, 1993), on 1.200–8: "The story of the deceived sailor was common and had been moralized"; also J. M. Evans, *Paradise Lost and the Genesis Tradition* (Oxford: Clarendon, 1968).

111 This is simply an allegory based on Jer.17:11 LXX.

112 On this stone cf. Pliny 30.130; 36.151; Wellmann, *Der Physiologos* (Philologus Supplement 22.1, 1930), 88–91.

113 Cf. Pliny 36.149.

114 This allegory is based on Job 4:11 LXX: "The ant-lion perishes from lack of food." More simply, Isidore 12.3.9.

115 A version of the story appears in the Epistle of Barnabas; see Chapter 1; contrast Isidore 12.3.3.

116 Cf. Aristotle *Hist* 499b18 (and the note of A. L. Peck, LCL, pp. 237–38); *Parts* 663a25; Pliny 8.76 (horn 3 feet long); perhaps sighted by Apollonius of Tyana (Philostratus *Life* 3.2). Virgin, Gregory *Moralia* 31.15.19 (PL 76.589D).

117 The "hunt" is Christian, like the hunt of the unicorn in Isidore 12.2.13. Cf. W. Richter, "Einhorn," *KP* 2 (1967), 213, and famous tapestries such as those in the Cluny Museum, Paris, and The Cloisters, New York. Richter notes that allegorically the unicorn sometimes means Christ or Christians, sometimes the devil, Jews, and the rulers of the world (earliest in Justin *Dialogue* 91 and 105 for the cross).

118 Galen *Temperament and Force of Simple Drugs* 11.15 (12.337–41 Kühn).

119 Pliny 8.109 accepts the story but rejects it in 32.26.

120 Aelian 6.34 (it stands up).

121 Deut. 14:8 refers to pig (*hyn*), not *hyaina*.

122 The basic source here is Barnabas. Pliny 8.105 notes that Aristotle (*Hist* 579b18) rejected this popular belief.

123 This is what Pliny says about the ichneumon (8.88, 90).

124 Aelian 3.22.

125 Aelian 3.9; cf. Horapollo 1.9.

126 So Pliny 10.104 (pigeon); Aelian 10.33 (3.44); Clement *Miscellanies* 2.139.4; Origen *Canticles Homilies* 2.12 (p. 59 Baehrens); Jerome *Against Jovinian* 1.30 (PL 23.263C–D), appealing to *physiologi*; partly in Isidore 12.7.60.

127 The gospels do not call this the Mount of Olives.

128 According to Aristotle *Hist* 589a10–32, frogs are hard to classify, but

Theophrastus (fr. 174, p. 219 Wimmer) argued for the spontaneous generation of both kinds. They appear often in Aesop's fables, strikingly in Exodus
8:1–15, and once in the Apocalypse of John (16:13). Origen says they make
noise pointlessly, perhaps recalling Aristophanes' *Frogs* (*Exodus Homilies* 4.6
[p. 178 Baehrens]). *Phys* provides an allegory of sorts.

129 The sources for this kind of tale go back to the Peripatetic school (Sbordone
97–98). Origen is not so explicit about the hostility.

130 Same as Horapollo 2.62 (from Apion–Chaeremon); a popular thought among
the early Fathers, Sbordone 101.

131 Six instances from the magical stones literature have a symbolic meaning
(Wellmann, *Physiologos*, 85).

132 This is proverbial: cf. Aristophanes *Knights* 419.

133 Aristotle says that wild birds breed once a year but the swallow and the
blackbird breed twice (*Hist* 544a25). Pliny agrees (10.147).

134 A Christian allegory (Sbordone 109), although snakes fear the shadow of the
ash tree "even in the morning or at sunset" (Pliny 16.64).

135 This seems based on a simpler story in Aelian 4.2 (Sbordone 112–13). For
"dove-keeper" see *Physiologus Syrus*, p. 37.

136 Perry 495 compares Oppian *Hunting* 2.445–88 on the oryx.

137 Common knowledge, but cf. Tertullian *Against Hermogenes* 44.2; Origen
Commentary on Matthew 10.19 (p. 25, 26 Klostermann).

138 Oppian *Fishing* 1.369–70; Aristotle *Hist* 566b3; Pliny 9.4–5.

139 Curley, *Physiologus*, cites Aristotle *Hist* 622b; Pliny 9.47; Aelian 9.34; and
Oppian *Fishing* 1.338, all on the nautilus.

140 Thompson, *Birds*, 62: Diodorus Siculus 1.97; Strabo 17.827; Pliny 10.40.
Unclean diet, Aelian 10.29 (Sbordone 123). Unclean water, Galen *Faculties of
Foods* 3.30 (6.721 Kühn).

141 This kind of analysis, as Sbordone 124 notes, begins with Justin *Apology*
1.55.

142 Elephant does flex legs, Aristotle *Hist* 498a2; Wellmann, *Physiologos*, 30.
Aelian (4.31) says it sleeps standing up because lying down and getting up
are so difficult.

143 Caesar *Gallic War* 6.27 (followed by Pliny 8.39) tells the same story about
the elk, but the elephant is already in Agatharchides (C. Müller, *Geographi
Graeci Minores* 1 [Paris: Didot, 1862], 146–47, from Photius and Diodorus
3.27) and Strabo 16.4, 772; cf. Ambrose *Hex* 6.5.32.

144 Cf. Aelian 6.61 (rescue when elephants fall into pits); 8.15 (rescue from
ditch). This account of the twelve and the child must be Christian allegory
once more.

145 Cf. Origen *Commentary on Matthew* 10.7 (p. 8, 8–10 Klostermann); cf. Pliny
9.107–9; Isidore 12.6.49.

146 Evidently continued from c. 9.

147 Obviously Egyptian in origin; Horapollo 1.16 ascribes hourly equinoctial
urination to the baboon.

148 Others tell of such a stone in the head of a hydra; see Sbordone 140–41.

149 Sbordone 142 notes that such a tale does not appear in ancient writers on
nature. It is an allegory against heresy.

5 ANTIOCHENES AND BASIL THE GREAT

1 Aelian Epilogue (LCL 3.386–87).

2 Clement *Miscellanies* 6.2.1; 7.111.

3 Tatian 15.3 (p. 32, 6–11 Marcovich).

4 Tatian 25, line 6 Marcovich. This may refer specifically to the "dog-marriage" of Crates, which Tatian mentions (3, line 26).

5 Ibid. 27, line 20.

6 Apollodorus *Library* 2.97 = 2.5.8.

7 Tatian 17, line 3.

8 Origen *Celsus* 4.74–99.

9 Cf. J. Geffcken, *Zwei griechische Apologeten* (Leipzig: Teubner, 1907), 108, 110.

10 Both *zōōsis* and *stoicheiōsis* (Tatian 9.1 [p. 22, 2]) are related to the Zodiac. Tatian soon rephrases the sentence (p. 22, 10) as "the diagram of the Zodiac circle is the work of the gods." Cf."they showed men a chart of the contellations" (8 [p. 19, 1]). Cf. A. Puech, *Recherches sur le Discours aux grecs de Tatien* (Paris: Alcan, 1903), 119 n. 2.

11 Tatian 9.1 (p. 22, 1–7).

12 Theophilus *To Autolycus* 2.16–17.

13 F. E. Robbins, *The Hexaemeral Literature. A Study of the Greek and Latin Commentaries on Genesis* (Chicago: University of Chicago Press, 1912).

14 Theophilus *To Autolycus* 2.18.

15 Ibid. 2.28.

16 Ibid. 2.23.

17 Ibid. 2.28.

18 Ibid.

19 S. Giet, *Basile de Césarée* (Paris: Cerf, 1950), 49–56; *Homily* 2.6 (p. 31, 10–18).

20 Irenaeus *Heresies* 5.33.4.

21 Hippolytus of Rome had already claimed that the Gnostic teacher Justin used Herodotus' fictional (4.9) "half-virgin, half-viper" as the basis of his system (*Refutation* 5.24–25).

22 *Heresies*, Preface 2.3.1 (p. 171, 6–12 Holl).

23 J. Dummer, "Ein naturwissenschaftliches Handbuch als Quelle für Epiphanius von Constantia," *Klio* 55 (1973), 289–99.

24 On Nicander's snake names cf. A. S. F. Gow and A. F. Scholfield, *Nicander* (Cambridge: Cambridge University Press, 1953), 19–21.

25 Basil *Epistle* 188.15 (3.44–47 LCL); cf. *Hex* 7.1–2, considerably more detailed and Aristotelian.

26 E. Amand de Mendieta, "La Préparation et la composition des neuf Homélies sur l'Hexaéméron de Basile de Césarée: le problème des sources littéraires immédiates," *TU* 129 (1985), 352–53. Basil's "attack on the abuse of allegory in exegesis could certainly apply to his brother Gregory's as yet unpublished doctrine" (J. Gribomont, "Basil of Caesarea," *Encyclopedia of the Early Church* [New York: Oxford University Press], 114). It would also apply to the homilies of Origen, or the *Physiologus*; cf. R. K. French, *Ancient Natural History* (London and New York: Routledge, 1994), 287–89.

27 *On Isaiah* 7:18–19 (PG 30.468B), cited by A. Hermann, "Fliege (Mücke)," *RAC* 7 (1969), 1120; cf. Aristotle *Hist* 539a23; 551a4. Basil's information about insects comes *ultimately* from Aristotle (Courtonne, *Saint Basile et l'hellénisme* [Paris: Firmin-Didot, 1934], 188–20).

28 J. Levie, "Les Sources de la 7e et de la 8e homélies de saint Basile sur l'Hexaéméron," *Musée Belge* 19–24 (1920), 142, notes that according to Aristotle (*Hist* 532b10) the grasshopper has no mouth (cf. Pliny 11.93). Basil worked in "demi-lumière, source ordinaire des méprises." On Basil's sources

cf. D. T. Runia, *Philo in Early Christian Literature* (Assen: Van Gorcum; Minneapolis: Fortress, 1993), 237.

29 Supplementum Aristotelicum 1.1. *Excerptorum Constantini de natura animalium libri duo. Aristophanis Historiae animalium epitome*, ed. S. P. Lambros (Berlin: Reimer, 1895). On the work cf. R. Pfeiffer, *History of Classical Scholarship* 1 (Oxford: Clarendon, 1968), 172–73.

30 On these homilies cf. W. Hengsberg, *De ornatu rhetorico, quem Basilius Magnus in diversis homiliarum generibus adhibuit* (Bonn: Universität, 1957), 196–229.

31 PG 44.61–124; see Giet 20–32.

32 *Homilies* 43.23.4–5 (PG 36.528A–B).

33 Giet 70–71; E. Amand de Mendieta and S. Y. Rudberg, *Eustathius. Ancienne version latine des neuf homélies sur l'Hexaéméron de Basile. TU* 66 (1958).

34 [Basil] *Structure of Man* 3 (PG 30.44D–45A).

35 Kinds of waters listed after Aristotle *Hist* 487a26.

36 Levie, "Sources", 142–45.

37 From Aristotle *Resp* 479b8.

38 But Aristotle (*Hist* 622a3) says the octopus is stupid because it comes toward a man's hand if he puts it under water.

39 Aristotle *Hist* 489a35–489b2.

40 Aristotle *Hist* 566b17.

41 Aristotle *Hist* 508b11.

42 Oppian *Fishing* 2.167–80 (crab and oyster); cf. Pliny 9.90 ("so clever are even the most stupid of animals," polyps).

43 Aristotle *Hist* 622a9.

44 Oppian *Fishing* 1.598–99 (cf. LCL 263 n. e); Aristotle *Hist* 597a14.

45 Simply for warmth in Aelian 9.46.

46 Aelian 7.33. Mentioned, 9.47.

47 Athenaeus 7.312D–E lists authorities pro and con.

48 Already a question for Irenaeus *Heresies* 2.28.2.

49 Mountains and islands again in *Hex* 7.6 (123, 18–19); cf. *Phys* 17.

50 Cf. Aelian 2.17; Oppian *Fishing* 1, 212–43; Plutarch *Convivial Questions* 641B; Pliny 9.41, 79 (GCS).

51 Compare Ambrose *Hex* 5.10.29: mute, deprived of reason.

52 GCS 129: Empedocles in Diogenes Laertius 8.77; Plutarch *Animals* 964D–E; Plato *Timaeus* 91D–92C.

53 This is purely rhetorical; cf. Giet 438 n. 1.

54 Aristotle *Hist* 487b21–32 (the two species, 487b27).

55 Aristotle classified birds into (1) flying animals with feathered wings, such as eagles and hawks, (2) those with membranous wings, such as bees and cockchafers, and (3) those with dermatous wings, such as various bats. Bloodless fliers include those with sheathed wings, e. g., cockchafers and beetles, and unsheathed (no examples). Aristotle *Hist* 487b22, with Peck's note (LCL, 1965, 12–13); 490a6–21; Aristophanes *Epitome* 1.18–21 (p. 4, 5–10 Lambros). Feathered fliers are divided into whole wings and divided wings. On the distinction cf. *Posterior Analytics* 96b39; *schizoptera* in *Parts* 697b11, *Progression* 710a5; *holoptera* in *Parts* 692b13, *Progression* 709b30. Basil fails to get Aristotle's terms quite right; cf. Courtonne, *Saint Basile et l'hellénisme*, 118; D. S. Wallace-Hadrill, *The Greek Patristic View of Nature* (Manchester: Manchester University Press, 1968), 6–7; Levie, "Sources," 118. On classifications cf. R. French, *Ancient Natural History*, 56–58.

56 The model for what follows is given by Aristotle *Hist* 487b33–488b28 (birds and other animals).

57 Ibid. 488b24.
58 Ibid. 614b23–26 (less detail); Aelian 3.13 (more).
59 Cf. Isidore 12.7.16.
60 Aristotle *Hist* 615b23; Aelian 3.23; cf. Isidore 12.7.17.
61 Aristotle *Gen* 774b32.
62 Cf. Isidore 12.7.25.
63 Aristotle *Hist* 612b31–34; Aelian 3.44.
64 Aristotle *Hist* 563a17–27; 619b23–34.
65 Cf. Isidore 12.7.52.
66 Aelian 2.46.
67 Ibid. 17.19: prayers and sacrifices charm these birds.
68 Aristotle mentions the sound of the grasshopper (*Resp* 475a8; *Hist* 535b7); cf. Pliny 11.266.
69 Clement's "circuminspire."
70 Cf. Clement *Tutor* 2.66.2 (oil harms bees and insects). Aristotle too says that insects die in oil (*Resp* 605b20), as does the epitome by Aristophanes (p. 32, 2–3) and Aelian 4.18 (nothing about vinegar).
71 Aristotle *Parts* 693a6–10.
72 Aristotle *Hist* 551b9–15.
73 From Placita in H. Diels, *Doxographi Graeci* (Berlin: De Gruyter, 1929), 376–77.
74 Posidonius in Strabo 2.2.2, 95; so Ptolemy *Geography* 1.7.1 and 7.5.12; cf. Giet 482 n. 1).
75 Cf. Aristotle *Parts* 646a31–646b5.
76 Aelian 2.56, 6.41.
77 Plato *Timaeus* 90a–b.
78 Christians since Justin (*Apology* 1.55.4) had emphasized man's standing erect.
79 Many items are paralleled in Aelian (GCS Basil, p. 149).
80 Plutarch *Cleverness of Animals* 472A; Aristotle *Hist* 612b4.
81 Cf. Prov. 6:6.
82 Plutarch *Cleverness of Animals* 967F; Aelian 2.25.
83 Eph. 6:1: "Children, *obey* your parents."
84 Plutarch *Cleverness of Animals* 969A–B; Sextus Empiricus, *Pyrrhonean Outlines* 1.69 (cf. *SVF* 2.726–27); Porphyry *Abstinence* 3.6; Aelian 6.59 (GCS Basil).
85 A similar notion in Aelian *Miscellany* 10.3 (called a myth in *Nature of Animals* 4.34).
86 Aristotle *Hist* 507a34–b11 (cf. Aelian *Nature of Animals* 5.41); Basil reverses second and third stomachs.
87 Aristotle *Parts* 658b34–659a36.
88 Appian *Syrian Wars* 32: "The appearance of the phalanx was like that of a wall, of which the elephants were the towers."
89 Aristotle *Hist* 596a11; cf. Pliny 8.28.
90 Mouse: Solinus 25.2, Isidore 12.2.16; elephant hates mouse, Pliny 8.29; scorpion, Aelian 9.4 (mice in 9.3).
91 Rejecting the complaint of Marcion against the Creator, as well as the rather simple explanation by Theophilus (2.17): when Master Adam sinned his slaves sinned too.

6 THE LATIN FATHERS AND ISIDORE: PORTENTS

1 *Octavius* 17.10, from Cicero *Nature of the Gods* 2.121, 127.
2 Ibid. 18.7; cf. Seneca *Clemency* 1.19.2–3.

3 Ibid. 20.3–4; Cicero *Divination* 2.49, 61.

4 Arnobius 7.26–27.

5 Vultures and eagles, Pliny 10.6–19; storks, 10.61–62; *immusuli* (unknown), 10.20; *buteones* (buzzards), 10.21; ravens, 10.30–33; sparrow hawks, night owls, 10.39; phoenix 10.3–5.

6 *On the Wrath of God* 13.9–12: A. S. Pease, M. *Tulli Ciceronis De Natura Deorum Libri III* 2 (Cambridge, MA: Harvard University Press, 1958), 1230–32.

7 In the late sixth century Gregory of Tours wrote eight books about miracles, four of them on Martin.

8 *Dialogues* 1.13.8 (CSEL 1.165–66).

9 Ibid. 1.14 (166–67).

10 Ibid. 1.15 (167–68). Cf. dead or sleeping cubs, *Phys* 1; Isidore 12.2.5.

11 Ibid. 1.16 (168).

12 Ibid. 2.9.6 (191).

13 Ibid. 3.9.4 (207); cf. 2.2.4–7 (182).

14 P. Courcelle, *Recherches sur les Confessions de saint Augustin* (Paris, 1950), 101–2.

15 Ambrose *Hex* 4.3.11, misunderstanding Basil *Hex* 2.8.

16 *On Penance* 2.2.8 (CSEL 73.161); *On the Death of Satyrus* 2.59 (CSEL 73.281–82).

17 Cf. Ambrose *On Luke* (CSEL 32.4.140–41). The sirens now appear in the text not of Palaephatus but of Pseudo-Heraclitus, *On Incredible Tales* 14 (p. 78 Festa). Cf. P. Courcelle, "L'Interprétation evhémériste des Sirènes-courtisanes jusqu'au xiie siècle," Monographien zur Geschichte des Mittelalters 11 (Stuttgart: Hiersemann, 1975), 35–48, esp. 35–41. Note especially D. Hagedorn, *Der Hiobkommentar des Arianers Jolian* (Patristische Texte und Studien 14; Berlin and New York: De Gruyter, 1973), 186, 14–187, 6, contrasting "hypotheses" with "the true account."

18 *Hex* 6.9.74.

19 *Clementine Homilies* 1.10 = *Recognitions* 1.9.

20 *Decretum Gelasianum* 6.11 (p. 53 von Dobschütz); E. Peterson, "Die Spiritualität des griechischen Physiologus," *BZ* 47 (1954), 72.

21 See J. Gribomont, "Jerome," *Encyclopedia of the Early Church* (New York: Oxford University Press, 1992), 431.

22 "S. Gerolamo e S. Ambrogio," *Studi e Testi* 235 (Mélanges E. Tisserant 5, 1964), 183–98; cf. J. N. D. Kelly, *Jerome* (New York: Harper and Row, 1975), 143–44.

23 *Famous Men* 124; tr. Kelly, *Jerome*, 177.

24 See E. Lucchesi, *L'Usage de Philon dans l'œuvre exégétique de saint Ambroise* (Leiden: Brill, 1977); H. Savon, *Saint Ambroise devant l'exégèse de Philon le juif* (Paris: Études Augustiniennes, 1977).

25 Eusebius-Jerome *Chronicle*, Helm pp. 50, 18 [Palaephatus 30]; 52, 13 [28]; 53, 19 [3]; 55, 17 [12]; 56, 21 [4]; 57, 15 [1]; 62, 24 [Heraclitus 14].

26 Orosius 1.12.7 (CSEL 5.62, 7); 1.13.4 (63, 10).

27 *Confessions* 6.4; cf. P. Brown, *Augustine of Hippo* (Berkeley: University of California Press, 1967), 79–87.

28 Cf. M. A. Vannier, "Le Rôle de l'Hexaéméron dans la pensée augustinienne de la création," *Studia Patristica* 22 (1990), 372–81 (375).

29 H.-I. Marrou, *Saint Augustin et la fin de la culture antique* (repr. Paris: Boccard, 1983), 135–36; the reference should be *On Christian Doctrine* 2.29.45 (CCL 32.64).

30 Ibid. 136–38; *CD* 21.4.

31 *GL* 1.18 (CSEL 28.1.26); Basil *Hex* 2.6.

32 Against Basil *Hex* 8.1 (128, 1).

33 Augustine *GL* 3.8 (CSEL 28.1.71); Marrou, *Saint Augustin*, 139. The story is not unlike Pliny 32.17.

34 *On Psalm* 102:9 (CCL 40.1459).

35 Marrou, *Saint Augustin*, 139–40; salamander, *CD* 21.4; dragon, *GL* 3.9 (CSEL 28.1.75); unicorn (allegorized), *On Psalm* 91:11 (CCL 39.1287); goat-stag (allegorized), *On Job* 39:1 (CSEL 28.3.616).

36 Augustine *Narrations on Psalms* 101, s. 1.7–8 (CCL 40.1430–31).

37 *CD* 16.8.

38 Ibid. 18.13.

39 Ibid. 21.4–5. Mare: Pliny 8.166; Solinus 23.7; salamander: "Those who have devoted themselves to the study of animals." The principal "other matter" he was considering was how to defend church doctrine against those who refused to "admit that flesh can burn but not be consumed or can suffer but not die."

40 Text in Migne, PL Supplement 4 (ed. A. Hamann, Paris: Garnier, 1967), 39–234; on him see P. Riché, *Éducation et culture dans l'occident barbare VIe–VIIe siècles* (Paris: Seuil, 1962), 82.

41 Commentary 2.11, c. 67; 4.17, cc. 138–39; 8.3, c. 194; 9.11, c. 210.

42 Ibid. 8.9, c. 200 (four *iugera*, Pliny 9.4; islands, Basil *Hex* 7.4; *Phys* 17). He also appeals to Josephus (*War* 6.208) for sons devoured by parents (ibid. 3.10, c. 109).

43 J. M. Petersen, *The Dialogues of Gregory the Great in their Late Antique Cultural Background* (Toronto: Pontifical Institute, 1984), 98, cf. 179.

44 Riché, *Éducation et culture*, 191–92; F. Boglioni, "Miracle et nature chez Grégoire le Grand," *Cahiers d'Études Médiévales*, 1 (Montréal: Bellarmin; Paris: Vrin, 1974), 19.

45 *On the Nature of Things* praef. 1 (p. 167 Fontaine).

46 Isidore *On Ecclesiastical Offices* 41 (40) (CCL 113.47). He follows Caesarius *Sermon* 192.2 (CCL 104.780) but removes a reference to transvestites.

47 Isidore *On Ecclesiastical Offices* 1.45 (44), pp. 49–50.

48 Isidore *On Ecclesiastical Offices* 2.3, p. 54; Vergil *Aeneid* 6.25, of the Minotaur.

49 Ibid. 2.12, p. 72; Pliny 34.166.

50 J. Fontaine, *Isidore de Séville Traité de la nature* (Bordeaux: Féret, 1960), 4–5.

51 Ibid. 9.

52 Ibid. 11–13.

53 The text of the *Etymologies* was edited by W. M. Lindsay (Oxford: Clarendon, 1911); also in PL 82, 73–728 (animals of Book XII, cols. 425–72).

54 *Etym* 1.44.5. These traditional distinctions appear in Cicero *On Invention* 1.27 (explicitly cited in *Etym* 2.6.2; 2.9.18; 2.29.15); for Greek parallels, cf. my *Earliest Lives of Jesus* (London: SPCK, 1961), 120–23.

55 N. Henkel, *Studien zum Physiologus im Mittelalter* (Tübingen: Niemeyer, 1976), 139–46 (144 n. 18). Weasel, *Etym* 12.3.3; pelican, 12.7.26; hearsay, 12.2.13, 12.4.43.

56 J. Fontaine, "Isidore of Seville," Encyclopedia of the Early Church 1.418.

57 Pliny *Natural History*, preface 22.

58 Pliny (Junior) *Epistles* 3.5; night work, Pliny (Senior) *Natural History*, preface 18; excerpting Livy, *Epistles* 6.16.7; 20.5.

59 *Natural History*, preface 17.

60 K. Sallmann, "Solinus," *KP* 5 (1975), 260.

61 Isidore refers to 16 verses from this book, none used by Vibius Sequester.

62 T. Mommsen (ed.), *C. Iulii Solini collectanea rerum memorabilium*, 2nd edn (1895; reprinted Berlin: Weidmann, 1958), 245–46 on Isidore *Etym* 12. Isidore names and cites Solinus, however, in his *On the Nature of Things*

(40.1, from Solinus 23.20–21); cf. A. Schenk, *De Isidori Hispalensis de Rerum Natura libelli fontibus* (Jena: Neuenharn, 1909), 60.

63 G. Thilo (ed.), *Servii Grammatici Qui Feruntur in Vergilii Carmina Commentarii*, 3 vols. Leipzig: Teubner, 1881–1887; repr. Hildesheim: Olm, 1961 (cited hereafter without Thilo's name).

64 Ambrose *On the Faith* 1.6.46 (CSEL 78.20) for heresy like a hydra (11.3.35); Dracontius (12.2.37); and Jerome (not named) for his *Life of Antony* (11.3.21).

65 A. Schmekel, *Isidorus von Sevilla. Sein System und seine Quellen* (Berlin: Weidmann, 1914), 55–58.

66 H. Philipp, "Isidor," *RE* 9 (1916), 2076–77 (especially *Etym* 14.8.39 for the interweaving of Servius and Solinus).

67 R. Gelsomino, *Vibius Sequester* (Leipzig: Teubner, 1967), xl–li. Ovid *Metamorphoses* 15.273–358.

68 *Phys* 22, *Etym* 12.2.13; Gregory *Moralia* 31.15.29 (PL 76.589C).

69 *Etym* 11.3–4; except 12.4.48 (snake in Ovid) and 12.7.28 (Diomedian birds).

70 Ibid. 11.3.28–39; also 12.4.23 (hydra fabulous).

71 Ibid. 12.6.57; Pliny 32.41.

72 *Etym* 12.7.44, 75.

73 PL 177.12–169.

74 F. J. Carmody, "De Bestiis et Aliis Rebus and the Latin Physiologus," *Speculum* 13 (1938), 153–59.

75 B. E. Perry, "Physiologus," *RE* 20 (1940), 1122.

76 Varro is mentioned, but what follows is a generalized "we say" (Augustine *CD* 21.8). Most of my references start from the notes of PL 82 (taken from the "editio Arevaliana").

77 Seneca *Natural Questions* 2.45.3; Pliny 2.27.

78 Compare Serv *Aen* 3.90 (p. 357): Stoics and Academics "say that events contrary to nature do not happen but seem to happen."

79 All this from Varro via Augustine.

80 Valerius Maximus 1.6 (*externa*). 1.

81 Julius Valerius (Pseudo-Callisthenes) 3.87–88.

82 Similar to Serv *Aen* 6.286 (p. 50, 4).

83 Lucan really says that terror arose because "the offspring were monstrous in size and number of limbs," but Pliny 7.34–35 also speaks of "monstrous births" and refers to the maidservant (not located) who gave birth to a snake as a portent.

84 Cf. Pliny 11.244.

85 Vergil *Aeneid* 6.596.

86 Solinus 1.71.

87 Daphne escaping from Apollo?

88 Aristotle says that the natural arrangement is liver/right, spleen/left, though "cases have been observed in some quadrupeds in which spleen and liver were transposed" (*Hist* 496b16).

89 Augustine *CD* 3.5, questioning a literal interpretation of Gen. 6:2–4.

90 Augustine *CD* 16.8 with Pliny 7.23; a similar point in Aelian 4.46.

91 A separate group in Solinus 30.6 (they eat panthers and lions).

92 *Blemmyae*, Pliny 5.46 (Solinus 31.5); others, Pliny 7.23.

93 Solinus 30.12–13; cf. Pliny 6.188.

94 Solinus 19.8 calls them *Phanesii* (an error).

95 Mostly in Pliny 7.10–30.

96 Jerome *Life of Paul the Hermit* 8 (PL 23.23B); *On Isaiah* 5.13.22 (CCL 73.166).

97 In India, Pliny 7.23; no location in Augustine *CD* 16.8.
98 Himalayan forests, Pliny 7.11; no location in Augustine *CD* 16.8.
99 Solinus 19.7.
100 *Etym* 11.3.7. *Macrobii*, Pliny 7.28 (5 cubits and 2 spans); Pygmies, 7.26 (3 spans) in "most outlying mountain region" of India.
101 Pliny 7.30.
102 Serv *Aen* 7.662 (p. 178), explained differently.
103 Ibid. 6.289 (pp. 51–52).
104 Ibid. 5.864 (pp. 654–55); cf. *Phys* 13 (pp. 51–52). Resembles [Heraclitus] 14 (p. 78 Festa) on prostitutes.
105 Cf. Palaephatus 20 (p. 28 Festa). Not the same as Serv *Aen* 6.286 (p. 50), though he explains why Vergil has plural Scyllas.
106 Serv *Aen* 6.395 (p. 62). No relation to Palaephatus 39 (pp. 58–59 Festa).
107 Serv *Aen* 6.287 (p. 51).
108 Ambrose *On the Faith* 1.6.46 (CSEL 78.20).
109 Servius contrasts *fabulae* with *res vera*.
110 Serv *Aen* 6.288 (p. 51); not close to Palaephatus.
111 Close to Palaephatus 1 (pp. 2–5). Minucius Felix (*Octavius* 20.3) lists Scylla, Chimaera, hydra, and centaurs as fictitious and uses Palaephatus' principle: "if they had been, they would exist; because they cannot exist, they did not" (cf. Cicero *Divination* 2.97).
112 Palaephatus 2 (pp. 5–8) gives another rationalization.
113 Jerome *On Isaiah* 14.51.20 (CCL 73A.571). Lengthy description in Aelian 17.9.
114 Augustine *CD* 18.17, from Varro; cf. Petronius 62. Augustine proves transformations by Italian hearsay about barmaids who gave customers drugs in cheese and turned them into pack-animals (18.18).
115 Augustine *CD* 18.16. Pliny 8.80–82 rejects such tales as "fabulous" and declares that "no lie is so shameless as to lack a supporter."
116 Cf. Petronius 63; Synod of Patrick, Auxilius, Isserninus, 16 (PL 53.825B): "A Christian who believes there is a Lamia, interpreted as a vampire, in a mirror, is to be anathematized"; Charlemagne, Capitular of Paderborn, 6 (year 785):

> If anyone, deceived by the devil, believes in pagan fashion that some man or woman is a vampire and eats human beings, and therefore he burns this person up or gives the flesh to others to eat or eats it himself, he is to suffer capital punishment.
>
> (PL 97.145B)

For the Lamia see Apuleius *Metamorphoses* 1.17 and 5.11; Horace (*Art of Poetry* 340) says she swallows children live.
117 As in Apuleius *Metamorphoses* 3.21–25.

7 ISIDORE OF SEVILLE, BOOK 12 *ON ANIMALS*

1 Tertullian *On Veiling Virgins* 5.2.
2 Cf. Augustine *CD* 16.11.
3 Augustine *GL* 3.11 (CSEL 28.1.75).
4 Serv *Aen* 1.435 (p. 143); cf. Augustine *GL* 3.11 (p. 75).
5 Serv *Georg* 4.168 (p. 333).
6 Jerome *On Psalms* 1.3 (PL 24.27A).

7 Serv *Aen* 3.540 (p. 434); *Aen* 1.185 (pp. 74–75); *Georg* 3.49 (p. 279).
8 Serv *Aen* 4.57 (pp. 472–73).
9 All quite unlike Varro *Latin Language* 5.98.
10 Sedulius 1.115 (CSEL 10.24).
11 Ambrose *Hex* 6.4.25 (*agniculus*).
12 Serv *Ecl* 3.8 (p. 31).
13 Cf. Solinus 52.59.
14 Cf. Festus p. 48, 14 Müller.
15 Origen *Canticles Homilies* 2, 11 (p. 56 Baehrens).
16 *Phys* 41.
17 Gregory *Moralia* 30.10.36 (PL 76.343D).
18 Serv *Aen* 1.184 (p. 73).
19 Solinus 19.15–16; close to Serv *Aen* 4.73 (p. 477); cf. Origen *Canticles Homilies* 2.11 (p. 56 Baehrens); other references in Sbordone 97. Deer kill snakes, Gregory *Moralia* 30.10.36 (PL 76.543D).
20 Solinus 19.11–12; Augustine *On Psalms* 41:4 (CCL 38.462); Verecundus *Commentary* 4.17, cc. 138–39 Hamann; cf. H.-I. Marrou, *Saint Augustin et la fin de la culture antique* (4th edn, Paris: Boccard, repr. 1983), 141 n. 1; rivers from Gregory, loc. cit. (n. 19). Chins-rumps of deer crossing sea, Aelian 5.56; teeth-tails of wolves crossing river, 3.6; bills-tails of cranes in flight, Cicero *Nature of the Gods* 2.125; Aelian 3.13; cf. 5.22; Pliny 10.63; Serv *Aen* 1.398 (p. 134).
21 Solinus 19.19 (more than in Pliny 8.120).
22 *Ginnus* from mare coupled with mule, Pliny 8.174.
23 Martial 13.94.
24 Varro *Agriculture* 3.12.6, from L. Aelius.
25 Aelian says the name is western Iberian (13.15).
26 I have moved swine here from 12.2.37. Morel emends to *psyllus*, mentioned in Lucan 9.894–937, and Pliny 21.78; 28.30; but these refer to an African tribe, not an animal (with snakes in Pliny 7.14, but not as here).
27 *Praises of God* 1.515. On Dracontius and Isidore cf. C. Moussy and C. Camus, *Dracontius Œuvres* 1 (Paris: Belles Lettres, 1985), 7 n. 1, 105–6, 178. I have moved the quotation (in 12.2.37) to follow *suillus*.
28 Varro *Agriculture* 5.96.
29 Serv *Aen* 3.21 (p. 340).
30 Solinus 52.36.
31 E. H. Warmington, *Remains of Old Latin* 2 (LCL, 1936), 120–21.
32 Ambrose *On the Death of Satyrus* 1.8 (CSEL 73.213), with advice about such examples in Menander *Rhetor* 2.16 (p. 206 Russell–Wilson – who in turn note the bull of Vergil *Georgics* 3.518 and Statius *Thebaid* 9.82–85).
33 Cf. Serv *Georg* 3.245 (p. 295); Isid 12.2.3.
34 Serv *Ecl* 3.30 (p. 34).
35 Solinus 20.5; Jerome *On Amos* 3.6 (CCL 76.309).
36 Solinus separates *bubali* from *uri*, after Pliny (8.38). Horns as cups, cf. Caesar *Gallic War* 6.28.
37 Cf. Serv *Ecl* 3.55 (p. 280).
38 Fairly close to Solinus 49.9.
39 Jerome *On Isaiah* 5.22.15/25 (CCL 73.215).
40 Serv *Ecl* 6.54 (p. 75).
41 Solinus 27.27; cf. *Phys* 9.
42 Palladius *Agriculture* 4.14.4 (p. 146 Schmitt).
43 Based on Vergil *Georgics* 3.87–88 (cf. *Aeneid* 8.596).

44 Partly from Solinus 45.6; cf. 45.12.

45 Pliny 8.157.

46 Irrelevant; due to Pliny's naming Centaretus (8.159)?

47 Palladius *Agriculture* 4.13.2 (pp. 142–43).

48 Solinus 27.18.

49 Schmitt prints this as a variant for Palladius *Agriculture* 4.13.3 (p. 143).

50 Palladius *Agriculture* 4.13.3 (p. 143).

51 Serv *Georg* 3.82 (p. 282), with *felinei* for *picti*.

52 Festus, p. 374, 25 Müller.

53 Jerome *Hebrew Questions on Genesis* 36:24 (CCL 72.44–45). Homer (*Iliad* 2.851–52) ascribes she-mules to the Paphlagonians, another remote tribe (reference from PL 82.433). Verecundus *Commentary* 9.11, c. 210 Hamann, reports the mating without comment.

54 Jerome *Hebrew Questions on Genesis* 30:41 (CCL 72.38).

55 Ibid.; cf. Augustine *CD* 18.5.

56 Pliny describes both cases (8.171).

57 Pliny 8.212–13.

58 A shepherd's name in bucolic poetry; cf. Serv *Ecl* praef. (p. 4).

59 Serv *Georg* 3.446 (p. 311). Ambrose *Hex* 5.3.9 insists that fish have no unnatural unions like these.

60 Augustine *GL* 3.11 (CSEL 28.1.75).

61 Serv *Aen* 1.215 (p. 83).

62 Serv *Georg* 3.245 (p. 295).

63 Solinus 27.13.

64 Ibid. 27.18.

65 Ibid. 27.20.

66 *Phys* 1, demythologized; cf. [Origen] *Genesis Homily* 17 (a homily used by Isidore: Baehrens, *TU* 42.1.75).

67 I have transferred the quotation from section 6 because it makes no sense there.

68 Serv *Aen* 12.6 (p. 575).

69 Based on Pliny 8.48.

70 Solinus 37.5.

71 Cf. ibid. 17.4–5.

72 Ibid. 17.8

73 Serv *Georg* 2.151 (p. 234), tells this of the lioness, from Pliny 8.43, "old popular belief" (i.e., Herodotus 3.108). Aelian 4.34 calls it a myth.

74 Cf. Pliny 10.202; i.e., the death of its prey.

75 Cf. Solinus 17.11; Pliny 8.42.

76 Solinus 52.40; Gregory *Moralia* 31.15.29 (PL 76, 589D).

77 Rhinoceros in Aelian 17.44.

78 Cf. rhinoceros (Solinus 30.21), unicorn (52.40).

79 *Phys* 22 is the "author on the nature of animals," but Isidore follows Gregory, loc. cit. (n. 76), who speaks of "those who worked hard with laborious investigation in describing the natures of animals."

80 Elephants are attracted by girls in Pliny 9.13–14 and Aelian 1.38 (women generally), but Isidore's hunt is Christian, like Gregory's hunt of the unicorn. According to *Phys* the virgin takes it to "the palace of the king."

81 Cf. Serv *Aen* 1.592 (p. 176).

82 Varro *Latin Language* 7.39–40; cf. Solinus 25.15.

83 Solinus 25.2.

84 Walk in herds, Pliny 8.11; greet sun, Solinus 25.2; flee from smell of mouse, Solinus 25.9 (fear mouse, Ambrose *Hex* 6.6.37); mate in secret, Pliny 8.13.
85 Cf. *Phys* 43 (p. 129), with Sbordone's note.
86 Solinus 25.8–9 (200 or 300, Pliny 8.28 after Aristotle *Hist* 596a12).
87 Cf. Serv *Georg* 1.57 (p. 147): "There were elephants also in Africa, but better ones in India."
88 Serv *Ecl* 8.27 (p. 96).
89 Jerome *On Zephaniah* 2.12 (CCL 86A.689).
90 Solinus 40.21–23 gives a more balanced account.
91 Close to Solinus 30.19.
92 Solinus 2.38 (from Theophrastus, fr. 175 Wimmer); cf. Pliny 8.137.
93 Serv *Aen* 4.551 (p. 562).
94 *Phys* 23 (p. 83); cf. Apuleius *Transformations* 1.9.
95 Serv *Georg* 1.58 (p. 148, 1–6). The story is denied in Pliny 32.26.
96 Serv *Georg* 3.247 (p. 295).
97 Solinus 26.4–5; Servius, loc. cit. (note above).
98 Close to Solinus 2.35–36 (cf. Pliny 10.80).
99 Ibid. 30.24.
100 Close to Varro *Latin Language* 7.32.
101 Solinus 15.8, 11.
102 Cf. ibid. 15.6–10.
103 Serv *Georg* 3.438 (p. 310); cf. Varro *Latin Language* 5.99.
104 Serv *Ecl* 3.18 (p. 33).
105 Pliny 8.148; cf. 150.
106 Varro *Latin Language* 5.101.
107 Gregory *Moralia* 19.1.2 (PL 76.96C).
108 *Phys* 15 (pp. 57–58); cf. Oppian *Fishing* 2.107–19.
109 Serv *Ecl* 10.7 (p. 119).
110 Solinus 27.57–58.
111 Almost all of cc. 32–33 comes from Solinus 27.59–60.
112 Solinus 27.21; Pliny 8.136.
113 Solinus 30.28; Pliny 8.125.
114 Solinus 32.25; Pliny 8.90.
115 Is this a confusion based on Pliny 8.91? I have moved swine (*suillus*) to follow 12.1.25 (p. 309); see discussion there.
116 Varro *Latin Language* 7.46.
117 Serv *Aen* 1.423 (p. 140).
118 Serv *Georg* 3.407 (p. 308).
119 *Mus* Iberian, F. Tietze in *Glotta* 28 (1939/40), 279; Greek (Hesychius), J. Friedrich, ibid. 29 (1941/42), 61.
120 Serv *Georg* 3.278 (p. 297): *saurex pro sorex.*
121 Serv *Aen* 9.747 (p. 376).
122 Contrast *Phys* 21 (pp. 76–77)
123 Solinus 4.3.
124 Jerome *On Psalms* 1.19 (PL 36.55A).
125 Serv *Aen* 12.9 (p. 576).
126 Cf. Pliny 8.224.
127 Ambrose *Hex* 6.4.20. Cf. *Phys* 16 (pp. 55–56) on *echinus*; Augustine *On Psalm* 103 c. 3, 18 (CCL 40.1515): *spinosum.*
128 Pliny 29.138.
129 Serv *Aen* 4.402 (p. 536, 1, 17).
130 *Phys* 12 (pp. 48–49).

NOTES

131 Solinus 30.23.
132 Gregory *Moralia* 5.20.40 (CCL 143.246); Sofer 102; not like *Phys* 20 (pp. 73–75).
133 Isidore like Solinus (27.28ff.) lays emphasis on African snakes (27.28), though his quotations on them come from the ninth book of Lucan (604–937) or the scholia (H. Usener, *M. Annaei Lucani Commenta Bernensia* [Leipzig: Teubner, 1869], 308–9). Lucan "took the names of the snakes either from Macro, from the books of *Theriaca*, for he edited two of them, or the obscure ones from snake-charmers" (Usener, op. cit., 308, on Lucan 9.701).
134 Serv *Aen* 5.85 (p. 603).
135 Lactantius *On the Creation* 7 (CSEL 17.26).
136 Serv *Aen* 2.474 (p. 292).
137 Isidore likes the rhymes and imitates them at *Etym* 12.4.39. A remote model: Cicero *Orator* 2.140: *quot homines, tot causae*; but directly, Tertullian *Scorpiace* 1: *tot venena quot et genera, tot pernicies quot et species, tot dolores quot et colores*.
138 Cf. Augustine *On Psalm* 148:9 (CCL 40.2172).
139 Solinus 30.15.
140 Pliny 29.67.
141 Lucan 9.733: needs no poison to inflict death; 732: *Nec tutus spatio est elephans.*
142 Cf. Lucan 9.730–33; Solinus 15.11; cf. Pliny 8.33.
143 Pliny 29.66.
144 Jerome *On Isaiah* 5.14.29 (CCL 73.173).
145 Solinus 27.53; Pliny 8.78–79.
146 Pliny 8.78–79; not close to Solinus 27.51.
146 Jerome *On Isaiah* 16.59.6 (CCL 73A.640).
148 So the basilisk of Lucan 9.725.
149 Serv *Georg* 3.416 (p. 309).
150 Pliny 10.169; cf. *Phys* 10 (p. 34).
151 The title of Nicander's second poem.
152 Augustine *On Psalm* 57.7 (CCL 39.715).
153 Cf. Lucan 9.718 ("parched *dipsas*") and the scholion on that line in Usener, op. cit., 309: "It makes those struck die of thirst"; Solinus 27.31; also Lucian *On the Dipsas* and Aelian 6.51. Because *dipsas* recurs in *Etym* 12.4.31, *seps* (17) in 12.4.32, and *ammodytes* (30) in 12.4.39, Schmekel considers 12.4.30–33 inserted later (p. 41 n. 2).
154 Solinus 27.31, with Cleopatra.
155 Ibid. 27.32a; cf. Lucan 9.709, 805–14; Aelian 15.13.
156 Solinus 27.32b, slightly changed.
157 Lucan 9.723, 774–88; Solinus 27.32. Cf. *Etym* 12.4.31.
158 Close to Solinus 27.28. Horns: Pliny 8.85; flexible: Lucan 9.716, "wandering about with twisting spine."
159 Solinus 27.30.
160 Cf. ibid. 27.29; Pliny 8.85.
161 *Hydri* in Pliny 29.72.
162 Festus p. 50, 13 Müller.
163 Serv *Aen* 6.287 (p. 51), with *excetra*. Palaephatus 38 (pp. 55–58 Festa) gives another rationalistic explanation.
164 Serv *Georg* 3.415 (p. 309).
165 J. Blänsdorf, *Fragmenta Poetarum Latinorum* (Stuttgart and Leipzig: Teubner, 1995), 275 (Aemilius Macer fr. 8).

166 Cf. Lucan 9.720: *natrix violator aquae*.
167 Solinus 2.33; cf. Pliny 8.37, 30.139.
168 Solinus 27.30 (Dressel 45 n. 1); cf. Lucan 9.822–27 who discusses the *iaculus* but does not use these words.
169 Solinus 32.33.
170 Only the second half of the sentence refers to the *ammodytes*, whose name recurs (from Solinus) in 12.4.39. Cf. Usener, op. cit., 309, on Lucan 9.716.
171 Already discussed in *Etym* 12.4.17.
172 Already discussed in *Etym* 12.4.13.
173 A venomous ant in Pliny 29.92; but a snake in Lucan 9.837: "Who would fear to tread on your lair, *salpuga*?"
174 Cf. *Caecilia*, a lizard in Columella 6.17.1, 4; Pliny 9.166 mentions *caeci serpentes*.
175 See Multipede, 12.5.6, and Pliny 29.136.
176 Called *batrachus* in Pliny 32.145; cf. Thompson, *Fishes*, 28–29. Frogs (*ranae*) in Isidore *Etym* 12.6.58.
177 Pliny affirms (10.188) and denies (29.76) this; Solinus leaves the animal out.
178 Pliny 29.74–75.
179 *Phys* 31 (p. 101).
180 Ibid. 2 (pp. 8–9).
181 Already discussed in *Etym* 12.4.30.
182 Solinus 27.33; cf. *Etym* 12.4.3.
183 Serv *Aen* 1.688 (p. 194).
184 Serv *Georg* 3.422 (p. 309). Cf. *Phys* 11.
185 Solinus 27.35.
186 Serv *Aen* 2.211 (p. 255).
187 Ibid. 7.354 (p. 154).
188 *Phys* 11, etymologized.
189 Serv *Aen* 5.95 (p. 604); cf. Pliny 10.188.
190 A warped development from 1 Cor. 15:21.
191 *Phys* 11.
192 Jerome *On Psalm 21* (PL 36.174).
193 Solinus 27.33: "scorpions, skinks, and lizards are classified with worms, not snakes." Tertullian begins his *Scorpiace* with an extended discussion, partly from Nicander.
194 Cf. Pliny 29.92–96; especially the Spanish fly.
195 Pliny 28.136; see *Etym* 12.4.33 (*multipes*).
196 Mentioned Pliny 29.113.
197 Cf. Pliny 11.75–78.
198 Jerome *In Amos* 2.4.9 (CCL 76.266).
199 Serv *Georg* 1.256 (p. 190).
200 Supposedly causes migraine: O. Keller, *Die antike Tierwelt* 2 (Leipzig: Engelmann, 1913), 504.
201 Cf. Pliny 30.39: *scarabaei terrestres ricino similes*.
202 Cf. Pliny 29.111.
203 The *Oxford Latin Dictionary* gives "woodworm" or "maggot" for *tarmes*.
204 See Pliny 30.39, noted above.
205 Ibid. 30.131.
206 See *Etym* 12.1.6.
207 Ambrose *Hex* 5.1.4.
208 Systematized from Ambrose *Hex* 5.2.5.
209 *Glaucus* (*umbra?*), *auratae*, Pliny 9.58; cf. Martial 13.90.

210 Cf. Ambrose *Hex* 5.3.7: "others generate eggs, like the larger *varii*, which they call trout." Cf. A. C. Andrews, "Greek and Latin Terms for Salmon and Trout," *Transactions of the American Philological Association* 86 (1955), 314 n. 43.
211 Orb, Pliny 32.14; sole, 9.72 (flat).
212 Sea-mouse in Pliny 9.71; with whale, 9.186; on Pliny's mixups cf. Jones, LCL *Pliny* 8.591.
213 Aristotle (*Hist* 547b18) said they were generated spontaneously in mud; cf. Oppian *Fishing* 1.764–66; Thompson, *Fishes*, 190.
214 Serv *Aen* 5.822 (p. 651).
215 Cf. Ambrose *Hex* 5.10.28 (*illa immensa genera piscium, aequalia montibus corpora, ut tradiderunt nobis qui videre potuerunt*).
216 Serv *Georg* 4.387, 394 (pp. 350–51).
217 Solinus 12.1, 3, 5–7.
218 Ibid. 32.26.
219 Text confirmed by Gregory of Tours (Sofer 158–59); cf. Pliny 32.19 from Apion (grunts when caught).
220 Confused with sea pig (*Etym* 12.6.12)?
221 Solinus 12.13 (Pliny 9.50).
222 Pliny 32.15.
223 Ibid. 20.120; cf. 32.55.
224 The *araneus* "wounds with the sharp point of its dorsal fin" (Pliny 9.155).
225 Solinus 32.22–26.
226 Ibid. 32.30.
227 Pliny mentions the *phagrus* (9.57) or *phager* (32.150).
228 Pliny 32.11–12, from Ovid *Fishing*.
229 Pliny 32.138.
230 From Pliny 32.8 (*echeneis*); according to 9.54 they leap over ships.
231 Mentioned by Ovid (*Fishing*), according to Pliny 32.152.
232 Ambrose *Hex* 5.2.6.
233 Pliny 32.11, citing Ovid *Fishing* (9–18).
234 Partly from Serv *Aen* 11.682 (p. 556).
235 Serv *Georg* 4.234 (p. 339).
236 Pliny 32.2, 6, slightly paraphrased; cf. 9.79 and Lucan 6.674–75. Discussion in Thompson, *Fishes*, 67–70 (examples).
237 Pliny 32.69.
238 Pliny 32.15 (*lolligo*) thus; Isidore confuses it with the *millago* here but goes on correctly, following Pliny, in *Etym* 12.6.47.
239 Cf. Pliny 9.40.
240 Serv *Georg* 2.506 (p. 268). Tyre called Sar [rock], Theodoret *Ezekiel Commentary* 26.1–2 (PG 81, 1068A); Thompson, *Fishes*, 213: *sardae // sardenai*, Galen *Faculties of Foods* 3.41 (6.746 Kühn); Edict of Diocletian 5.12 (T. Frank (ed.), *Economic Survey of Ancient Rome* 5 [Baltimore: Johns Hopkins, 1940], 329.
241 *Allex* (= *allec*) is actually a sauce ("sediment of *garum*") or derived from a worthless small *aphye* (Pliny 31.85–96). On such small fry see Thompson, *Fishes*, 21–23, and on *garum* Keller, *Antike Tierwelt* 2.337–38.
242 Pliny 9.4; Solinus 52.41.
243 Pliny 32.138; cf. *Etym* 12.6.25.
244 Pliny 32.148.
245 Pliny 32.14; cf. Ambrose *Hex* 5.7.18 (viper hisses).
246 Pliny 32.12.
247 Pliny 32.7 (*ex eodem mari*, not Indian).

248 Pliny 32.141 ("some" = Anaxilaus).
249 Pliny 32.15, exactly copied. Cf. *Etym* 12.6.36.
250 Palladius *Agriculture* 13.6 (p. 259).
251 Ambrose *Hex* 5.11.33 (oysters).
252 *Phys* 44. Pearls, also *Etym* 16.10.1. Conceived from heavenly dew, Pliny 9.107.
253 Vitruvius 7.13.3, slightly garbled.
254 Ambrose *Hex* 5.8.21–22. This is what Pliny (9.90) says of polyps and shellfish.
255 Repeated from *Etym* 12.6.17.
256 Serv *Georg* 1.207 (p. 179); cf. Pliny 10.189.
257 Cf. *Etym* 12.6.6 and notes.
258 Pliny 9.184.
259 Kinds: Pliny 32.32–41; ships (incredible); 32.41.
260 Ambrose *Hex* 5.9.24.
261 Ibid. *Hex* 5.1.3 with Origen *Exodus Homily* 4 (p. 178, 13 Baehrens).
262 Salpe(s) in Pliny 32.140.
263 Cf. Pliny 9.149; also 31.124–30.
264 Name in Pliny 9.148.
265 Ambrose *Hex* 5.14.45–49. Only the "swan song" is sweet, 5.12.39. See *Etym* 12.7.18.
266 Cf. Pliny 10.3.
267 Cf. Serv *Aen* 6.198 (p. 39).
268 Jerome *On Obadiah* 2/4 (CCL 76.357), from "those who discuss the nature of birds." Cf. Aelian 2.26, and the osprey (*haliaëtus*) in Pliny 10.8.
269 Gregory *Moralia* 31.47.94 (PL 76.625D); also in *Phys* 6.
270 The osprey in Pliny 10.10. Cf. Ambrose *Hex* 5.18.60; Augustine *Deeds of Pelagius* 6.18 (CSEL 42.71); *Exegesis of John* 36.5 (CCL 36.327); Marrou, *Saint Augustin*, 140; Verecundus *Commentary* 2.11, c. 67 Hamann.
271 Ambrose *Hex* 5.20.64; *On the Death of Theodosius* (PL 16.1447–48). Like Origen he likens the female vulture to the Virgin Mary (*Hex* 5.20.65); not so, *Phys* 19.
272 Reading *bradipes* for *gradipes*. Pliny 10.57 calls *tarda* a Spanish name.
273 Based on Pliny 10.58–59 and Serv *Aen* 1.398 (p. 134). Same story in Aelian 3.13. Cf. Ambrose *Hex* 5.15.50; stones of urchins, 5.9.24, and pebble ballast of bees (Aelian 1.11 [5.14]). Flying wedge, Cicero *Nature of the Gods*, 2.125. (notes by Pease).
274 In line, Ambrose *Hex* 5.15.53.
275 Cf. Basil *Hex* 8.5.
276 Solinus 40.25–26; cf. Basil *Hex* 8.5.
277 Juvenal 6.165 treats it as an impossibility.
278 Serv *Aen* 7.700 (p. 165), referring to Pliny – who however rejects "swan song" (10.63). Cf. Ambrose *Hex* 5.22.75; Isidore *Etym* 12.7.1.
279 Serv *Aen* 11.580 (p. 547).
280 Ibid. 1.393 (p. 132); Blänsdorf, *Fragmenta Poetarum Latinorum*, 274 (Aemilius Macer fr. 4).
281 Gregory *Moralia* 31.21.37, on Job 39:13.
282 Serv *Aen* 7.412 (pp. 156–57): "that is, great and noble," with Lucan 5.553.
283 Ambrose *Hex* 5.13.43.
284 Serv *Georg* 1.364 (p. 204).
285 Not from *Phys* 7.

286 Solinus 33.15 (expanded from Pliny 10.97); ultimately from Aristotle *Hist* 616a6; cf. Herodotus 3.111 and Aelian 2.34; 17.21.
287 Solinus 52.43, 45.
288 Martial 14.73.
289 *Cyanea* means "sea-blue" (Pliny 10.89).
290 Cf. Basil *Hex* 8.6, p. 137; Ambrose *Hex* 5.13.40; Serv *Georg* 1.399 (p. 208).
291 Augustine *On Psalm* 101.7 (CCL 40.1430), likewise questioning veracity.
292 Cf. e.g. Hyginus *Fables* 30.6 (p. 32 Rose).
293 Solinus 2.45 (Pliny 10.126–27).
294 Serv *Aen* 11.271 (pp. 512–13).
295 Cf. Pliny 10.74 (not Solinus 40.19).
296 Solinus 20.3, expanded from Pliny 10.132.
297 Jerome *On Zephaniah* 2:12 (CCL 76A.689). Isidore rejects *Phys* 4 on the pelican.
298 Solinus 32.32. *Phys* 40 calls it "unclean" apparently because it frequents polluted waters.
299 Sofer, op. cit., 134–36.
300 Cicero *For Flaccus* 76, but probably from a commentary (Fontaine, 745 n. 2).
301 Ambrose *Hex* 5.24.87; Jerome *On Isaiah* 1:2.19 (CCL 73.39); cf. Pliny 10.168.
302 Ambrose *Hex* 5.2.39.
303 Cicero cites this line from his lost translation of Aratus in his treatise *On Divination* 1.14; see Pease's commentary (pp. 84–85).
304 Serv *Ecl* 8.55 (p. 101).
305 Serv *Aen* 4.462 (p. 548) says this of the *bubo*.
306 Brief reference to Ovid in Serv *Aen* 4.462.
307 Ambrose *Hex* 5.24.86; unlike Serv *Georg* 1.403 (p. 208).
308 Solinus 11.14; Pliny 10.74.
309 Cf. Jerome *Epistles* 106.63 (CSEL 55.279), a review of words in Psalm 101:7; *Phys* 5.
310 The Greek name is *koronē*, not *cornix*.
311 Partly from Serv *Georg* 1.388 (p. 207).
312 Martial 14.76.
313 Pliny 10.40.
314 Serv *Aen* 7.190 (p. 141).
315 Augustine *CD* 21.4 (his own experience).
316 Pliny 29.79.
317 Ambrose *Hex* 5.13.44.
318 Serv *Aen* 8.652 (p. 293); cf. Pliny 10.51 (Aelian 12.33); Basil *Hex* 8.7 (p. 466 Giet).
319 Ambrose *Hex* 5.13.44; Vergil *Georgics* 1.363; Augustine *On Psalm* 103, s. 3.17 (CCL 40.1514–15; cf. 1490).
320 Serv *Georg* 1.360 (p. 204).
321 Cf. Serv *Aen* 10.145 (p. 403).
322 Jerome *On Zechariah* 1.5:9–11 (CCL 76A.790).
323 Jerome *Against Jovinian* 1.30 (PL 23.263C); Origen *Canticles Homilies* 2.12 (p. 59 Baehrens).
324 Cf. Serv *Aen* 6.193 (p. 38: *Veneri consecratus, propter fetum frequentem et coitum*); Steier, "Taube," *RE* 4A (1932), 2496–98.
325 Serv *Ecl* 1.57 (p. 13).
326 Ambrose *Hex* 6.3.13; cf. *Phys* 18; Hippolytus *On Christ and Antichrist* 55 (p. 36, 17—37, 3 Achelis).

327 Pliny 10.66–67, 69.
328 Jerome *On Zechariah* 1.5:9–11 (CCL 76A.790); Pliny 10.86; different in *Phys* 8.
329 Text emended by Sofer, op. cit. 11–12.
330 Not close to Servius, Schmekel 51 n. 1.
331 Serv *Georg* 3.338 (p. 303).
332 Festus p. 197, 8–14 Müller.
333 Definitions in Serv *Aen* 3.246 (p. 385); Dressel 54 n. 2.
334 Divisions in Serv *Aen* 3.359 (pp. 405–6); almost as here.
335 Cf. Serv *Ecl* 10.20 (p. 122).
336 Serv *Georg* 4.257 (p. 340); 4.310 (p. 344).
337 Ibid. 4.284–86 (p. 342), with reference to Pliny 11.70; cf. Serv *Georg* 4.309 (p. 344); *Aen* 1.435 (p. 143).
338 Palladius *Agriculture* 6.10 (p. 166), rearranged.
339 Serv *Aen* 1.435 (p. 143); Blänsdorf, *Fragmenta Poetarum Latinorum*, 278 (Aemilius Macer fr. 18).
340 Serv *Georg* 4.168 (p. 333); reference to Pliny 11.27.
341 Pliny 30.39.
342 Ibid. 30.30: rare in Italy.
343 Ibid. 18.250–53; cf. 11.98.
344 Vergil *Georgics* 4.243 (*lucifugis . . . blattis*) and Servius on the verse (p. 340); Pliny 11.99 (*lucem fugiunt*).
345 Cf. Pliny 11.101: "the hind feet of locusts are longer and curve outward."
346 Solinus 2.40.
347 Ashes sprinkled on the fly revive it (Lucian *Fly* 7).
348 Cf. Aelian 4.51 on these flies.
349 Augustine *On Psalms* 148.10 (CCL 40.2172–73).
350 Augustine *On the Trinity* 3.7 (CCL 50.139).
351 Serv *Georg* 3.148 (p. 289).
352 O. Ribbeck, *Scaenicae Romanorum Poesis* (*Fragmenta*) (repr. Hildesheim: Olms, 1962), 2.216 (Afranius, 3): *bibones*.
353 Serv *Georg* 1.186 (p. 174).

BIBLIOGRAPHY

Ancient works and discussions of them

Acta Apostolorum Apocrypha, ed. R. A. Lipsius and M. Bonnet. 3 vols, Leipzig: Mendelssohn, 1891–1903; cf. E. Plümacher, "Apokryphe Apostelakten," *RE* Supplementband 15 (1978), 11–70; cf. also E. Hennecke, W. Schneemelcher and R. McL. Wilson, *New Testament Apocrypha*. Philadelphia: Westminster, 1963, 1965.

Acts of John. Acta Iohannis, ed. E. Junod and J. D. Kaestli. Corpus Christianorum, Series. Apocryphorum. vols. 1–2. Turnhout: Brepols, 1983.

Acts of Paul. PRAXEIS PAULOU, ed. C. Schmidt. Hamburg: Augustin, 1936.

Acta Sanctorum. Antwerp: Cnobarus, 1675; repr. Brussels: Culture et civilisation, 1968.

Aelian *On Animals*, tr. A. F. Scholfield. LCL, 1958–59.

—— *Varia Historia*, ed. M. R. Dilts. Leipzig: Teubner, 1974; tr. N. G. Wilson. LCL, 1997.

—— *Claudi Aeliani Epistulae et Fragmenta*, ed. D. Domingo-Foresté. Stuttgart/Leipzig: Teubner, 1994.

Afranius. In O. Ribbeck, *Scenicae Romanorum Poesis Fragmenta*. Repr. Hildesheim: Olms, 1962.

Aisōpeiōn Muthōn Sunagōgē. Ed. C. Halm. Leipzig: Teubner, 1852 and later. Tr. L. W. Daly, *Aesop without Morals.* New York and London, Yoseloff, 1961.

Alexander of Lycopolis. *Contra Manichaei opiniones disputatio*, ed. A. Brinkmann. Leipzig: Teubner, 1895.

Ambrose. *On the Deaths of Satyrus, Theodosius, Valentinian* CSEL 73; *On the Faith* CSEL 78; *Hexaemeron* CSEL 32. 1; *Letters* CSEL 82. 2; *On Luke* CSEL 32. 4; *On Penance* CSEL 73; Kasser, R. "Acta Pauli 1959," *Revue d'histoire et de philosophie religieuses* 40 (1960), 45–47; Lucchesi, E. *L'Usage de Philon dans l'œuvre exégétique de saint Ambroise.* Leiden: Brill, 1977; Savon, H. *Saint Ambroise devant l'exégèse de philon le juif.* Paris: Études Augustiniennes, 1977.

Anthony of Padua. *Liber miraculorum. Analecta Franciscana* 3 (1897), 121–58.

Apion. Jacoby, F. *Die Fragmente der griechischen Historiker* III C. Leiden: Brill, 1958.

Apocryphon of John. W. C. Till, *Die gnostischen Schriften des koptischen Papyrus Berolinensis 8502, TU* 60, 1955; M. Krause and P. Labib, *Die drei Versionen des Apokryphon des Johannes.* Wiesbaden: Harrassowitz, 1962.

Apostolic Fathers. Barnabas: H. Windisch, *Der Barnabasbrief.* Tübingen: Mohr,

1920; R. Kraft, *The Didache and Barnabas*. Garden City NY: Nelson, 1967; Clement: J. B. Lightfoot, *The Apostolic Fathers* I ii. London: Macmillan, 1890; R. Knopf, *Lehre der Zwölf Apostel, Zwei Clemensbriefe*. Tübingen: Mohr, 1920; J. J. Thierry, "Note sur *ta elachista tōn zōōn* au chapitre xx de la Clementis," *VC* 14 (1960), 235–44; Hermas, ed. M. Whittaker, *Der Hirt des Hermas*. Die apostolischen Väter, I: Berlin: Akademie, 1956 (GCS 48); Ignatius in *Die Apostolischen Väter*, ed. K. Bihlmeyer and W. Schneemelcher. Tübingen: Mohr, 1956; commentary by W. R. Schoedel, *Ignatius of Antioch*. Philadelphia: Fortress, 1985.

Aristeae Ad Philocratem Epistula, cum ceteris de origine versionis LXX interpretum testimoniis, ed. P. Wendland. Leipzig: Teubner, 1900.

Aristophanes, *Epitome. Supplementum Aristotelicum* 1. 1. *Excerptorum Constantini de Natura Animalium Libri Duo. Aristophanis Historiae Animalium Epitome*, ed. S. P. Lambros. Berlin: Reimer, 1895.

Aristotle. *Generation of Animals*, tr. A. L. Peck. LCL, 1943; *History of Animals*, tr. A. L. Peck and D. M. Balme. 3 vols. LCL, 1965–91; *Parts of Animals*, tr. A. Peck. LCL, 1937; *Movements of Animals, Progression of Animals*, tr. E. S. Forster. LCL, 1937; *On the Soul Parva Naturalia On Breath*, ed. W. S. Hett. LCL, 1957 (*Prophecy in Sleep*, 374–85).

Athenagoras Legatio pro Christianis, ed. M. Marcovich. Berlin and New York: de Gruyter, 1990; *Athenagoras Legatio and De Ressurectione*, ed. W. R. Schoedel.

Augustine. *On Christian Doctrine*. CCL 32; CSEL 89; *On the City of God*. CCL 47–48; *On the Customs of the Catholic Church*. CSEL 90; *On the Deeds of Pelagius*. CSEL 42; *On Genesis to the Letter*. CSEL 28. 1; *On Job*. CSEL 28. 3; *On John*. CCL 36; *Letters*. CSEL 34. 1–2, 44, 57–58, 88; *On Psalms*. CCL 38–40; *On the Trinity*. CCL 50–50A. Other texts from Migne, PL. P. De Vooght, "La Notion philosophique du miracle chez saint Augustin dans le 'De Trinitate' et le 'De Genesi ad litteram'," *Recherches de théologie ancienne et médiévale* 10 (1938), 317–43; "Les Miracles dans la vie de saint Augustin," ibid. 11 (1939), 5–16; "La Théologie du miracle selon saint Augustin," ibid., 197–222; H.-I. Marrou, *Saint Augustin et la fin de la culture antique*. 4th edn. Repr. Paris: Boccard, 1983; P. Brown, *Augustine of Hippo*. Berkeley: University of California Press, 1967; Courcelle, P. *Recherches sur les Confessions de S. Augustin*. Paris: Boccard, 1950; Vannier, M. A. "La Rôle de l'Hexaéméron dans la pensée augustinienne de la création," *Studia Patristica* 22 (1990), 372–81.

Babrius and Phaedrus, ed. B. E. Perry. LCL, 1965.

Barnabas. See Apostolic Fathers.

Basil of Caesarea, *Hexaemeron*, ed. E. Amand de Mendieta and S. Y. Rudberg, *Basilius von Caesarea Homilien zum Hexaemeron* (GCS N.F. 2; Berlin: Akademie, 1997). PG 29. 3–208; ed., tr. S. Giet. *Basile de Césarée Homélies sur l'Hexaéméron*, Paris: Cerf, 1950; J. Levie, "Les Sources de la 7e et de la 8e homélies de saint Basile sur l'Hexaéméron," *Musée Belge* 19–24 (1920), 113–29; Y. Courtonne, *Saint Basile et l'hellénisme*. Paris: Firmin-Didot, 1934; W. Hengsberg, *De ornatu rhetorico, quem Basilius Magnus in diversis homiliarum generibus adhibuit*. Bonn: Universität, 1957; E. Amand de Mendieta, "La Préparation et la composition des neuf Homélies sur l'Hexaéméron de Basile de Césarée: le problème des sources littéraires immédiates," *TU* 129 (1985), 349–67 (article from 1975 promises a commentary, now basically provided in the 1997 edition); Robbins,

F. E. *The Hexaaemeral Literature. A Study of the Greek and Latin Commentaries on Genesis*. Chicago: University of Chicago Press, 1912.

Cicero M. *Tulli Ciceronis Academica*, ed. J. S. Reid. London: Macmillan, 1885 (useful commentary).

—— *De Divinatione*, ed. A. S. Pease. University of Illinois Studies in Language and Literature 6. 2–3 (1920); 8. 2 (1923).

——*De Natura Deorum Libri III*, ed. A. S. Pease. 2 vols. Cambridge MA: Harvard University Press, 1955, 1958.

Clement of Alexandria, ed. O. Stählin. 4 vols. Leipzig: Hinrichs, 1905–36. GCS 12, 15, 17, 39; *Clément d'Alexandrie, Les Stromates: Stromate*, ed. A. Le Boulluec. V, 2. Paris: Cerf, 1981; *Miscellanies Book VII*, ed. F. J. A. Hort and J. B. Mayor, London: Macmillan, 1902; A. Deiber, *Clément d'Alexandrie et l'Égypte*. Mémoires de l'Institut français du Caire 10, 1904; M. G. Murphy, *Nature Allusions in the Works of Clement of Alexandria*. Washington: Catholic University of America, 1941.

Clement of Rome. See Apostolic Fathers.

Cornutus. *Theologiae Graecae Compendium*, ed. C. Lang. Leipzig: Teubner, 1881.

De Bestiis et Aliis Rebus. PL 177. 12–169.

Decretum Gelasianum, ed. E. von Dobschütz. *TU* 38. 3–4, 1912.

Didymus. *Didyme l'Aveugle Sur la Génèse*, I, ed. P. Nautin. SC 233. Paris: Cerf, 1976.

Dionysius of Alexandria. *The Letters and Other Remains of Dionysius of Alexandria*, ed. C. L. Feltoe. Cambridge: Cambridge University Press.

Doxographi Graeci, ed. H. Diels. Berlin: De Gruyter, 1929.

Dracontius. *Œuvres*, 1, ed. C. Moussy and C. Camus. Paris: Belles Lettres, 1985.

Epicurea, ed. H. Usener. Leipzig: Teubner, 1887.

Epiphanius. *Panarion*, ed. K. Holl. 3 vols. Leipzig: Hinrichs, 1915–33. GCS 25, 31, 37; J. Dummer, "Ein naturwissenschaftliches Handbuch als Quelle für Epiphanius von Constantia," *Klio* 55 (1973), 289–99.

Eustathius (translator of Basil). PL 53. 867–966. B. Altaner, "Eustathius, der lateinische Übersetzer der Hexaëmeron-Homilien Basilius des Grossen," *ZNW* 39 (1940), 161–70; E. Amand de Mendieta and S. Y. Rudberg, *Eustathius. Ancienne version latine des neuf homélies sur l'Hexaéméron de Basile. TU* 66 (1958).

Evangelia Apocrypha, ed. C. Tischendorf, 2nd edn, Leipzig: Mendelssohn, 1876.

Festus. *Sexti Pompei Festi De verborum significatione quae supersunt*, ed. C. O. Müller. Leipzig: Weidmann, 1839.

Firmicus Maternus. *De Errore Profanarum Religionum* (CSEL 1); commentary by A. Pastorino. Florence: "La Nuova Italia", 1956.

Fulgentius. *Fabii Planciadis Fulgentii V.C. opera*, ed. R. Helm. Leipzig: Teubner, 1898 (*Mitologiae*).

Galeni opera omnia, ed. C. G. Kühn. 20 vols. Repr. Hildesheim: Olms, 1967; *De Usu Partium Libri XVII*, ed. G. Helmreich, 2 vols. Leipzig: Teubner, 1907–9.

The Attic Nights of Aulus Gellius, tr. J. C. Rolfe, 3 vols. LCL, 1927.

Geminus. *Elementa Astronomiae*, ed. C. Manitius. Leipzig: Teubner, 1898.

Geographi Graeci Minores 1, ed. C. Müller. Paris: Didot, 1862.

Geoponica, ed. H. Beckh. Leipzig: Teubner, 1895.

Gregory of Nyssa. *On the Christian Vocation*, in *Gregorii Nysseni opera*, ed. W. Jaeger et al. 8. 1 (Leiden: Brill, 1952), 129–42.

Gregory the Great. *Moralia on Job.* CCL 143; PL 75–76. F. Boglioni, "Miracle et nature chez Grégoire le Grand," Cahiers d'études médiévales, 1. Montréal: Bellarmin; Paris: Vrin, 1974, 11–102; J. M. Petersen, *The Dialogues of Gregory the Great in their Late Antique Cultural Background.* Toronto: Pontifical Institute, 1984.

[Heraclitus]. *Peri apistōn,* in *Mythographi Graeci* III 2, ed. N. Festa (Leipzig: Teubner, 1902), 73–87.

Hermas. See Apostolic Fathers.

Hippocrates. *Œuvres complètes d'Hippocrate,* 6, ed. É. Littré. Paris: Ballière, 1849.

Horapollo. *Hori Apollinis Hieroglyphica,* ed. F. Sbordone. Naples: Loffredo [1940].

Ignatius. See Apostolic Fathers.

Irenaeus. *Irénée de Lyons. Contre les hérésies.* Édition critique. 10 vols, ed. A. Rousseau et al. SC 100, 152–53, 210–11, 263–64, 293–94. Paris: Cerf, 1965–82; R. M. Grant, *Irenaeus of Lyons.* London: Routledge, 1997.

Isidori Hispalensis Episcopi Etymologiarum sive Originum Libri XX, ed. W. M. Lindsay. 2 vols. Oxford: Clarendon, 1911; also in PL 82, 73–728 (Liber XII *On Animals,* 423–72); H. Dressel, *De Isidori Originum Fontibus.* Turin: Vincentius Bona, 1874; A. Schenk, *De Isidori Hispalensis de Rerum Natura libelli fontibus.* Jena: Neuenhahn, 1909; A. Schmekel, *Isidorus von Sevilla. Sein System und seine Quellen.* Berlin: Weidmann, 1914 (but see B. Altaner, "Der Stand der Isidorforschung," *Miscellanea Isidoriana.* Rome: Gregorianum, 1936, 1–32 (esp. 12–14)); H. Philipp, "Isidorus von Sevilla," *RE* 9 (1916), 2076–79 (Arbeitsweise, Etymologiae, Quellen); J. Sofer, *Lateinisches und Romanisches aus den Etymologiae des Isidorus von Sevilla.* Göttingen: Vandenhoeck & Ruprecht, 1930; J. Fontaine, *Isidore de Séville et la culture classique dans l'Espagne wisogothique.* Paris: Études augustiniennes, 7 (1958); O. Hiltbrunner, "Isidoros (8)," *KP* 2 (1967), 1461–62; Fontaine, "Isidore de Séville," *Dictionnaire de spiritualité* 7 (1971), 2104–16; H.-J. Diesner, "Zeitgeschichte und Gegenwartsbezug bei Isidor von Sevilla," *Philologus* 119 (1975), 92–97 (not on animals); J. N. Hillgarth, "The Position of Isidorian Studies: A Critical Review of the Literature 1936–1975," *Studi Medievali* 24 (1983), 817–905; Fontaine, "Isidore of Seville," *Encyclopedia of the Early Church,* ed. A. Di Berardino. New York: Oxford University Press, 1992, 418–19.

—— *De Ecclesiasticis Officiis.* CCL 113.

—— *Traité de la nature,* ed. J. Fontaine. Bordeaux: Féret, 1960.

Jerome and Eusebius. *Chronicle,* ed. R. Helm. GCS 47.

Jerome. *Hebrew Questions on Genesis.* CCL 72; *Letters.* CSEL 54–56; *Lives of Hilarion, Malchus, Paul.* PL 23; *On Christian Doctrine.* CCL 32; *On the Major Prophets.* CCL 73–75; *On the Minor Prophets.* CCL 76–76A. J. N. D. Kelly, *Jerome.* New York: Harper & Row, 1975.

John Moschus. *Spiritual Meadow.* PG 87. 3, 2851–3116; French tr., M.-J. Rovët de Journel, *Jean Moschus: Le Pré Spirituel.* Paris: Cerf [1946].

Joseph's Bible Notes (Hypomnestikon), ed. G. Menzies and R. M. Grant. Texts and Translations 41, Early Christian Series 9. Atlanta: Scholars, 1996.

Julius Africanus. *Les "Cestes" de Julius Africanus,* ed. J.-R. Vieillefond. Florence: Sansoni/Paris: Didier, 1970.

Justin Apologies. ed. A. Wartelle. Etudes Augustiniennes, 1987.

Justin Dialogus cum Tryphone, ed. M. Marcovich. PTS 47, 1997.

Lives of the Saints. *Butler's Lives of the Saints*, ed. H. Thurston and D. Attwater. 4 vols. New York: Kenedy, 1956.

Lucan, tr. J. D. Duff. LCL, 1928.

—— M. *Annaei Lucani Commenta Bernensia*, ed. H. Usener. Leipzig: Teubner, 1869.

Menander Rhetor, ed. and tr. D. A. Russell and N. G. Wilson. Oxford: Clarendon, 1981.

Minucius Felix. *Octavius*, ed. W. A. Baehrens. Leiden: Théonville, 1912.

Nepualii fragmentum, ed. W. Gemoll. Striegau: Städtisches Realprogymnasium, Tschörner, 1884; W. Kroll, "Nepualios," *RE* 16 (1935), 2535–37.

Nicander. A. S. F. Gow and A. F. Scholfield, *Nicander: The Poems and Poetical Fragments*. Cambridge: Cambridge University Press, 1953.

Oppian Colluthus Tryphiodorus, tr. A. W. Mair. LCL, 1928.

Origen Contra Celsum, tr. H. Chadwick. Cambridge: Cambridge University Press, 1953; *Homilien zum Hexateuch*, etc. ed. W. Baehrens et al. Leipzig: Hinrichs, 1920–. GCS 29, 30, 33; Baehrens, *Überlieferung und Textgeschichte der lateinisch erhaltenen Origineshomilien zum Alten Testament. TU* 42. 1 (1916); *Matthäuserklärung*, ed. E. Klostermann. GCS 40. Leipzig: Hinrichs, 1935; *Origène Traité des Principes*, tr. and comm. H. Crouzel and M. Simonetti, 5 vols, SC 252, 253, 268, 269, 312. Paris: Cerf, 1978–84.

Orosius. CSEL 5.

Orphicorum Fragmenta, ed. O. Kern. Berlin: Weidmann, 1922.

[Ovid]. *On Sea-Fishing (Halieuticon)*, in J. K. Mozley, *Ovid The Art of Love and Other Poems*. LCL, 1929, 310–21.

Palaephatus. *Peri Apistōn*, in *Mythographi Graeci* III. 2, ed. N. Festa. Leipzig: Teubner, 1902, 1–67. *On Unbelievable Tales*, repr., tr. and comm. J. Stern. Wauconda IL: Bolchazy-Carducci, 1996; A. von Blumenthal, "Palaiphatos, 2–4," *RE* 18 (1942), 2451–55.

Palladius. *Opus Agriculturae*, ed. J. C. Schmitt. Leipzig: Teubner, 1898.

Paradoxographi. Scriptores Mirabilium Graeci, ed. A. Westermann. London: Black & Armstrong, 1839.

Philo of Alexandria, tr. F. H. Colson and G. H. Whittaker et al., 12 vols. LCL, 1929–62.

—— *Philonis Alexandrini De Animalibus*, tr. A. Terian. Chico CA: Scholars Press, 1981.

Physiologus, ed. F. Sbordone. Milan: "Dante Alighieri", 1936 (review by B. E. Perry, *American Journal of Philology* 58 [1937], 488–96); *Physiologus Syrus seu Historia animalium XXXII. In S.S. Memoratorum, Syriace*, ed. and tr. N. G. Tychsen. Rostock: Libraria Stilleriana, 1795; M. Wellmann, *Der Physiologos*. Philologus, Supplement 22. 1, 1930; F. J. Carmody, "De Bestiis et Aliis Rebus and the Latin Physiologus," *Speculum* 13 (1938), 153–59; *Physiologus Latinus*, ed. F. J. Carmody. Paris: Droz, 1939; B. E. Perry, "Physiologus," *RE* 20 (1941), 1074–1129 (commentary, 1078–96); E. Peterson, "Die Spiritualität des griechischen Physiologus," *BZ* 47 (1954), 6–72; U. Treu, "'Otterngezücht.' Ein patristischer Beitrag zur Quellenkunde des Physiologus," *ZNW* 50 (1959), 113–22; id., "Zur Datierung des Physiologus," *ZNW* 57 (1966), 101–4; D. Offermanns, *Der Physiologus nach den Handschriften G und M*. Beiträge zur klassischen Philologie 22, 1966; O. Hiltbrunner, "Physiologus," *KP* 4 (1972), 840–41; R. Riedinger,

"Der Physiologus und Klemens von Alexandreia," *BZ* 66 (1973), 273–307; id., "Seid klug wie die Schlange und einfältig wie die Taube. Der Umkreis des Physiologus," *Byzantina* 7 (1975), 11–32; N. Henkel, *Studien zum Physiologus im Mittelalter.* Tübingen: Niemeyer, 1976; *Physiologus*, tr. M. J. Curley. Austin: University of Texas Press, 1979.

Pliny Natural History, tr. H. Rackham et al. 10 vols. LCL, 1938–62; F. Capponi, *Entomologia Pliniana* (*N.H. XI,1–120*). Università di Genova, Facolta di lettere, 1994.

Pliny Letters and Panegyricus, tr. B. Radice. 2 vols. LCL, 1969.

Plutarch's Moralia, tr. F. C. Babbitt et al. 15 vols. LCL, 1927–69.

Rerum naturalium scriptores graeci minores, ed. O. Keller. Leipzig: Teubner, 1877.

Scaenicae Romanorum Poesis Fragmenta, ed. O. Ribbeck. Repr. Hildesheim: Olms, 1962.

Servii Grammatici Qui Feruntur in Vergilii Carmina Commentarii, ed. G. Thilo. 3 vols. Leipzig: Teubner, 1881–87; repr. Hildesheim: Olms, 1961; J. F. Mountford and J. T. Schultz, *Index rerum et nominum in scholiis Servii et Aeli Donati tractatorum.* Cornell Studies in Classical Philology 23 (1930).

The Sentences of Sextus, ed. H. Chadwick. Cambridge: Cambridge University Press, 1959.

C. Iulii Solini collectanea Rerum Memorabilium, ed. T. Mommsen. 2nd edn. Berlin: Weidmann, 1958; Sallmann, K. "Solinus," *KP* (1975), 260.

Stoicorum veterum fragmenta, ed. H. von Arnim. 4 vols. Leipzig: Teubner, 1905–24.

Sulpicius Severus. *Libri qui supersunt*, ed. C. Halm, CSEL 1; *Vie de saint Martin*, ed. J. Fontaine. SC 133–35. Paris: Cerf, 1967–69.

Tatiani Oratio ad Graecos, ed. M. Marcovich. Patristische Texte und Studien, ed. H. Chr. Brennecke and E. Mühlenberg, 43. Berlin and New York: De Gruyter, 1995; *Tatian Oratio ad Graecos*, ed. M. Whittaker. OECT, 1982; Puech, A. *Recherches sur le Discours aux grecs de Tatieen.* Paris: Alcan, 1903.

Tertullianus. CCL 1; *De Anima*, ed. J. H. Waszink. Amsterdam: Muelenhoff, 1947.

Theon. *Progymnasmata.* In *Rhetores Graeci*, ed. L. Spengel. 3 vols. Leipzig: Teubner, 1853–56 (2.59–130).

Theophili Antiocheni Ad Autolycum, ed. M. Marcovich. Patristische Texte und Studien, ed. H. C. Brennecke and E. Mühlenberg, 44. Berlin and New York: De Gruyter, 1995; *Theophilus of Antioch To Autolycus*, ed. R. M. Grant. OECT, 1971.

Timotheus of Gaza On Animals, ed. M. Haupt, *Opuscula*, ed. U. Wilamowitz, repr. Hildesheim: Olms, 1969. Vol. 3, 274–302; tr. F. S. Bodenheimer and A. Rabinowitz, Leiden: Brill, *c.* 1948.

Verecundus. *In Cantica Ecclesiastica*, ed. A. Hamann. PL Supplement 4, Paris: Garnier, 1967, 39–234.

Vibius Sequester, ed. R. Gelsomino. Leipzig: Teubner, 1967.

Vita Leutfredi, in B. Krusch and W. Levison, *Passiones vitaeque sanctorum* (Monumenta Germaniae historica, Scriptorum Merovingiorum 7, Hanover and Leipzig: Hahn, 1919), 1–18.

Modern works

Andrews, A. C. "Greek and Latin Terms for Salmon and Trout," *Transactions of the American Philological Association* 86 (1955), 308–18.

Bammel, C. P. "Adam in Origen," in R. Williams (ed.), *The Making of Orthodoxy . . . in Honour of Henry Chadwick*. Cambridge: Cambridge University Press. 1989, 62–93

Bauer, J. B. "Novellistisches bei Hieronymus Vita Pauli 3," *Wiener Studien* 74 (1961), 130–37.

Bauer, W. "The 'Colt' of Palm Sunday," *JBL* 72 (1953), 220–9.

Bernand, A. and Bernand, E. *Les Inscriptions grecques et latines du Colosse de Memnon.* Cairo: Mémoires de l'Institut français d'archéologie orientale du Caire 49, 1950.

Betz, H. D. *Galatians.* Philadelphia: Westminster, 1979.

Blänsdorf, J. B. *Fragmenta Poetarum Latinorum.* Stuttgart and Leipzig: Teubner, 1995.

Brandenburg, H. "Einhorn," *RAC* 4 (1959), 840–62.

Brewer, E. C. *Dictionary of Miracles.* Philadelphia: Lippincott, 1885 (especially 357–67).

Brightman, F. E. *Liturgies Eastern and Western* I *Eastern.* Oxford: Clarendon Press, 1896.

Bultmann, R. *Die Geschichte der synoptischen Tradition*, 2nd edn. Göttingen: Vandenhoeck & Ruprecht, 1931.

Carlston, C. E. "Proverbs, Maxims, and the Historical Jesus," *Journal of Biblical Literature* 99 (1980), 87–105.

Cazzeniga, I. "Il supplizio del miele e delle formiche: un motivo novellistico nelle metamorfosi di Apuleio (VIII, 22)," *Studies in Philology* 46 (1949), 1–5.

Chadwick, H. "Enkrateia," *RAC* 5 (1965), 343–65.

—— "Origen, Celsus and the Stoa," *JTS* 48 (1947), 34–49.

Coulter, C. C. "The Great Fish in Ancient Story," *Transactions of the American Philological Association* 57 (1926), 32–50.

Courcelle, P., "L'Interprétation evhémériste des Sirènes-courtisanes jusqu'au xiie siècle."

—— Monographien zur Geschichte des Mittelalters II (Beiträge Luitpold Wallach), ed. K. Bosl (Stuttgart: Hiersemann, 1975), 35–48.

—— *Late Latin Writers and their Greek Sources.* Cambridge, MA: Harvard University Press, 1969.

—— *Recherches sur les Confessions de S. Augustin.* Paris, 1950.

Daly, L. W. *Aesop without Morals.* New York and London: Yoseloff, 1961.

Davies, M. and Kathirithamby, J. *Greek Insects.* New York: Oxford University Press, 1986.

Delehaye, H. *Les Légendes hagiographiques.* Brussels: Bollandistes, 1906; English translation, *The Legends of the Saints.* New York: Fordham University Press, 1962; "Passio sancti Mammetis," *AB* 58 (1940), 126–41.

Dibelius, M. *Die Formgeschichte des Evangeliums.* 2nd edn. Tübingen: Mohr, 1933.

Dickerman, S. O. "Some Stock Illustrations of Animal Intelligence in Greek Psychology," *Transactions and Proceedings of the American Philological Association* 42 (1911), 123–30.

Diels, H. "Laterculi Alexandrini aus einem Papyrus ptolemaeischer Zeit,"

Abhandlungen der königlich preussischen Akademie der Wissenschaften, 1904, II, 1–16.

—— and W. Kranz. *Die Fragmente der Vorsokratiker.* 6th edn. Berlin: Weidmann, 1951.

Dierauer, U. *Tier und Mensch im Denken der Antike. Studien zur Tierpsychologie, Anthropologie und Ethik.* Amsterdam: Grüner, 1977.

Dittenberger, W. *Orientis Graeci Inscriptiones Selectae.* 2 vols. Leipzig: Hirzel, 1903, 1905.

Dölger, F. J. *ICHTHYS. Das Fischsymbol in frühchristlicher Zeit.* 1. Rome: Herder, 1910.

Douglas, Mary. "The Abominations of Leviticus," *Reader in Comparative Religion. An Anthropological Approach.* 4th edn, ed. W. A. Lessa and E. Z. Vogt. New York: Harper & Row, 1979, 149–52.

Duchesne, L. *Le Forum chrétien.* Rome: Cuggiani, 1899.

Engemann, J. "Fisch, Fischer, Fischfang," *RAC* 7 (1969), 959–1097.

Fonck, L. "Hieronymi scientia naturalis exemplis illustratur," *Biblica* 1 (1920), 481–99.

Forbes, A. P. *Lives of S. Ninian and S. Kentigern.* The Historians of Scotland, 5. Edinburgh: Edmonston and Douglas, 1874.

Frank, T. (ed.) *Economic Survey of Ancient Rome.* 5 vols. Baltimore: Johns Hopkins, 1937–40; repr. Paterson NJ: Pageant, 1959.

French, R. K. *Ancient Natural History: Histories of Nature.* London and New York: Routledge, 1994.

Geffcken, J. *Zwei griechische Apologeten.* Leipzig and Berlin: Teubner, 1907.

Geisau, H. von. "Drakon," *KP* 2 (1967), 158; "Echidna," 193; "Kentauroi," *KP* 3 (1969), 183–84.

Grant, R. M. *Earliest Lives of Jesus.* London: SPCK, 1961.

—— "Dietary Laws Among Pythagoreans, Jews and Christians," *HTR* 73 (1980), 299–310.

—— *Heresy and Criticism.* Louisville: Westminster/John Knox, 1993.

—— "Insects in Early Christian Literature," in *Biblical and Humane: A Festschrift for John F. Priest.* L. Bennett Elder et al. (eds), Atlanta: Scholars, 1996, 215–24.

—— *Irenaeus of Lyons.* London: Routledge, 1997.

—— *Miracle and Natural Law in Graeco-Roman and Early Christian Thought.* Amsterdam: North Holland, 1952.

—— "One Hundred Fifty-Three Large Fish," *HTR* 42 (1949), 273–75.

—— "Paul, Galen, and Origen," *JTS* 34 (1983), 533–36.

—— "Ptolemaic Geography in Origen and Hippolytus," in G. Sfameni Gasparo (ed.), *Agathē elpis: studi in onore di Ugo Bianchi.* Rome: "L'Erma" di Bretschneider, 1994, 291–303.

Grün, J. "Affe," *RAC* 1 (1950), 158–60.

Halkin, F. "Un émule d'Orphée: la légende grecque inédite de saint Zosime [of Anazarbus]," *AB* 70 (1952), 249–61.

Hanfmann, G. M. A. "Satyrs and Sileni," *Oxford Classical Dictionary* (2nd edn, Oxford: Clarendon, 1970), 956.

Harnack, A. von. *Der kirchengeschichtliche Ertrag der exegetischen Arbeiten des Origenes,* 2. *TU* 42.4, 1919.

—— *Marcion: Das Evangelium vom fremden Gott. TU* 45, 1924.

Harpaz, I. "Early Entomology in the Middle East," in R. F. Smith et al., *History of Entomology*, 21–36.

Haussleiter, J. *Der Vegetarismus in der Antike*. Religionsgeschichtliche Versuche und Vorarbeiten 24 (1935).

Haynes, Sybille. *Land of the Chimaera*. New York: St. Martin's Press, 1974.

Hermann, A. "Fliege (Mücke)," *RAC* 7 (1969), 1110–24.

Jaeger, W. *Aristotle*. Oxford: Clarendon Press, 1934.

Käsemann, E. *An die Römer*. 4th edn. Tübingen: Mohr, 1980.

Keller, O. *Die antike Tierwelt*. 2 vols. Leipzig: Engelmann, 1909–13.

—— *Thiere des classischen Altertums in culturgeschichtlichen Beziehung*. Innsbruck: Wagner'sche Universitäts-Buchhandlung, 1887.

Kerval, L. de. *L'Évolution et le développement du merveilleux dans les légendes de S. Antoine de Padoue*. Paris: Fischbacher, 1906.

Kleberg, T. *Hôtels, restaurants et cabarets dans l'antiquité romaine*. Uppsala: Almqvist & Wiksells, 1957.

Klingender, F. *Animals in Art and Thought to the End of the Middle Ages*, ed. E. Antal and J. Harthan. Cambridge: M.I.T. Press, 1971.

Ladner, G. B. *God, Cosmos, and Humankind. The World of Early Christian Symbolism*. Berkeley: University of California Press, 1995.

Lagrange, M.-J. *Évangile selon Saint Matthieu*. Paris: Gabalda, 1923.

Leach, E. R. "Anthropological Aspects of Language: Animal Categories and Verbal Abuse," in W. A. Lessa and E. Z. Vogt (eds), *Reader in Comparative Religion: an Anthropological Approach*, 4th edn. New York: Harper & Row, 1978, 153–66.

Linzey, A. *Animal Theology*. London: SCM, 1994.

Lloyd, G. E. R. *Greek Science after Aristotle*. New York: Norton, 1973.

Loth, H.-J. "Hund," *RAC* 16 (1994), 773–828.

Malherbe, A. J. "The Beasts at Ephesus," *JBL* 87 (1968), 71–80.

Mayor, A. "Mad Honey!" *Archaeology* 48.6 (1995), 32–40.

Marx, A. *Griechische Märchen von dankbaren Tieren und Verwandtes*. Stuttgart: Kohlhammer, 1889.

McDermott, W. C. *The Ape in Antiquity*. Baltimore: Johns Hopkins, 1938.

Metzger, B. M. "St. Paul and the Lion," *Princeton Seminary Bulletin* 20 (1945), 11–22.

Miller, P. C. *Dreams in Late Antiquity*. Princeton: Princeton University Press, 1994.

—— "Jerome's Centaur: A Hyper-Icon of the Desert," *Journal of Early Christian Studies* 4 (1996), 209–23.

Mommsen, T. *Römisches Strafrecht*. Leipzig: Duncker & Humblot, 1899.

Morge, G. "Entomology in the Western World in Antiquity and in Medieval Times," in R. F. Smith et al., *History of Entomology*, 37–80.

Morin, G. "Le Dragon du forum romain: sa légende et son histoire," *Revue Bénédictine* 31 (1914), 321–26.

—— "Pour l'authenticité de la lettre de S. Jérome à Présidius," *Bulletin d'ancienne littérature et d'archéologie chrétienne* 3 (1913), 51–60.

Neusner, J. *Genesis Rabbah* I. Atlanta: Scholars, 1985.

Nock, A. D. "The Vocabulary of the New Testament," *JBL* 52 (1933), 131–39 =

Essays on Religion and the Ancient World, ed. Z. Stewart. Oxford: Clarendon, 1972, 342–47.

Opelt, I. "Elefant," *RAC* 4 (1958), 840–62.

Orth. "Katze," *RE* 11 (1921), 52–57.

Paredi, A. "S. Gerolamo e S. Ambrogio," *Studi e Testi* 235 (Mélanges E. Tisserant 5, 1964), 183–98.

Parsons, W. "Lest Men Like Fishes . . .," *Traditio* 3 (1945), 380–88.

Pervo, R. "The Ancient Novel Becomes Christian," in G. Schmeling (ed.), *The Novel in the Ancient World*. Leiden: Brill, 1996, Mnemosyne Supplementum 159 (1996) 685–711.

Pfeiffer, R. *History of Classical Scholarship* 1. Oxford: Clarendon, 1968.

Plümacher, E. "Paignion und Biberfabel. Zum literarischen und popularphilosophischen Hintergrund von Acta Iohannis 60f. 48–54," *Apocrypha* 3 (1992), 69–109.

Plumpe, J. C. "Vivum Saxum, Vivi Lapides. The Concept of 'Living Stone' in Classical and Christian Antiquity," *Traditio* 1 (1943), 1–14.

Pohlenz, M. *Die Stoa*. 2 vols., 2nd edn, Göttingen: Vandenhoeck & Ruprecht, 1955.

Pollard, J. *Birds in Greek Life and Myth*. London: Thames and Hudson, 1977.

Priest, J. F. "The Dog in the Manger: In Quest of a Fable," *Classical Journal* 8 (1985), 49–58.

Prinz and Ziegler, [K.], "Gryps," *RE* 7 (1912), 1902–29.

Puech, H.-C., "Le Cerf et le serpent," *Cahiers archéologiques* 4 (1949), 17–60.

Rech, P. and Stemplinger, E. "Ameise," *RAC* 1 (1950), 375–77.

Remus, H. *Pagan–Christian Conflict over Miracle in the Second Century*. Philadelphia: Patristic Foundation, 1983.

Riché, P. *Écoles et enseignement dans le Haut Moyen Age. Fin du Ve siècle–milieu du XIe siècle*. Paris: Picard, 1989.

—— *Éducation et culture dans l'occident barbare VIe–VIIIe siècles*. Paris: Seuil, 1962.

Richmond, J. *Chapters on Greek Fish-Lore*. Hermes Einzelschriften 28 (Wiesbaden: Steiner, 1973).

Richter, W. articles in *KP* on "Affe," "Ameise," "Einhorn," "Esel," "Fischereigewerbe," "Fliege," "Frosch," "Fuchs," "Gans," "Hyäne," "Hund," "Katze," "Krebs," "Löwe," "Maus," "Nashorn," "Schaf," "Schlange," "Schwan," "Schwein," "Spinnentiere," "Tiergarten," "Wanze," "Wespe," "Wolf," "Würmer".

—— in *RE* Supplementband 14–15 on "Wespe," "Wolf".

Robert-Tornow, W. *De apium mellisque apud veteres significatione et symbolica et mythologica*. Berlin: Weidmann, 1893.

Runia, D. T. *Philo in Early Christian Literature*. Assen: Van Gorcum; Minneapolis, Fortress, 1993.

Sallinger, A. and Bocher, O., "Honig," *RAC* 16 (1994), 433–73.

Schoeps, H. J. *Aus frühchristlicher Zeit*. Tübingen: Mohr, 1950.

——*Theologie und Geschichte des Judenchristentums*. Tübingen: Mohr, 1949.

Schrot, G. "Fischereigewerbe," *KP* 2 (1967), 555–56.

Scobie, A. "Some Folktales in Graeco-Roman and Far Eastern Sources," *Philologus* 121 (1977), 1–23.

Shepard, O. *The Lore of the Unicorn*. Repr. New York: Barnes & Noble, 1967.

Smith, R. F., Mittler, T. E., and Smith, C. N. (eds), *History of Entomology*. Palo Alto: Annual Reviews, 1973.

Sorabji, R. *Animal Minds and Human Morals*. Cornell Studies in Classical Philology, 54. Ithaca NY: Cornell University Press, 1993.

Stein, E. (*Alttestamentliche Bibelkritik in der späthellenistischen Literatur*. Lvov, 1936.

Stoessl, F. "Silenos-Satyros," *KP* 5 (1975), 191–93.

Strack, H. L. and P. Billerbeck, *Kommentar zum Neuen Testament aus Talmud und Midrasch* 1. Munich: Beck, 1926.

Swift, L. J. "Basil and Ambrose on the Six Days of Creation," *Augustinianum* 21 (1981), 317–28.

Telfer, W. "'Bees' in Clement of Alexandria," *JTS* 28 (1926–27), 167–78.

Thompson, D'Arcy W. *A Glossary of Greek Birds*. Oxford: Clarendon, 1895.

—— *A Glossary of Greek Fishes*. London: Oxford University Press, 1947.

Trencsényi-Waldapfel, I. "Sprichwort oder geflügeltes Wort?" *Acta Antiqua Academiae Scientiarum Hungaricae* 12 (1964), 365–71.

Van den Hoek, A. *Clement of Alexandria and his Use of Philo in the Stromateis*. Leiden: Brill, 1988.

Van Winden, J. C. M. "Hexaemeron," *RAC* 14 (1988), 1250–69.

Wagner. "Drakon (6)," *RE* 5 (1905), 1646–47.

Wallace-Hadrill, D. S. *The Greek Patristic View of Nature*. Manchester: Manchester University Press, 1968.

Walzer, R. *Galen on Jews and Christians*. London: Oxford University Press, 1949.

Warmington, E. H. *Remains of Old Latin* 2. LCL, 1936.

Weber, M. "Frosch," *RAC* 8 (1972), 524–38.

Wellmann, M. "Die Stein- und Gemmenbücher der Antike," *Quellen und Studien zur Geschichte der Naturwissenschaften und Medizin* 4.4 (1935), 86–149.

Westermann, C. *Biblischer Kommentar Altes Testament* I. 1. *Genesis*. Neukirchen/Vluyn: Neukirchener Verlag, 1974.

Witek, F. and Brakmann, H. "Hyäne," *RAC* 16 (1994), 893–904.

Ziegler, K. "Greif," *KP* 2 (1967), 876–77.

INDEX OF ANIMALS AND
MYTHOLOGICAL
CHARACTERS

INDEX OF ANCIENT
PERSONS, GROUPS,
AND WRITINGS

Abercius 25
Acts of John 27–8; *Paul*, 17, 19–20
Aelian 9, 18–19, 22, 26, 28, 30, 37, 41, 73
Aesop 44–5, 73
Aetius 113
Afranius 150, 162
Ambrose of Milan 11, 23, 41, 43, 78, 108–9, 113, 120
Amos 15
Androcles/Androclus 18–19
Androcydes 13
Antony of Egypt, Saint 119
Antony of Padua, Saint 25
Apion 18–19, 73
Apollonius of Tyana 37
Apostolic Constitutions 41
Apuleius 23
Aquila 42
Aristeas, Epistle of 8, 13, 48
Aristides 8
Aristophanes (poet) 28
Aristophanes of Byzantium 46, 73, 77
Aristotle 22, 23, 24, 26, 27, 30, 42, 45, 47, 48, 73, 77, 113, 118
Arnobius 107–8
Artemidorus 28
Athenaeus 22, 24
Athenagoras 8, 48
Augustine 12, 22, 32–3, 78, 110–11, 113

Barnabas, Epistle of 45–6, 48
Basil of Caesarea 24, 30, 76, 77–106, 108, 110
Beasts and Other Subjects 116
Braulio of Saragossa 113

Celsus 10–11, 41, 74
Chrysippus 30
Cicero 10, 107, 108, 133, 150, 156
Clement of Alexandria 8, 12–13, 22, 24, 29, 37, 41, 42, 46–8, 74
Clement of Rome 30, 39–41, 48
Clementine Homilies/Recognitions 48, 113
Colman, Saint 30
Commodian 20
Cosmas Indicopleustes 43
Cyril of Jerusalem 41

Deuteronomy 13, 41, 42, 45
Didascalia Apostolorum 41
Didymus of Alexandria 50–1
Diogenes Laertius 12
Dionysius of Alexandria 50
Donatus of Euroaea 37

Elijah 26
Epicharmus 22
Epicurus 8
Epiphanius 41, 76–7
Euripides 12
Eusebius of Caesarea 41, 42
Ezekiel, poet 40

Fabian of Rome 27

Galen 10, 17, 24, 37
Geoponica 30
Gellius, Aulus 19
Genesis 1, 11, 50–1, 77–106, 108, 142
George of Cappadocia 38
Gnostic tractate 42
Gospel of John 23
Gregory of Nazianzus 41, 77
Gregory of Nyssa 77

INDEX OF MODERN AUTHORS